Sex, God, and Church

Sex, God, and the Conservative Church guides psychotherapy and sexology clinicians on how to treat clients who grew up in a conservative faith—mired in sexual shame and dysfunction—and who desire to both heal and hold on to their faith orientation. The author first walks clinicians and readers through a critique of Western culture and the conservative Christian church, and their effects on intimate partnerships and sexual lives. The book provides clinicians a way to understand the faulty sexual ethic of the early church, while revealing the hidden mystical sex- and body-positive understanding of sexuality of the Hebrew people. The book also includes chapters on strategies for a new sexual ethic, on clinical steps to heal religious sexual shame, and on specific sex therapy interventions clinicians can use directly in their practice. Finally, it offers a four-step model for healing religious sexual shame and actual touch and nontouch exercises to bring healing and intimacy into a person's life.

Tina Schermer Sellers, PhD, is a licensed marriage and family therapist and certified sex therapist, as well as a professor of sexuality and medical family therapy in the graduate Family Therapy Department at Seattle Pacific University.

"Dr. Tina Schermer Sellers' provocative book addresses the sex-negative doctrine in the conservative Christian church that instills in many people deep shame about their body and discomfort with the opposite sex, making them ill-prepared for marriage. Showing how notions of Christianity and sexuality are complementary, Dr. Sellers offers both therapist and lay reader examples of working with clients to heal the soul-body split, reduce shame, and deepen a couple's loving connection."

—**Stella Resnick, PhD**, author, *The Heart of Desire: Keys to the Pleasures of Love*; couples and sex therapist, private practice, Beverly Hills, CA

"This book is powerful medicine for anyone who has ever suffered religious shame about sex. You will find compassion for your dilemmas of conscience, wisdom regarding the teachings of the church, and best of all—explicit practices for opening your mind, nurturing your heart, touching your body, and celebrating the spirit of all that is truly erotic."

—**Gina Ogden, PhD, LMFT**, author, *Expanding the Practice of Sex Therapy* and other books

"Masterfully integrating psychology and theology, Sellers gives us a ground-breaking, razor-sharp view into conservative Christian culture and its shame-inducing sexual ethic. As a psychologist, I am impressed by the precision, validity and robustness of her research. As a theologian, I am grateful for the Christian sexual ethic—rooted in justice, mutuality, and an infinitely relational God—that she introduces. As a millennial who grew up in the conservative Christian purity culture that Sellers describes, the practices in this book lit my pathway to greater freedom from shame and more authentic connection to God, myself, and others. I hope therapists and Christian leaders—pastors, parents, and youth workers—will read this insightful book with an open mind."

—**Christena Cleveland, PhD**, Duke Divinity School

"This is an enlightening, well-written, and clinically useful book on the problems and potential of conservative Christianity for clients dealing with sexual problems. Tina Sellers is uniquely positioned to make this unique contribution to therapy for a population often misunderstood by clinicians. Whether you're new to the field or highly experienced, I promise you'll learn a lot."

—**William J. Doherty, PhD**, professor, director, Minnesota Couples on the Brink Project, University of Minnesota; author, *Take Back Your Marriage*

"Most clinical programs—whether they are based in psychology or marriage and family therapy, social work or medicine, pastoral counseling, or any number of other fields in the 'helping professions'—do not adequately prepare trainees to work with individuals or couples who have been indoctrinated with Church-driven messages of sexual guilt and shame. As a therapist and educator, I have struggled to find resources that help guide clients on a path in healing and growth—and to do this in a way that simultaneously embraces their sexuality(ies) and religious/spiritual faith. The wisdom and counsel that Dr. Tina Sellers offers in this book should be in every training curriculum, on every providers' bookshelf, and in every couple's home."

—**Tai J. Mendenhall, PhD, LMFT**, Couple and
Family Therapy Program, The University
of Minnesota, Twin Cities

"This book is a practical and yet deeply theological path towards healing for those wounded by a shame-based purity culture. Dr. Schermer Sellers has researched and written a roadmap towards a sex-positive Gospel ethic of intimacy. I will be recommending it to pastors and counsellors and teachers everywhere."

—**Sarah Bessey**, author, *Jesus Feminist* and *Out of
Sorts: Making Peace with an Evolving Faith*

Sex, God, and the Conservative Church

Erasing Shame from Sexual Intimacy

Tina Schermer Sellers, PhD

Routledge
Taylor & Francis Group

NEW YORK AND LONDON

First published 2017
by Routledge
711 Third Avenue, New York, NY 10017

and by Routledge
2 Park Square, Milton Park, Abingdon, Oxon, OX14 4RN

Routledge is an imprint of the Taylor & Francis Group, an informa business

© 2017 Tina Schermer Sellers

Library of Congress Cataloging-in-Publication Data
A catalog record for this title has been requested

ISBN: 978-1-138-67497-4 (hbk)
ISBN: 978-1-138-67498-1 (pbk)
ISBN: 978-1-315-56094-6 (ebk)

Typeset in Bembo
by Apex CoVantage, LLC
Printed and bound by CPI Group (UK) Ltd, Croydon, CR0 4YY

To my beloved who inspires the poetry of my body
To Christian, Chloë, and Gary, who inspire the poetry
   of my heart
To Yahweh, who inspires the poetry of love
To Annette, whose inspiration is poetry

Contents

Acknowledgments

Some things incubate longer than others. This project cooked a long time.

I began this journey almost ten years ago, shortly after publishing that first article in 2006 ("Christians Caught between the Sheets—How 'Abstinence Only' Ideology Hurts Us"), exposing what I was learning from my students and clients about the cost of religious sexual shame and trauma on their lives and relationships. I think I needed to cook along with it. I needed to work through the academic side of what had happened in history, and I needed to understand and talk to many others, to learn how to see the puzzle in its entirety and to understand all the pieces. Ultimately, I wanted to *help* my clients and my students, to guide them toward hope in a sex-positive, all-loving God, who filled them with passion and desire *on purpose* so that they might "feel" life and live life abundantly (cf. John 10:10). And I wanted to be able to provide that map to other therapists, clergy, or any person who felt lost as they walked in this forest of religious sexual shame themselves, or alongside someone they loved or served. It all took time amid teaching, running a clinical practice, getting my PhD, launching an institute, getting married, and raising children.

Along the way, I've had hundreds of conversations with people who have struggled with their sexuality, and I am forever indebted to all of my "teachers"—my clients and students—for all that they've taught me, for the sacred stories they've shared, and for the privilege of allowing me to keep walking alongside them as they heal and craft the lives they desire to live. While the stories and case studies in *Sex, God, and the Conservative Church* are taken from the lives of real clients, most of the stories you'll read are compiled from various stories to further disguise and protect privacy. Even though sections are adapted, the ideas presented are drawn from the experiences of actual people in my clinical practice and the conversations I've had with countless individuals over the years in the course of my work.

Over this past decade, so many wonderful, passionate graduate students, colleagues, and friends have done research, called with ideas, cocreated new paradigms, and shared their stories. Each step, each narrative, inched this project forward in some important way. While I whined and fretted on more than one occasion, and pined for more time, I truly believe this book was not meant to be done a moment sooner. To all my graduate assistants who helped me over the years, I say this: your research, enthusiasm, and inspiration propelled me and this project, and I absolutely could not have done this without you. To Mícheál Roe, my dean for the bulk of this project, and Claudia Grauf-Grounds, my chair throughout most of it as well, thank you for having my back. To teach at a Protestant university, even if the graduate programs are given more leeway, is not easy on a chair and dean when a faculty member is openly researching, writing, and speaking nationally and internationally on the impact of religious sexual shame caused by the conservative Christian church. You two ran interference for me from the beginning and believed in the work from the moment I published that first article. Thank you from the bottom of my heart.

To all my varied readers over the years who suffered through the many drafts and iterations as I tried to navigate the academic and narrative forests, my gratitude to you as well. Academia has a way of bypassing the story and leaving you without much that's exciting to read. I can't always tell when my writing is boring, and I am so grateful that I have colleagues and friends who can and who are brave enough to tell me. Thank you to Bill Doherty, Tai Mendenhall, Jim Wellman, Kathleen Schiltz, Cissy Brady, Alissa Bagan, my writing group at CFHA, Charity Laughlin, and Chloë Sellers. To Annie Mesaros, Randall Ajimine, Lauren Pallay, and Taylor Ulrey, your insider knowledge and writing prowess were invaluable! Thank you.

I want to also thank the Thank God for Sex team (www.ThankGod ForSex.org). You all have been remarkable in bringing light to the sexual pain and trauma described in this book. You have all inspired me with your grace, activism, sense of justice, and love. I hope this book helps support your work around the globe.

Along the path, I have walked with mentors whose wisdom has left an indelible mark on my life. I want to thank Bill Doherty for taking the time to read two different iterations of this book and to guide both my thinking and my writing process. Your wisdom, experience, and encouragement over the years have been invaluable. To Gina Ogden, thank you for taking me into your life, introducing me to your tribe (and publisher), and helping me sort through the muck and mire at a time when I was about to round-file the project. You are a mighty sage, and I felt like God gave you to me in that exact moment to catapult this project into existence again.

To John Harrell, you gave me my first experience of what it is to fall in love with your editor! I remember the first time I got the first couple of chapters back from you all cleaned up. I called Gary and said, "I think I'm in love with my editor! He makes me sound so good!" To have an opportunity to work with someone who knows this audience, knows the theology, and is an editor and a remarkably fabulous person, all in the same human, is almost too much to ask for. You were literally a God-send! Working on this project with you has been so much fun, and I hope we get to do many more together.

The people closest to you physically, the ones strung most tightly to your heart, often get the lion's share of your musing, moaning, and out-loud processing. In my life, that is my daughter, my son, and my beloved. They are my sounding board: they read articles and books with me, put up with me reading articles to them, or humor me by reading an article when I say, "You have got to read this!" Thank you, Chloë and Christian, for putting up with my talking sexuality and spirituality from before you could speak and for letting me bring you into the lines of this book. Your truth about the lives of kids your age has been invaluable. How I got kids so wise and insightful is beyond me.

The person for whom there was no escape route was my sweet husband, Gary. He has read more books with me and been to more conferences and retreats on spirituality and sexuality than I am sure he'd like to admit. He is a champion partner in every sense. He is my muse and best friend, my most patient ally, my editor-in-chief, and he has saved me from sending more than one cranky e-mail when I've been tired (in fact, I think it happens every week). I have learned to run everything by him, and I couldn't do half of what I do without him, nor would I want to. As Bette might say, he is my wind.

Reference

Schermer Sellers, Tina. 2006. Christians Caught between the Sheets—How "Abstinence Only" Ideology Hurts Us. *The Other Journal* 7. http://theotherjournal.com/2006/04/02/christians-caught-between-the-sheets-how-abstinence-only-ideology-hurts-us/.

Figures

Introduction

To love another person is to see the face of God.

—Les Misérables

It's a sunny Tuesday morning and the sexual tension between Justin and Marta is still on my mind.

In my initial therapy session with them last night, I learned that this pair, a couple in their midtwenties who have been dating for a year, met in law school and each have a passion to make a difference in the world and to engage deep moral questions. Marta grew up with a Jewish mother and a Roman Catholic father, but she describes her family as more culturally religious than practicing. She told me that lively, spirited conversations were an everyday occurrence in her childhood and an important form of sharing affection in her family system, since both of her parents were professors at the local university. Justin, on the other hand, grew up in a conservative Christian home in Cincinnati. His grandfather had been a pastor and his family had attended the same church for generations. Prior to leaving for law school, Justin had been a worship leader in his high school and college group, playing guitar and occasionally teaching. He found it a challenge to be living several states away, but he was enjoying his new wingspan and the friends and activities that life was now bringing him.

Looking at one another sheepishly in that first session, the couple described the problem, cautiously and with an obvious sense of awkwardness. Marta went first, her voice soft but her words packing a punch.

"Justin has never had sex before and believes sex before marriage is wrong," she said. "I can respect that he has a different worldview, but frankly, I think this idea is a manipulation by the patriarchy, and an attempt to control women by making women's bodies the fulcrum on which their value hinges.

"I think it's bullshit," she continued, "and I know that on some level, he believes this, too. He is a feminist at heart, which is what confuses me about it all."

Looking a little ashamed and confused, Justin looked at Marta and then turned to me. "I know it may sound weird," he said after a moment, "but my whole life, this is what I have believed. Everyone I know from back home who has confessed to having sex before marriage regrets it. All my life, I have fought the urge. I have not wanted to regret my actions or to hurt my future marriage. I'm honestly just afraid of doing the wrong thing. But I look around me now, and all of our friends from law school who are in good relationships are having sex or living together, and they're good people, doing great things. All of a sudden, I feel like everything I believe is being thrown up in the air. But when I talk to my Christian friends back home I immediately feel convicted and ashamed, even when I just talk about Marta and me, without sharing any details.

"I'd like to feel as comfortable and clear as Marta," Justin continued. "Really, I would. But what if I'm wrong? What if having sex before marriage really *is* wrong? Can you help us figure this out, please? I don't want to lose our relationship, but I don't want to hurt our relationship, either. I think we have a really good thing here."

Building a Bridge of Spiritual Intimacy

How would you handle this case? Where would you begin? How would you hold these contrasting sexual, sociopolitical, and spiritual histories and commitments? How would you help them to draw a bridge to each other, something on which to craft an intimate relationship that could nourish them, both erotically and spiritually? Is it even *possible* to do this, given the tension between Justin's religious background and Marta's feminist convictions, with the electric crackle of healthy, mutual sexual attraction animating the space between them all the while?

Even if you're not a therapist, keep reading, because there's plenty to be gained here for anyone who has ever wrestled with questions like these:

- How did Christianity take the gift of sexuality and turn it into something people seem so afraid of?
- How has Christianity contributed to our culture's ignorance surrounding things like eros, sacred sexuality, and the human body?
- How can we help people to heal from years of religious sexual shame and faulty teaching, while still respecting their faith traditions?
- What does a cohesive, faith-based picture of intended sexuality look like?
- What are actual, intimate sexual practices that couples can share that will build a sex life that is wholly integrated with their spirituality?
- And what practices can single people do to heal and develop a loving and celebratory relationship with their body and with God?

One of the challenges I believe we face as therapists is helping our clients who seek to integrate their spiritual selves with their sexual selves, especially if their religious upbringing is foreign to us. As a sex therapist who also teaches at a Christian university, I have seen firsthand the floundering of young couples who grew up steeped in a religious culture that has historically treated the body and its desires with suspicion, and how often they have no idea how to live as sexual beings in their relationships and daily life. This book is designed to help therapists and others who encounter people like Justin and Marta who are being confronted with the power of their erotic yearnings on the one hand, and a long history of body-suspicion in their religious background on the other. In these pages, I hope to offer steps toward integrating their sexual selves and their religious selves. As we'll see, these two elements of human life aren't *nearly* the mutual contradictions that pop culture and the Christian church's history have often assumed them to be. In fact, they go hand in hand.

In North America, many conservative strains of Christianity have kept sexuality and spirituality separate for centuries, often rigidly so. Thankfully, the "purity" movement, one of the more ascetic and toxic eras in sexual ethics in the last 100 years, seems to be waning. But like Justin in our story, many young people are still struggling to find a way to reconcile their sexual desires with the religious elements of their lives.

Mass media doesn't help. In many of the pop-culture expressions of our body-obsessed and yet body-hating culture, it's as if bodies, sex, and people are commodities—never quite good enough, always one step away from the ideal. The perfect body, the perfect mate, the perfect sexual encounter, are available for sale 24 hours a day, seven days a week, 365 days a year—if only we'll try one, simple, quick fix or cosmetic improvement. In this body-focused version of sex, there is no room for humanness or spirituality, a vacuum that often leaves people failing to find meaning and depth in their connection to themselves and to those around them.

People sometimes turn back to conservative Christianity for answers to that quest for something meaningful, but here's the irony: they're promised a "happily ever after" if they'll wait for sex until marriage, marry another Christian, and raise children in the church, but they usually discover that the rules fail to deliver the goods. As we will see in this book, regulations like the ones that were taught to Justin actually make the situation worse for everyone—for individuals, for the church, and for culture. They underscore a fundamental presupposition that the spirit and the body are completely separate things. That assumption deprives us of some of the key tenets of the Judeo-Christian faith structure. For example, what if the body is a vehicle by which we can experience the transcendent? What if the body's experiences in the world are actual, bona fide means of divine communication, and the body, with all its desires, pleasures, pains, struggles, yearnings, challenges, climaxes, and difficulties, can lead us not *further away* from a fuller relationship with God but *closer*? What if the abundant life God desires for all to experience is found not only outside the body but also inside sensual and sexual experiences of love?

In that kind of framework, our bodies become more than just impulsive, suspicious things in need of control more than anything else. Instead, they become primarily something to be celebrated—the means by which we experience life in all of its fullness and freedom, including dimensions of love, sexuality, eros, and the very God who Judeo-Christian culture says invented those things in the first place. The body, the spirit, and sexuality become inextricably woven together, a tapestry of God-given humanness that cannot be unraveled or ripped apart without damaging the whole artwork that is the integrated human self. When we therapists, or the church, or popular culture, try to live in a false narrative that splits them apart, we do so to our own peril and to the harm of those we're tasked with helping.

A Model for Healing Religious Sexual Shame

The separation of body from spirit affected how America constructed medicine as well, which in turn affected how we built the field of psychotherapy. Descartes demythologized the body and handed over its study to the science of medicine through the study of physiology and anatomy. This led to the scientific method, which, due to its rigid methodology, initially freed the scientific community of the moral responsibility of the real health concerns of human beings (Mehta 2011). Human beings became biological organisms to be studied, and disease was seen as a deviation from the norm. A person was turned into an "infected host."

I remember beginning my training in the late 1980s when the first articles on spirituality were being published in the field of marriage and family therapy. I remember the hushed conversations between the family therapists in my department and the psychologists. At that time, it was almost seen as heresy in the field of clinical psychology to talk about spiritual matters in the context of psychotherapy. It simply was not seen as "scientific enough" to be valuable. Gina Ogden, PhD, a pioneer from as early as the late 1970s in the fields of sex therapy, spirituality, and psychotherapy, and Rachel Naomi Remen, MD, a pioneer since the early 1980s in the fields of medicine, spirituality, and physician work-life balance, have both done extensive research looking at the interface of comprehensive systemic health—emotional, spiritual, physical, and sexual. When I was first in training, their ideas were still seen as novel and they were fighting uphill in clinical culture. That's all changed now. Today, the fields of both medicine and psychotherapy recognize the role that spiritual health plays in our overall wellness, but we still have a long way to go. We need models for healing religious sexual shame in those places where religion has caused harm.

As one early step on that road toward integrating therapy with spirituality toward wholeness and wellness, this book offers a pathway to understand how culture and Christianity may have influenced clients' sexual and relational health. It also will offer alternative stories, taken right from the pages of Judeo-Christian history, that point to God's love of the human body and God's intention in sexual love. Many of these stories will be new to your clients, and the narratives will provide a launchpad from which they can begin to explore a new paradigm of spiritual intimacy. Along the way, you'll receive guidance on how to relieve the pain of a toxic culture of religion and

[Handwritten margin note: the splitting of emotional, spiritual, physical, sexual personhood causes holistic damage. left feeling like incomplete artwork.]

sexuality, so that you will be able to walk gently with your clients, carrying a new awareness as themes of vulnerability, shame, isolation, fear, and silence emerge. You will have a context to understand how these religious narratives formed, and best of all, you will be equipped with alternative storylines that *celebrate* the body, sexual touch, love, and God.

Plus, I believe that as we gain competence to help couples like Justin and Marta find healing and wholeness, we will be helping to heal the larger fabric of *cultural* pain, too. Anytime one couple, or even one person, begins to share their story of sexual healing and decides to step into a new narrative that combines love of God, enjoyment of sex, and celebration of the body all at the same time, then we all step a little closer to healing.

Definitions

Talking about sexuality and religion, especially when the two are discussed in the same space, can be very difficult unless we understand what we mean by the words we use. Before we go any further, I want to pause and offer some guidance about how I'll use particular words throughout this book, in the hope that our conversation together, as well as your conversations with your clients, can be as clear as possible.

Eros/Erotic

The words *eros* and *erotic* are used throughout the text, and they're by far the most misunderstood words I use. Plato, the earliest philosopher to define the concept of eros, described it as a coming-to-life in beauty in relation to both body and soul. Living in America, however, I have learned that just as the word *sex* has become a reduced vernacular for "intercourse," the word *erotic* has come to mean "pornographic." In their book *Holy Eros: Pathways to a Passionate God*, James and Evelyn Whitehead, both Christians, offer wonderful examples of how eros shows up in daily life:

- Our God is a God of life—of exuberant, surprising, extravagant vitality. Creation testifies to the overflowing energy of God's presence in our world. Our own generosity, our surprising ability to forgive, and our endless desire for more life all witness to this God-given energy within us. Eros, once used to identify a god in ancient Greece, now serves as a metaphor that names the vital energy Christians recognize as God's gift.
- Eros is the vital energy that courses through the world, animating every living thing. It is the force that turns the flower to the sun, the energy that stirs humans to be in touch, to reach out and link their lives in lasting ways. Eros is the raw energy that impels an infant to seize a bright marble lying in the dirt and put it into her mouth. Eros wants to touch, to taste, and even to consume.

- Eros is the force that quickens our hearts when we encounter suffering and moves us to help and heal. Sex, curiosity, compassion— Eros moves through our lives in delightful and bewildering ways. To live a responsible life we will have to name and at times tame this ambiguous force.
- Eros is our desire for closeness, the visceral hope that moves us out of solitude and motivates us to chance the risky relationships of friendship and love. Eros is about union—with the beautiful other, with a suffering person, with the world of nature waiting to be embraced and protected.

(Whitehead and Whitehead 2008, 9–10)

When I use the word *eros* (or *erotic*), I am speaking of the force of life within us—our passion, our deepest hopes and desires, our creativity and creation. Eros is that sense within us that inspires us to create, to love, to heal, to care, to experience the fullest of life through the embodied experience of our senses. This breath of life is our hint of the God of all creation, lodged deeply in the soul and psyche of every human.

When it's received well, this life force has the potential to give us our clearest experience of our divine Creator. At the same time, if eros is mismanaged, misdirected, or separated from what Judeo-Christian heritage claims is God's intent, it can cause enormous damage. In this text, I will invite you to develop a curiosity with your clients about the erotic mysteries in life, how they show up in their lives, and how they inspire the imagination and nourish the spirit, heart, and relationship.

Sex

In American culture and in Christian culture, "sex" has been reduced to mean penis-in-vagina intercourse (coitus). I will address a host of problems with this definition in various places throughout this book, but for now, it's important to know that I define sex as *any* intimate touch between people with the mutual intent to share connection and pleasure. When I talk about sex, the body, mind, heart, and soul are engaged and involved, not just the genitals.

Sacred / Sacred Sexuality

Sacred is another word I use throughout this book to mean "set apart by God, worthy of respect, and love-inspiring." When I say, "sacred sexuality," I'm referring to a form of sexuality and sexual expression that is worthy of being known in an intended way, one that has the ability to inspire awe in a person or a couple spiritually, emotionally, and physically. This form of sexuality also increases eros between the people involved.

helpful redefining Penetrative
sex is not a helpful
definition of this conversation

Conservative Christianity

Throughout the text I will refer to "conservative Christianity," a difficult concept to describe, since there are so many different variations and styles of Christian living in North America, with every form of social, political, and theological commitment imaginable. Let me offer some broad strokes, though, that can help to describe the types of Christianity that are at the heart of where this book is coming from.

"Conservative Christianity," as I use the term in this book, tends toward a literal view of the Bible, rather than a metaphorical one, and typically views an as-is, plain-sense reading of the biblical text as the rule for life and practice. The preaching and teaching in conservative Christian churches tend to center very heavily around expounding on the Bible (often instead of speaking on given topics), and in many families and churches, there are few higher premiums than the one placed on reading, meditating on, and (in some circles) memorizing Scripture, "God's Word," in an effort to get to know God more closely.

Most of all, there's usually a very heavy emphasis on a personal relationship with Jesus Christ to forgive a person for their sins and teach them to live a new life. "Being saved" is often the central moment in a conservative Christian's life, as it is the moment in time that a person made their "decision to follow Christ," often (though not always) marked by a prayer asking Jesus into one's heart. This is a conscious choice to follow Jesus and his teachings.

Many young adults who grew up in conservative Christian circles spent their teen years attending church youth groups, usually weekly, which often featured fun social games in addition to Bible lessons and chances for kids to be in positions of spiritual leadership. These experiences were often important social events, too, and many Christians met dating partners or lifelong friends on youth outings or at church social functions, mission trips, or summer camps.

For those who are now young adults, especially Millennials, many people who grew up in conservative Christian circles have a very developed sense of social justice. They may describe wanting to help make the world a better place, because they find the teachings of Jesus and of the entire Christian Bible to be opposed to injustices like racism, sexism, homophobia, and economic oppression. For that reason, it's often difficult to guess a conservative Christian's (or ex-conservative Christian's) political affiliations, because their consciences on various issues may propel them to different places on the political spectrum. But the attention to understand "God's will for my life" or "God's plan for the world" will probably be there in any case, and you may hear phrases like those emerge in the way they describe themselves and their commitments.

One thing that is especially important for this book is the common emphasis on "purity" among conservative Christians—the ideal of "saving oneself" sexually for marriage and holding premarital virginity as an important ideal. Some Christians go even further and opt not even to kiss before they are at the altar on their wedding day.

What I do *not* mean by "conservative Christianity" is a kind of hard-core, militant fundamentalism—the sort that might appear picketing at major news events, or that actively seeks to disparage those who disagree with them. Instead, I'm referring to a kind of "gentle conservatism" that, even though it might have strong social or political convictions, is rooted in a theology that believes that God *loves* humanity, and a commitment to treating people decently and with good humor, even when they disagree.

Asceticism

When I speak of the purity movement or particular times in Christian history, I may use the word *ascetic*. Asceticism is a lifestyle marked by a withdrawal from worldly pleasures, usually for a spiritual purpose or a type of spiritual goal. Time or energy that might otherwise have been spent pursuing material possessions or physical pleasures (including sexual desire and behavior) is instead spent in prayer, fasting, and religious reflection (Finn 2009, 94–7). When I speak of a particular time in history as being ascetic, I am referring to the religious rules of the day requiring the people to deny or treat as suspect bodily desires and bodily pleasures, especially as they related to sexual desire.

Religious Sexual Shame

You will see me use this phrase throughout this book, and I want to be clear what I am referring to when I use it. Brené Brown defines shame as the intensely human feeling that we are unworthy of love and belonging (Brown 2012, 11). Shame researchers differentiate shame, the feeling that *I am bad*, from guilt, which is the sense that I have *done* something bad. Shame researchers say that the feeling of shame is attributed to the whole self, not to a particular action or to a particular time. That is why shame is so lethal an emotion. It means the person feels bad, wrong, unworthy, or condemned, right to the core of who they are. Shame does not motivate change like guilt does; rather, it induces depression and can often lead to suicidal ideation.

Religious sexual shame is prompted by particular religious messages about the sexual self, innate sexual desire, natural sexual curiosity, natural sexual thoughts, and sexual actions. Children who express natural sexual curiosity, for example—who might touch their genitals as toddlers while in the bath, only to have some beloved authority become angry with them—will feel shamed and condemned and will not understand why they're in trouble. Then, if a parent or authority figure mentions God or religion while chastising the child, the shame becomes religious in nature. For example, if a parent were to say, "That's yucky, and God wouldn't want you touching your body that way," there's a good chance that now the child feels badly about herself and feels that the God of the universe is ashamed of her as well.

It's not hard to imagine other possible examples of religious sexual shame in the making. A set of five-year-old playmates who are playing "Doctor" and touching each other's genitals are also likely to feel deep shame if an adult overreacts on finding them and tells them that God wouldn't want them touching each other's private parts. The youngster who accidentally walks in on their parents as they are making love may be scolded by a mother and father insecure about their own sexuality as it relates to being people who try to follow Christ. The adolescent whose youth group leader condemns masturbating may wonder what to do with an erect penis and feel ashamed for wanting to touch it. When a religious, sexual component is added to an experience of condemnation, it becomes religious sexual shame, which only amplifies the shame impact.

A Sex-Positive Gospel Ethic

As we move through this book I will raise the notion of a sex-positive Gospel ethic. When I do, I am referring to a sexual ethic that is marked by mutual power, love, and justice, and invites people of faith to experience intimacy not only with a beloved but with all of creation. It is an ethic that seeks to love ourselves and our beloved with the kind of attention, intention, presence, and fullness of senses that Jesus had for his followers. It serves to strengthen people's well-being and self-respect. It touches our senses powerfully, enhances our self-worth, and increases our desire to connect with more love and grace with others. It moves from an old ethic, which required one person to be powerful and the other to be vulnerable, to an experience where both parties know power *and* vulnerability. The merging of the male and female energies that is within each person is released into the relationship, satiating the couple and spilling over to bless the community. It is a creation of mystery and interdependence, a thing of mystery that is worth celebrating.

In the Company of Friends

For readers who are Christians, especially those who aren't therapists themselves, I strongly encourage you to take a copy of this book and read it together with friends or colleagues, discussing it as a group along the way. This can be a wonderful healing experience. Many people have felt profound isolation in their sexual development and have never experienced the kind of grace, love, and community that can emerge when they share the impact of their isolation in a safe and trusting group. It can be enormously healing for a person to be held in prayer and grace among others who can attest to their pain or confusion, because doing so can bring a realization that they're not the only ones who carry sexual-spiritual hurt.

To therapists, regardless of faith commitment: let me encourage you to consider whether reading this book with your clients could be of added benefit to the healing and learning process. Particularly when we get to Chapter 8 and explore actual sexual practices that you can assign as homework between sessions, you'll find it helpful to talk through the exercises together as the couple tries them at home.

A Road Map

This book is designed so as to give both context and practical help. It is intended both for clinicians who sit with clients every day, and also for readers who are simply interested in integrating their sexuality with their faith commitments. The first three chapters will describe how religious sexual shame commonly manifests itself in the lives of clients today. We'll talk about how to recognize shame when it appears and how to begin to treat it, and I'll offer a wider history of how the Christian church inadvertently made decisions that set itself up to become sex-negative and how this pattern continued throughout history through many sociopolitical influences. We will then explore the role that American consumerism has played as an actor on our sexual health and dysfunction. In Chapter 8 we will turn a corner away from the problem and look at some beautiful, sex-positive Judeo-Christian stories that have gotten little recognition in the development of the Christian church, thus contributing to the problem of an unintegrated sexuality and spirituality. These stories provide a basic scaffolding so that clients can start to build a new story. Chapter 5 will propose a sex-positive Gospel by constructing a sexual ethic on the core values of the ministry of Jesus himself. I will demonstrate how Jesus's ministry was centered around guidelines on how to experience an abundant life, of which connection and pleasure were as central to the fabric as justice, grace, and love. I will then offer reflection questions for you to consider using with your clients.

Chapters 6 through 8 will offer varying degrees of interventions in the healing of religious sexual shame. Some can be done with individual clients, some with couples; some can be done in the office during treatment, and some you'll want to assign as homework. The interventions create change through both reflection and intimate touch.

We close with an epilogue, which offers a challenge to the field of psychotherapy. How can we integrate the elements of relational, sexual, and spiritual competency more fully? What added training do we clinicians need in order to increase our abilities in the areas of spirituality, sexuality, spiritual intimacy, and emotional health? Are we where we need to be?

The Messenger

Finally, I think it's important to lay some of my cards on the table from the outset. I have consulted many scholars and read a great deal of literature in the writing of this book, but I realize that there are old, entrenched controversies embedded within any discussion of religion. If you have a background in the Christian church, you'll know that many of us have been taught one particular flavor of Christianity over another—whether it is in regard to sacraments, or gender roles, or church authority, or which Bible translation to use, or sexual orientation, or a million-million other details that Christians have disagreed about across the millennia. As a Christian family, we do have our differences and preferences. But even as you recognize your history and the lessons you learned (or hear things that are completely foreign to your own background), try to bear with me. Try not to get stuck on a particular detail or a particular slant to church history or teaching. In the end, weaving a coherent, useful tapestry requires me to choose threads, which I've tried to do in a way that is thoughtful and supported by scholars, experts in their field. But scholars are known to disagree with one another, which is the nature of what happens whenever people try to explore existential truths.

As a Christian myself, I've come to believe that we can get pretty close, but that we'll probably never get it completely and absolutely right. I'm convinced that God remains vast and knowable only in parts, but not in entirety, and that with all of our understanding and searching, we ultimately stand in the mystery of a loving God—a God who encourages our questions and wants to be known, a God who wants our company and welcomes our wonder and awe when we don't understand God's nature or character fully. People of faith may not agree on all the nuances of Christian expression, but hopefully we can agree at least on that much.

A Tapestry Within a Tapestry

It's important to know, too, that the material in this book is personal for me, not just academic. Some of the same religious aspects of conservative Christianity that we will explore in this book had a negative impact on my young adult life, which is part of why I've become such a proponent for helping people to find a more liberating, more fulfilling, and (honestly) more *fun* sex life than they've known before.

My family was a Swedish American immigrant family that was largely non-religious except for two great aunts whom I adored. My whole extended family demonstrated an open and ongoing conversation about sexuality and gender as I grew up. This is typical of Scandinavian homes. For me, it meant entering junior high school informed about my body, sexual development, and some gender issues from many conversations with parents, aunts, and grandparents. True to our family's culture, some of those conversations were serious, some teasing, but all of them were good-natured and helpful. We were a very affectionate and embodied family, too, so hugs were frequent and all-encompassing. That was the backdrop for me as I moved to California from the Pacific Northwest and joined the junior high youth group at our local Protestant church, which was known for its fun weekly events and summer trips.

[handwritten margin note: these expectations cause guilt, shame, self hate. This is just another way woman are majorly deminished in church.]

As a teenager in the late 1970s, I started to notice a new form of patriarchy emerging inside the conservative church. Slowly, women began to lose what footing they had gained in the previous decade to teach or speak from the pulpit. It also slowly became suspect for men and women to be on leadership teams together. So while I had the good fortune to grow up with some sexual openness in my Swedish American family, the church was teaching me that my voice and rights were not as important as those of men, and that what made me valuable was to put everyone else's needs in front of my own. In sexuality and in intimate relationships, I was learning that to be a good Christian, I was supposed to defer to my partner, to discount my needs, to not listen to my gut, and to give the benefit of the doubt to others, even to my own peril.

[handwritten margin note (left): This is the form of splitting i do often. what is biblical about these actions & what is damaging?]

I got married fa ~~ y my church culture to engage in the dyn: ~~ r even to speak for my own needs—a perfect storm that came packaged with the full catastrophe of family-of-origin issues (like most families, we had our shadows and closets) and a great deal of naïveté. It's safe to say that the marriage became toxic, and my lack of confidence in my own voice and resources only made it more painful to endure.

[handwritten note overlaid: Do i actually believe my voice + rights + person hood is = ? No! Probably not.]

It wasn't until years later that I started to realize that I was a person of inherent, infinite worth—body, mind, soul, and spirit—with an intended purpose to give and receive connection and pleasure, justice, and grace, and that I had nothing to feel ashamed for. That realization came in my forties, and if I could do it again, I wish I had been taught those things much earlier than I had been. It was out of this desire, to help people to learn how precious they are, that I taught my children the value of their voice and their belovedness in God's eyes so much earlier than I had learned it myself. I also taught my son the equal value of the woman's voice, agency, and intelligence in the world. It took lots of therapy for me to be freed from the grip of the patriarchal thinking that the conservative church had taught me, and hard emotional work to whittle my life into something that allowed me to be proud of who I was, sexuality and all. Hopefully, my kids are learning something along the lines of this—and hopefully your clients and mine can, too. After all, my saving grace was that Jesus stood as a feminist, the rock of my faith—the one who elevated women, spoke with outcasts, and served the God who created sexuality to be abundant, beautiful, and fulfilling. My hope is that you'll get a glimpse of that grand design for sex through reading these pages.

[handwritten margin note (left): Jesus THE FEMINIST.]

The Journey of Justin and Marta

As Justin and Marta started to explore their relationship, they were embarking on a journey that illustrates many of the concepts we'll explore through this book.

We talked about what they wanted for their intimate life, what they believed were the ingredients that went into a dynamic sexual and intimate life, and how such a life would be built and sustained. We explored their sex histories, talking about what they had learned and who had taught them, and I asked them to think about what had been helpful and what hadn't been. We explored their relationship to pleasure and to their bodies, and I assigned them some reading to do with each other in order to grow their base of information on sexuality, male sexual pleasure, and female sexual pleasure. Through it all, they were gaining in their ability to "talk sex together" through the act of reading out loud and discussing with each other. I gave them plenty of homework, often asking them to talk through their preferences and ideas, expressing it verbally and specifically with each other.

That was just the biological and emotional part. Next came the theology. Together we slowly went through a lot of the material in this book— separating Jesus's ministry from the ministry of Paul, the formation of the Christian church, the ascetic movements throughout the last 2,000 years, the separation of the body from the spirit, and the impact of shame and condemnation on how conservative Christians have come to think about sexuality. Most importantly, we talked about sex-positive Hebraic stories, including (and in Justin's case, especially) the ones found right there in the Old Testament, and what they might mean if we were to bring them forward to be applied in the present day.

I then invited Justin and Marta to design a sexual ethic that supported the development of a lifelong intimacy and dynamic sexual life like the one they wanted. In time, they formed a sexual ethic that felt deeply rooted in their faith, aligned with justice and their values, and appropriately independent from a conservative doctrine while still retaining the core elements of its Christian character. In the end, they felt clear about how to keep building on their love for each other and their commitment to their relationship, and to keep learning about the integration of sexuality and spirituality. Two years after they were married, they came to one of our Passion for Life™ Couples Intimacy Retreats. It was so much fun not only to see how far they had come but also to watch them take their love to a whole new level at the retreat.

Come With Me

So here we go! I invite you to venture with me, and with your clients, into the mystery of God and sex. As we'll see, there's a vast, overflowing garden of eros to explore if we're willing to take an imaginative and courageous first step into who we are and what Judeo-Christian tradition has to say about eros. The question before us is simply whether we're willing to learn how to live fully and lavishly into a God-centered, profound erotic joy, and to help our clients get there too.

References

Brown, Brené. 2012. *Daring Greatly: How Courage to be Vulnerable Transforms the Way We Live, Love, Parent, and Lead.* New York, NY: Gotham.

Finn, Richard. 2009. *Asceticism in the Graeco-Roman World.* Cambridge, UK: Cambridge University Press.

Mehta, Neeta. 2011. Mind–Body Dualism: A Critique from a Health Perspective. *Mens Sana Monographs* 9 (1): 202–9.

Schonberg, Claude–Michel, and Alain Boublil. 1980. *Les Misérables.* Musical.

Whitehead, James D., and Evelyn Eaton Whitehead. 2008. *Holy Eros: Pathways to a Passionate God.* Maryknoll, NY: Orbis.

1 Christianity and Sex

What's Going On?

John, a newly married, 28-year-old youth pastor, was about to come to one of our couples retreats with his wife, Becky. Both were excited to have a chance to deal with problems that were emerging early in their marriage and not to have to wait for things to get worse.

As a young couple involved in the church, neither had had any sex education, and both had grown up in sexually silent and reactive homes, with an abstinence-only, generally sex-negative view of sex. Both had felt shame about their sexual desire with each other while dating, and even though they managed to be virgins when they got married, up until that point they had felt horrible after every small "transgression" of feeling and action and every dalliance into masturbation.

Neither had found very many people safe to talk with about intimacy issues before or after marriage, so finding a safe place to ask questions seemed next to impossible. When John and Becky would try to raise sexual conversations to seek insight, one of two things would typically happen: either they would talk with their friends, who were people too closely involved in their community or circle to feel comfortable talking about these issues with them (many of them had grown up in conservative Christian circles, too), or John and Becky would consult a therapist, only to find that the therapist wasn't able to respect their faith tradition. They were at their wits' end, but they were willing to try at least one more time, which is how I met them.

As we talked together, John and Becky described their sexual frustration. For starters, Becky had never had an orgasm "during intercourse," and John "had never learned to 'go down' on a woman." Plus, Becky couldn't shake the knowledge that John had had a porn habit before they were married, and fretted that John was comparing her to the women he had seen online. The fact that neither John nor Becky was comfortable talking frankly about sexual issues in the first place only compounded the silence and increased their anxiety.

John communicated his own frustration this way. "No matter what I say to her, she doesn't believe me," he said in exasperation. "She thinks I am comparing her to pornography and that I'm a pervert! She doesn't understand that porn is not the same thing to me as she is, or that I don't want to have any involvement with porn—or that I haven't even been watching it for over two years now. Now she thinks it must be what I am fantasizing about when we are sexual, which I'm not. Becky is my everything!

"I feel like the church instilled in her to be deeply suspicious of men and their sexual drives," he continued. "Now, that same suspicion is in bed with us every night. I hate it, and I wish we could just enjoy having sex without all the suspicion about who's thinking what."

What Is Religious Sexual Shame and Why Does It Matter?

My clinical practice and academic teaching career have been on the campus of a Christian university. While the graduate program I teach for doesn't require students to espouse any particular faith perspective, we nonetheless attract many students from conservative Christian backgrounds. In the early 2000s, I began to notice profound levels of sexual shame and dysfunction among many of the conservative Christian couples I treated and in the sexual autobiographies of family therapy students who had grown up in conservative Christian families. I began to wonder what we in the church had been teaching people about sexuality and Christian faith, and how this narrative had changed in the previous 20 years. Somehow or other, these young men and women in my office had adopted narratives about their bodies and their sexuality that were hindering their development as erotic beings. But how did it happen? When in history did these messages of sexual condemnation arise, fostering such an atmosphere of silence and shame around issues of sexuality, eroticism, and desire? And whatever we Christians had been teaching them, how did those ideas lead these young adults to such an all-encompassing ignorance about sexual matters?

I started to realize that a pervading sense of sexual illiteracy was infusing the stories and sex lives of so many who had grown up in conservative Christian homes. But why? And if these ideas were causing sorrow and suffering, as I saw that they were, were these narratives truly "Christian" at all? If they weren't, what was? Furthermore, it seemed to me that in Jesus's day, the very author of the Christian faith led his ministry not with lecture, warning, and condemnation but with *compassion* and *grace* when people brought their questions and wrestlings. When I looked at conservative Christianity's teachings on sex and the body, why was I seeing the opposite of Jesus's model? Was anyone else asking these questions?

A Journey of Questions—A Habitat of Suffering

As I dug in and did some research, I found that the ministry of Jesus was built on faith, justice, love, mutuality, equality, and care for those less fortunate. His ministry called religious leaders to account for the ways they were marginalizing, abusing, and discounting those not in power—the poor, women, children, the sick, the disabled, the socially outcast and shunned, and those of other races or creeds. His example taught that all people were precious creations of God, and over and over again in the Gospels we see Jesus's guidance and grace as he walked with those who sought his company, or who brought an open heart and honest questions. He wasn't ashamed, like his contemporaries apparently were, by the Samaritan woman at the well (John 4), even though she was a foreigner, an outsider, and a victim of sexism, classism, and xenophobia. Jesus not only spent time with her but also commended her for her spiritual insight. The woman caught in adultery in John 8 had every reason to expect religious law to fall on her like a ton of bricks, but Jesus not only speaks to her but also goes so far as to defend her dignity and worth, and to chastise the religious leaders for their hypocrisy.

And it wasn't just women. Jesus held up children as spiritual exemplars when his disciples told them to go away (Matthew 19:13–15, Mark 10:13–16, Luke 18:15–17). He invited Zacchaeus and Levi, both tax collectors, to be his companions (see Mark 2:14, Luke 5:27–28, 19:1–10). He defended the criminal dying on the cross next to him (Luke 23:43). He even prayed for the forgiveness of those who had framed and crucified him, in the very moment that he was dying (Luke 23:34). And these are just to name a few.

If we talk to those who have followed Jesus throughout their lives, we gather countless stories of how he is still affecting people's lives in our own day and age. Kris and Sue, a married couple, clung to each other and to their faith community as they went through the illness and death of their ten-year-old daughter, Lillie. Glenn, a husband, described his faith as giving him a rock-like foundation of courage as he endured the pain his wife, Cherri, caused when she had an affair. In my own life, it was my faith and community that held me together 20 years ago when I went through a very painful divorce from a deeply wounding marriage, and then nine years of single parenting. Only love and justice of the magnitude of Jesus himself could transform pain into beauty.

Jesus's example was one of self-giving, of deep love, and of setting people free from the things that imprisoned them, and I and others had experienced his healing and liberating power. So why was it that each year I would hear so many stories of sexual pain and suffering from family therapy students, many of whom were Christians actively seeking to follow Jesus's example? If they were trying to order their lives around the teaching of someone as liberative as Jesus of Nazareth, why were they hurting so badly? Why were they so deeply frustrated and despairing in their sexuality? True, some of the situations I encountered had originated from poor choices or from unusual challenges in their current sexual relationships. But on balance, what seemed pervasive was a deep distrust of the body and of sexuality, and for many, a deep distrust in the other gender, or even in intimacy and marriage itself.

As I explored these questions, I began to learn that much of that sexual suffering was generally rooted in either of two primary venues, or sometimes both. One was a culture of silence or of punishment around forms of sexual curiosity, and the other was a social culture that defined sex and the body as objects for pleasure without any consideration for relationship and mutual care. My clients, both men and women, expressed feeling ashamed of their sexual desires or experiences. They told of long histories of seeing sexual desire as something wrong, impure, or problematic about them. Women described a sense of disdain for their bodies—how they looked, how they felt, their desire or lack of it. Men spoke about feeling entitled to sex and then disappointment in their sexual relationships, or a sense of confusion and naïveté around what to expect from their partner, or even around rudimentary skills like how to love, how to touch, or what was needed to bring their partner pleasure. In nearly all cases, there was an obvious lack of grounding in any form of sex education—positive or spiritually rooted—a scarcity that was compounded by conservative Christianity's pervasive, sex-negative message of what *not* to do with each other. All in all, it was a toxic mixture, one that left men and women ill-prepared for eroticism and physical pleasure with each other.

In many cases, clients had spent their formative years wanting, shaming, repressing, secretly touching, engaging in recreational sex, and living in a culture that objectified sex and bodies. They felt at odds with their bodies, with their partner (if they had one), and with their faith, *all at the same time.* With couple after couple, client after client, the pervasive question seemed to be, "Is there a greater purpose in sex, or is it merely about feeling good in the moment or fulfilling some expectation in marriage? Is there anything more than this suffering, or is this all there is?"

Janet had experienced some of these things firsthand. At age 54, having been married a little over three decades, she knew all about the sexual dysfunction that conservative Christianity can cause. "My husband and I both came from good Christian homes and were virgins when we married at 21 years old," she said. "Both of our families hadn't talked about sexual matters when we were growing up. For most of the first 30 years of our marriage, I had low sexual desire and my husband was the constant initiator. It set up a bad dynamic between us. All I knew was what I 'should' do and nothing about what I really wanted as a wife or a sexual person.

"This pattern finally began to change as our kids grew older," she continued. "After they left home, I began to work on my own reactions and lack of autonomy. It helped tremendously in my ability to exercise more freedom within our sexual relationship. I found that the more I grew sexually, the more intriguing our relationship became. I am just now discovering how sexuality is linked to spirituality in my life. My husband has helped me to feel free to experiment and find new ways to be intimate with him."

Stories like Janet's invite us to ask questions about the how, the what, and the why of sexual and spiritual nourishment or starvation. What kept this husband and wife from discovering how sexuality is linked to their faith? What set them up to spend the first 30 years of their marriage in constructed roles

[handwritten margin note:] male-centric sexual pleasure. It is the womans job to please not to be over.

of "Christian husband" and "Christian wife" that inhibited the gift of sexual communion? What would they have needed while growing up that might have helped them to be nourished by the gift of sexuality at the outset of their relationship and through raising children? And what was it about time or the circumstances of life that finally allowed them to experience a more mutual and enjoyable sex life together?

Sex Is a Vital Part of Life

The vast majority of couples in our culture, both those who claim a faith and those who do not, have one thing in common: they want something more. A 2010 study found that while the majority of couples believe that sex is a vital part of life, 43 percent of Americans are sexually satisfied, down from 51 percent just six years prior (Fisher et al. 2010, 36). Some of the factors for our culture's increased dissatisfaction are physical, like the challenge of living with pain or illness, while some have to do with life-style, like working long, exhausting hours, depleting the time and energy necessary to foster intimacy. Other factors may have to do with the quality of the relationship in areas like trust, support, playfulness, or respect. Yet if what I've heard in my practice over the years is any indication, beneath each of these factors lie the foundational sexual narratives that were absorbed growing up, and the ways in which those messages affect what people have come to believe about their sexual selves.

This chapter is going to take us on a journey to better understand the messages that have infiltrated traditional conservative Christian teachings, as well as the ideas that inform our culture's views on sexuality. We'll explore how those ideas have helped and hindered the discovery of God's gifts of eros, sexuality, sensuality, pleasure, and the body, especially for people who grew up claiming a Christian faith. Those of us who practice therapy know firsthand that the ideas and narratives that our clients carry with them into treatment did not come from a vacuum. They have actual, historical origins and represent a tangled jumble of overt and covert messages about gender and sexuality, delivered to us over time through family, friends, culture, and community. But many clients who grew up in conservative Christian homes, living with silence and condemnation around sexuality and sexual knowledge, come seeking clarity, guidance, and a newfound freedom to be fully human, made in God's image (see Genesis 1:27). These are the people whom we'll have in mind as we explore these ideas further.

We've Been Here Before

As I've treated and taught people over the last 20 years, it's become clear to me that while so much has changed in our culture, the ways in which sexuality is discussed in the traditional Christian church are about the same now as it was back then. In fact, if I have seen any trend over that time, it is that those now in their twenties and thirties who grew up in a conservative Christian church community describe an even more rigid, condemning, and fear-based message about sexual desire, their bodies, and sexual behaviors than was present from the 1960s through the 1980s. The examples that follow will offer a glimpse into how these common, faith-based sexual messages have been handed down over the last several decades.

Common Threads

Here are the themes repeated in the vast majority of sexual stories I hear from the Christians whom I have served and taught:

- "Sex was a silent, loaded topic in my family while I was growing up."

In stories like these, whenever a child in the family did bring up a topic involving sex or sexuality, an adult in the family would likely get upset and say something like, "How could you bring that up at the dinner table?" or "We don't talk about those sorts of things," or "Where are your manners?" Typically, the adult, who would now be visibly uncomfortable, would make a quick move to change the subject or postpone discussion until some later time. Even though the child's question or comment may have been made in complete innocence and curiosity, the parent's response communicated that the young person had done something wrong by bringing it up (embarrassment), that they should have known better (shame), and that this was very bad, or secret, or inappropriate for conversation (humiliation).

The words in parentheses are strong feelings that mark the memory in the body. The young person's physical reaction to the emotion creates a meaning for them, usually that "something must be wrong with me, I must be bad, or there is something very bad about sex."

"My parents never talked about sex when I was little," a 28-year-old woman once told me, echoing many other stories I've heard from Christians over the years. "They didn't even talk with me about sex when I had my first menstrual period in the fifth grade. Throughout my childhood, when issues around sexuality or the body came up, my parents reacted in a way that implied that it was something bad or something not to be curious about or to discuss."

"Everything about sex was kept a secret," wrote a young man. "The absolute dearth of information about sexual matters in my family and during my parents' childhood tells me that these families probably viewed sex as something dirty and forbidden. In order to maintain the family honor anytime something related to sex came up, sexual matters were covered up and buried. The result was a family existence that was dark and uncompromising in its moral tone."

"Sex and sexuality," echoed Jane, a 25-year-old grad student, "was not overtly talked about, or if it was addressed, it was with a negative comment or admonition to 'not do' or 'want' something (anything) considered sexual."

Many Christian couples have told me similar stories over the years, and they usually go something like this: the child had asked a sex-related question or made a comment about the body, and the parent had responded reactively, often giving instructions about what not to do, and usually by way of a monologue. These things were not open for discussion. "Where did you hear such a thing?" the parent might have asked. "I don't ever want to hear you say that again."

"Our family never talked about sex or sexual development," wrote Jasper, "so I wasn't aware of what was going on with my body when I first began to explore masturbation. I must have been eight or nine years old when this first began to happen. I remember asking my mom about what was going on with my body when I touched myself in a certain way. I can't remember exactly what she said—only that I felt extremely shamed by her response and became afraid to touch myself ever again."

• "'Sex' is for marriage, and that's all you need to know."

The focus of this type of discourse is solely on behaviors, on what a decent person cannot or should not do. There would be scant discussion, if any, about what kinds of sexual expression might be beneficial and why, and which times and occasions might be more appropriate than others for exploring them. There were no conversations to help youth to understand how to honor sexual desire as a gift from God, both before marriage and during marriage. Conversations about gender and culture were absent, too, so the clients I heard from often had no idea how the tendencies and hormonal expressions of adolescent boys and girls vary from culture to culture. Equally important and silenced were conversations about what skills and practices are necessary for growing into a loving partner and for choosing a partner who can be loving and attentive.

At its very worst, I've seen examples of how this void of unanswered questions and conversations has created unprecedented ignorance about sexual and relational desire, the body and emotions, wants and expectations, knowledge about self, knowledge about the other person, awareness about sexual complexity in culture, and the language for how to talk about sexuality with a partner. I've heard hundreds of disaster stories, many I will share throughout these early chapters, but one I will share came from a recent supervision of a young couple who came in for premarital counseling.

MacKenzie and Forrest, both conservative Christians and virgins, were about to graduate from college and had been dating for three years. They each carried heaps of shame around their desires, and they had no history of sex education to guide them in understanding how their bodies worked and why. Their families of origin were very loving, but like many conservative Christian families, they had been silent and shaming around sex, sexuality, and bodies.

The two of them had dabbled in some physical contact during their dating, but the guilt and shame they felt at wanting the other person sexually had actually been suffocating their sexual desire for each other and with only two months left before their wedding. For her part, MacKenzie felt that her desire was disappearing as the sense of "wifely expectation" approached, and Forrest felt pressure to perform but was very anxious because he realized he wouldn't know how when the time came. Forrest also disclosed that he felt compulsive with his porn use, something that MacKenzie saw as a sexual betrayal of *her*. Altogether, Forrest's and MacKenzie's levels of self- and other-awareness, of intimacy, sexuality, gender, emotional intelligence, and relational development, were virtually nonexistent. The two of them were at an almost paralyzing deficit as they began one of the most complex and demanding relationships of their lives. It would take a lot of hard work, and very frank conversations together, to move their relationship to the fullness of its potential to nourish them and to expand their adult development.

Without embarking on an intentional journey to understand sexuality or relational intimacy, confusion and pain, rather than freedom, expressivity, and fullness of life, seem to dominate the sex lives of many Christians. They are then left to try to understand their sexual desires in an absence of crucial information about who they are and how their bodies work.

That's not a neutral silence, especially for teens and young adults. Faced with a void like this in sexual literacy, young people become predisposed to look elsewhere for information. Often, they turn to the media, a source only too ready to commodify their healthy erotic desires, objectify their bodies, and teach them to treat potential mates as products rather than persons. In general terms, they learn that a human is merely a body, a thing to be used to give or take pleasure at will. At best, when they do learn something from the media about sexual connection, its sexuality is no-strings-attached entertainment, devoid of negative consequences. This may be truer in heterosexual media, where all genders often learn that women are to please men for attention or status. Women learn that to get what they want (attention, money, or pseudo-love) they have to use their bodies for sexual favors, and men learn that they have the right to expect this. Both men and women are taught that the best sex is wild, spontaneous, risky, free, and unattached. But disillusionment ultimately sets in, and people find themselves wanting something more substantial, more intimate, and more enduring. Here again, they are met with silence.[1]

At this point, one of the basic hindrances to conservative Christians' sexual development should be clear. By the time these persons walk into my office, they have already spent years floundering between two conflicting messages about sexuality. On the one hand, their conservative Christian background has insisted that sex belongs in marriage—*period*. But on the other hand, pop culture has insisted that wild, unattached, recreational sex is the best there is—*period*. The impossible task of trying to live amid both narratives at the same time breeds despair, both for married people and for singles alike. How can a couple cultivate a sexual relationship that is intimate, erotic, relationally nourishing, rooted in God's love and mutuality, and bubbling over with pleasure and connection, when the highest virtue is either heeding the church's call toward sexual suffocation or the culture's call to unrealistic, untrained sexual abandon? Who can blame young Christians for being disillusioned under circumstances like that?

Jules, 30, knew the frustration personally. "As I grew into my adolescence," she wrote, "I began to associate sex with sin, and I imagine that it had to do with being surrounded in a conservative religion in my home, church, and school. My attitude about sex and sexuality was that it was something that only married or sinful people engaged in. Other than that, I didn't have much information, and because I was shy, the only place where I could learn about sex and sexuality was from TV, magazines, and books."

Andrea, another young woman, explained how her lack of knowledge and understanding created vulnerability when she finally did begin dating. "Because I hadn't really pursued physical intimacy in high school (kissing or making out) and didn't really understand much about the dating scene," she wrote, "I became physically involved with people my age, postcollege, who were at a different stage of experience and understanding than I was. That meant that my experience of sexual interaction suddenly and significantly accelerated.

"I pretty much immersed myself in a more advanced sexual and intimate climate without realizing it and without being prepared," she continued. "Because it all felt considerably more intimate for me, I assumed that it was intimate for the guy I was with as well, a presumption that came at a bitter cost. Just because it was new and intimate for me did not mean it was new or intimate for him! Because so much of my conception of sexuality was unclear, I fell into the trap of confusing sex and affection. Had I been taught better ways to meet that yearning for affection and to recognize that sexual interaction does not reflect emotional affection or investment, I could have been spared a lot of anguish."

These stories, and countless others, have illustrated for me just how damaging silence and shame can be, and how ignorance contributes to a dearth of awareness: self-awareness, sexual awareness, gender awareness, other-awareness, emotional awareness, even cultural awareness, as well as how and where to protect oneself. But one of the biggest costs is in what we might call "pleasure imagination." None of these youth were guided to see their natural tendencies and curiosities in sexual pleasure as a gift from a loving God or given appropriate information about the gift of *their* bodies and the gift of *others*' bodies, which means that they never developed a sense of sexual play and enjoyment. Put simply, it means that when sexual encounters do happen, they're a whole lot less fun than they could be, and they miss out on the sense of joy, creativity, and delight that they might otherwise have.

• "Agapae is the only form of love that is truly Christian."

In many stories from the young people I've met, there's a tendency to pick and choose the *kinds* of love that they are willing to let themselves feel.

Many young women and men want to feel only *agapae* love (self-giving or unconditional love, offered openly), which they believe to be holy or "Godly," along with *philia* (the nonsexual, brotherly love of friendship), and they can become confused or feel ashamed when they notice the desire of *eros* (romantic and sexual love) welling up within them. In my experience, Christians today seem to think that agapae is the most Christian form of love, that philia is allowed, and that eros will lead you astray—a kind of ranking of forms of love, with some more desirable than others.

Drawing distinctions around types of love may be useful for understanding the multidimensional nature of human affection and desire, but to rank them over and against each other is to misunderstand and misapply them. "This dichotomy cannot be justified or explained by careful biblical and historical scholarship," writes James Nelson, a Christian ethicist. "The more likely reason for its pervasiveness is simply the pervasiveness of our experience of the alienating sexual dualism"—referring to the spirit/body split of Christianity (Nelson 1992, 23). This distortion has plagued Christians who have been taught to see agapae as morally acceptable and eros as morally corrupt. This did not stop people from feeling desire, of course: it just stopped them from talking about it openly and approaching their desires from an understanding of God's love, rather than suspiciously.

As a result, even all these decades later, the culture of silence, confusion, and ignorance leads people to isolate, and they often find themselves trapped in pain with nowhere to turn. "Human emotions, desires, and sexual feelings," writes Nelson, "have remained unintegrated into Christian understandings of selfhood. The manner in which our sexuality underlies and informs all of our loving has been left unappreciated and unclarified" (Nelson 1992, 23). Not surprisingly, many earnest young Christians are mired in silence and confusion as to why they have these varied desires and longings, wondering to themselves what it means that they have so many desires that are morally corrupt. What else could they conclude then that something is wrong and unholy with them?

- "Be pure."

In the early 1990s, the no-sex-before-marriage discourse was expanded to include the idea that Christians must remain "sexually pure" before marriage, which many Christian youth understood to mean refraining from *any* expression of sexual desire: no masturbation, kissing, longing, touching, fantasizing, and so on. This movement, which began in the South and spread to over two million youth in several countries, involved purity pledges that were signed, purity rings, and for some girls, purity dances (balls) with their fathers. This is what has become known as the purity movement. The vagueness of phrases like "purity" and "sexual abstinence" used in teaching and in the pledges these youth were asked to sign left young people confused and overly self-restrictive in the development of their erotic selves.

What does "purity" look like, anyway? And by implication, what are the "impurities" that a person is supposed to avoid? Are my romantic and sexual desires bad? Perverted? What does "sexual abstinence" refer to? Is it abstinence from vaginal intercourse, or does it also refer to other forms of sexual intimacy, like fellatio, cunnilingus, or anal sex? Is masturbation wrong? Is mutual masturbation okay as long as neither person has an orgasm? What, precisely, are we supposed to "abstain" from? As we learned later, there were sociopolitical forces that set the stage for the purity movement, which are chronicled in books like *Sex, Mom, and God* by Frank Schaeffer (2011).

What is stunning to me is how this "purity message" resembles the most extreme ascetic movements of the first centuries of the early church, where to serve God was to master renouncing *all* sexual thoughts, feelings, and actions. I have heard many say they were told that when they even desired someone, whether in real life or in fantasy, they were impurely "lusting" after them and thus "sinning against themselves, the other, their future mate and God." In fact, I recently found a quote out of a current book on Christianity and sexuality describing a person's *experience* of sexual attraction, regardless of whether he or she consciously notices it, as "the very existence of such atmospheric erotic intentionality [that] subtly stains you. It is yet another aspect of our battle with darkness" (Powlison 2005, 100). Schools of thought that fail to differentiate between feelings (which naturally occur outside of our control) and thoughts and actions (which we *can* control) are a great way to lead from biology straight into shame. But because desire is as naturally human as breathing, these teachings only encouraged youth to hide what they felt or did from those around them and to condemn themselves for feeling things they were supposedly wrong for feeling.[2]

A further tragedy for many of these earnest young Christians was that their aversion to desire did not lift when they got married. Many young men and women developed significant sexual dysfunction and chronic low desire issues that persisted well into their marriages. Some of this may have had to do with the purity pledges themselves. Research on the effect of the purity pledge indicated a slight delay (12 to 18 months) in the onset of sexual activity, a reduced use of contraception when young persons did engage in intercourse, and a significant increase in shame, condemnation, and self-loathing (McClintock 2001, 30; SIECUS 2005). Donna Freitas, in her groundbreaking book *Sex and the Soul*, interviewed over 2,500 students at public, Catholic, and evangelical Christian colleges around the United States about their sexual beliefs, attitudes, and behaviors. "Of all the students I interviewed at all three types of institutions," she writes, "the only students who spoke of pregnancy scares and having unprotected sex came from the evangelical colleges. Katrina Tan, [an evangelical student] who also had a pregnancy scare, confirms this tendency, which is supported by statistics about Christian students, who are more likely to delay sex, yes, but when they do engage in sex, they are more likely to have unprotected sex" (Freitas 2008, 124–5).

I spent some time talking to students who grew up inside the purity culture to learn what they experienced and had been taught. "From my personal experience, the message was hard-core," wrote Jamie in an e-mail. "Along with 'sexual purity,' there was 'emotional purity' and living within certain boundaries so that you didn't give pieces of yourself away by going 'too far' physically, or even so that you didn't have serious emotional connections or conversations with the opposite sex. You were told to have clear relationship boundaries—but this was never clearly defined and was hard to understand.[3] A lot of the pressure came from my parents and certain church groups and parachurch organizations. This quote kind of describes the overall idea and concept that was constantly driven home:

"'Imagine for a moment one of those huge lollipops, the kind that you buy at an amusement park candy store. Take off the wrapper, and pass it around to ten people. Allow them to lick as much as they want. The leftover is saved for the husband or wife, the rightful owner of the lollipop.' Yuck! Who would want that?[4]

"Imagine being described as a lollipop like that. Now you feel dirty, unwanted, yucky, and worthless. If I have given anything away, even just 'emotionally,' this is how I am supposed to feel about myself."

To add to the message of purity, at once both vague and unforgiving, is the added, covert message that the body is a thing to be owned by someone else. Probably as a result, there is a strong culture among female students at Christian colleges to find validation in a husband. "The idealization of sexual purity is powerful at evangelical colleges," writes Donna Freitas,

> and it exacts demands on students that can be severe, debilitating and often unrealistic. The pressures to marry are extreme for women, and college success is often determined by a ring, not a diploma. Because of the stronghold of purity culture, many students learn to practice sexual secrecy, professing chastity in public while keeping their honest feelings and often their actual experiences hidden. Students are aware that officials at evangelical colleges see it as their duty to monitor male-female romantic relationships and to strictly enforce campus rules about visitation in the residence halls.
>
> (Freitas 2008, 219)

The Effect of These Messages on Sexual, Spiritual, and Esteem Development

Beliefs Versus Actions

Thanks to the National Survey of Family Growth, conducted every few years by the Centers for Disease Control and Prevention, we know that traditional religious teaching about sexuality changes attitudes, but not behaviors. When participants were asked if they think it is okay for an 18-year-old to have sex with someone they love, 74 percent who claimed no religious affiliation said "yes," along with 54 percent of Catholics and 29 percent of fundamentalist Protestants. But when the questions dealt with actions, rather than attitudes, the differences were much, much smaller. Those who claimed no religion on average lost their virginity at 16.4 years old, while those with a Catholic affiliation were 17.7 years old and those with a fundamentalist Protestant affiliation were 16.9 years old (Daugherty and Copen 2016, 8). Similarly, according to this research, while conservative Christians might believe that sex before marriage is wrong, of people who actually were virgins at marriage, 12 percent had no religion, 15 percent were Catholic, and 17 percent were fundamentalist Protestant (Centers for Disease Control and Prevention, referenced in Russell 2006).

"A series of studies have shown that young Christians find it difficult to keep the covenant these ["purity rings"] symbolize," writes Freitas, referring to the rings many Christian women wear to symbolize a commitment to abstinence from intercourse until marriage. "In many cases, abstinence pledges do little more than postpone sexual intercourse for a few months or turn those who try to keep them in the direction of other sexual activity" (Freitas 2008, 77).

Nowhere to Turn

Along with purity rings, and adding to an overall sense of sexual illiteracy, many Christian young adults may have grown up in a culture of abstinence-only sex education, which research shows does *not* lower the incidence of sexual intercourse and *increases* the incidence of unwanted pregnancy, thanks to the decreased use of contraception in this population (Kirby 2007, 15). "Children of sexually ignorant or silent parents, in school systems with poor or nonexistent sex education programs, without the health resources of the middle class, will grow up to have sexually ignorant children like themselves," writes Christine Gudorf (1994, 23). Rather than helping teenagers to navigate the newfound sexual desire that they are experiencing in this stage of life, abstinence-only education actually removes some of the tools that could help students understand how they feel and to make good decisions in spite of what's happening to their bodies.

For many Christian young people, making the jump from high school to college only brings a new layer of sexual proscription. Evangelical colleges, writes Freitas,

> often combine monitoring with legislation about sexual activity on campus (including, in some instances, requiring students to sign agreements that, under penalty of expulsion, they will not have sex during their college years). Such monitoring can create an unfortunate communications breakdown—a campus atmosphere akin to a high school environment that fails to recognize and trust that students are already

powerfully bound by the sexual tenets of their faith traditions, particularly in the area of restrictions on premarital sex. As a result of this oversight, many students feel compelled to hide their sexual practices not only from friends but also from all adults with whom they come into contact, including clergy. This stops them from seeking adult advice about sex and helps to create a culture of fear regarding sexual activity and identity on campus.

(Freitas 2008, 219)

The chief complaint of students on evangelical campuses, including mine, is that there is too much silence and taboo about sex, which leaves students feeling as though there is nowhere to turn for help or advice. After counseling many conservative Christian students over the last two decades (or students who had previously inhabited conservative Christian culture), I've come to realize that they need an environment that is safe and grace-filled, a forum where they are invited to share their histories and desires, ask questions, and wonder together. They also need guidance through mutual dialogue (not lectures) that can help them connect their spiritual desires with their sexual choices—integrating sexuality and spirituality—and to be invited into conversations about God's abundant purpose for giving humans sexual desire in the first place. This change must happen for these students to deal with sexuality in a healthy way and to affirm that their sexual desire is a God-given life force, that it is *good*. Learning about sexuality—how to channel it, manage it, and appreciate it—is an important part of human development. Given how the wider culture and the church both tend to miss the importance of walking young people through these developmental steps, there is an urgent need for mature counselors and mentors to support Christian young adults through the process of understanding their desires and living them out in vibrant, faith-honoring ways.

Ring by Spring

In the meantime, the age of marriage is lower among conservative Christians than among non-Christians, which increases the risk that a Christian will couple before an adequate understanding of self or of "other" has been developed. In response to the purity message, many Christians choose not to date or court, or to delay those processes in pursuit of marital partners. This essentially halts the developmental "teacher" that the process of dating has historically been. In Freitas's research we see that students at evangelical colleges are in a culture that nearly obliterates dating while putting extreme pressure to have found one's mate before graduation. In this research and in my office, I hear young adults talking about this pressure to marry. One young woman shared with me that within a month of starting to date someone, people begin to ask if they are planning on getting married.

It is important to appreciate the impact that Joshua Harris's books (*I Kissed Dating Goodbye*, 1997, and *Boy Meets Girl*, 2000) had on the sexual and spiritual health of the conservative youth that came of age after the 1990s. Libby Anne, a well-known blogger now married and in her thirties, describes in detail the impact these books had on her life, and her stories have been echoed hundreds of times in my office. She describes how some youth leaders, having read Harris's books, used the information to encourage adolescents not to invest emotionally or physically in another person unless they were sure they would marry them. If they dated and the relationship didn't move to marriage, then it was as if they had given something of their heart and body away to another person that they could never retrieve, something that should ultimately have belonged to whomever they would eventually marry. Libby Anne vividly describes how she and others were terrified to feel or do anything for fear of destroying their future. "I was afraid to think about guys for fear of cheating on my future spouse," writes Libby Anne. "I wish I'd realized that love is infinite. I wish I'd realized that my girlhood crushes were harmless. I wish I could have enjoyed those feelings instead of feeling eternally guilty" (2012).

Purity movement teachings also dealt with lust and modesty in such a way that women were made responsible for how men behaved. They were to wear modest clothing in order to keep men from "stumbling." This taught women to distrust men and taught men that they were not responsible for their behavior or sexual drive. Further, it caused women to see their own sexual desire as dangerous as well as their bodies and the reactions they elicited as even more powerful. As a result, many women drove their sexual feelings even further underground. This fear of being blamed for men's behavior invited many women to become controlling of the men in their lives, since men were given permission to accuse women for their out-of-control behavior. It also set up a dynamic where women expected men to misbehave sexually. As Libby Anne described, "I feel like what I was taught was, 'Your husband will cheat on you no matter what. Be ready to resent him for it, and also to resent those sluts that set him up for this by their appearance.'" She talked about how long it took before she could finally hear how much her husband loved her, how unreasonable she was being, and how wrong Harris's teaching about lust had been about men, about sexuality, and about women. Libby Anne goes on to say how different her life would have been if she had not been taught to see dating as something wrong, but instead as an opportunity for learning, and if she had been allowed to just grow up instead of focusing so much of her dating on the goal of marriage and the fear of slipping up (2012).

Interestingly enough, Joshua Harris recently has been revisiting the impact of his books and he is seeking to hear the stories. He wrote *I Kissed Dating Goodbye* as a 21-year-old man, and from 1997 forward, youth leaders from across the country used his *young and untested* wisdom to cement the purity message. Now at 40, he has begun compiling narratives of individuals frustrated with the impact that his books had on them (Harris n.d.).

With my clients, I talk about dating as a relational learning process, the gathering of many experiences with someone who is a romantic interest. In dating, you learn about yourself, what kind of person fits well with you, and what is important to you in romantic partnership, all while gaining experience in truly knowing another person. During the dating process, the jury stays out, allowing you to stay in a place of curiosity and information-gathering. The pressure is off since you haven't decided you are getting married to a particular person, and in the meantime, there is an appreciation for the learning itself. Dating is a time of discovery with the options of "learn and stay" and "learn and get out" both available.

All of that changes at the precise moment when a person decides, either formally or informally, that they will marry the person they have been dating. The minute one decides that this is who they are going to marry, even if it is only two months into a relationship, the dynamics of learning and observing change considerably. Whatever creates serious doubt is typically either ignored or placed under the category of "things that will change." Plus, young adults are still in the process of forming their identities—who they are, what they like, where they're going in life—and conservative Christians in particular often have little or no dating experience at that time anyhow. For those reasons, when they are expected to make one of the most important decisions of their lives, they often choose based in romance but not in realism, without accounting for the seriousness of the choice they're making.

It's not that they don't *think* that they know things—which can actually make the situation worse. Often, Christian young adults, not having been trained in their relational development, subscribe to popular but naïve ideas like these:

- this is their *only chance* to find a suitable spouse, so they need to make a move on the opportunity *now*;
- all of their friends think that it's true, too, and they can't all be wrong;
- a wedding would be fun, and not primarily a source of frustration, pain, and exhaustion;
- he or she is a perfect match for me.

These are hardly adequate points of evidence or rationale for committing one's entire life to a person, let alone someone whose prefrontal lobe may not be fully formed until age 25–28 and who is consequently in a sea of identity-formation processes the whole time. The research bears this out: people who marry before the age of 25 are twice as likely to divorce as those who marry after that time (Centers for Disease Control and Prevention 2015; McKinley Irvin 2012).

Romance Versus Sex

Adding to all of the complication and risk of poor decision making, conservative Christians have often been given a sexual ethic that incorrectly conflates "sex" with "intercourse," and makes "sex" (so defined) out to be the "thing" you are to avoid at all costs before marriage. Having learned that "sex" and "intercourse" are one and the same, that intercourse is all that really counts, and that sex should happen only after you are married, young Christians often separate *romance*, which has acceptable limits, from *sexual expression*, which they believe to be unacceptable.

As evidence, many men and women I've spoken with have had no trouble describing romantic experiences, crushes, and dates they've had, and some have described hand-holding or kissing without noticeable shame. But as the conversation has moved into more physical expressions of loving and sexual touch, the stories have often begun to take on a shameful and hushed tone. Sexual expression, all of it, has typically been seen as a manifestation of their weak will, their carnal desires, some kind of perceived perversion, and selfishness. Romance and crushes are good; sexuality in any form is bad.

The problem, of course, is that within a marriage, any sexual relationship that is separated from romance and tender affection is set up for failure from the start. Having learned to suffocate or suppress their sexuality over the years of their development, including with the person they love, many young Christians find themselves unable to bring their sexuality into the light when they finally *are* married. They have trouble seeing it as a good, God-given thing after so many years of shaming themselves for feeling their natural erotic impulses. Sexuality is not nearly as easy as many Christian couples seem to think it will be before they tie the knot.

If it's common to believe that sexual expression is a lesser form of self-disclosure, then it's not hard to make the jump to feeling like they have to choose their faith *over and against* their sexuality. "Many college students seem to encounter religion and sex as if they are two powerful and jealous gods," writes Freitas. "When they interact, as they do among evangelicals, it is a battle to the death. Either religion wins, and sex withers away (until marriage, theoretically), or sex wins, and faith flounders" (Freitas 2008, 215). Freitas interviewed one student who said they felt that sex

> can have an effect on your spiritual or religious life. . . . Like, you're torn between the social pressures of having sex and . . . the [religious] pressure to not have sex. I feel like it can . . . sever anyone's connection to a religion because they don't know which way to go. They don't know which is the lesser of two evils.
>
> (Freitas 2008, 209)

The Gender Web

Part of the issue, even if couples do figure out how to integrate their sexuality and their faith, is one of simple ignorance: they don't know what they like or even where to begin. Women raised in conservative religious homes often find themselves at odds with their husbands because they don't know what kinds of touch they like, or that they have any right to want or ask for multiple forms of physical intimacy. It actually makes a sad kind of sense: having been silenced for so many years by a sex-negative culture, a Christian woman is likely to bring more emotional baggage into the bedroom than a non-Christian would. Thanks to the church, she's likely to have spent years turning off her sexual desire, and thanks to pop culture, she's been treated as an object by the media and by men in general. Consequently, she might find that she judges herself by how pretty *she* thinks she is, and by how much she thinks her *husband* desires her. On a deeper level, even if she has come to the point of admitting that she has a sexual character of her own, she might simply write herself off as "damaged goods" or a "Jezebel"[5] for whatever thoughts, feelings, or sexual actions she has experienced or silently desired, not realizing how healthy and normal it really shows her to be. Added to self-loathing and socially constructed shame, a powerful form of diminishment can arise and encourage her to abdicate her own wishes to his, setting up a sexual dance of obligation, transaction, and misery. When sex becomes dominated by the *husband's* desires, and absent hers, her sexual desire will probably diminish by an enormous margin.

Men raised in conservative religious environments are at a disadvantage, too. Throughout their postadolescent lives, they have been taught that intercourse is an erotic pinnacle, some kind of "real deal" of intimacy. This can leave them feeling entitled to intercourse in marriage, having paid the dues of "waiting" to get it. Plus, they have grown up in a social culture that portrays women as objects, rather than sexual beings also deserving of pleasure, further adding to men's neglect of the women they love and contributing to women's sexual boredom within marriages.

Just like women, men have also been taught by conservative Christian culture to suppress their sexual thoughts and actions. As a result, many men isolate themselves when they do find sexual outlets, be it through masturbation, pornography, or some other means. Long-term sexual isolation and shame cause men to feel insecure about their abilities as a lover and even more awkward when sexual conversations arise with their partner, leaving them unable to navigate a crucial element of learning to live and love together. Neither their church nor their culture has taught them the *art* of loving a woman, how women differ from men in sexual expression and desire, or how a flesh-and-blood woman is different from the porn they may have been watching on a screen. No one has given these men a mandate to make sure that their wife is receiving pleasure, nor has anyone taught them that good sex is measured by *more* than just how often intercourse happens and whether they both had an orgasm. Young Christian men and women don't know that erotic and sacred sexual experiences consist of much more than intercourse. Theologically, they've never been trained to reflect on *why* God might have given men and women their desires for sexual intimacy at all, what it might say about God's character that God invented sex, or even how men and women are wired differently as sexual creatures. They almost certainly haven't been trained in how to use sexuality as a vehicle for expressing God's love—God's *eros*—to the person who shares their bed. And they've not been directed to understand how the discipline and eroticism of sexual touch in a committed relationship is one of the most profound ways to practice and experience God's love in their *own* lives. In short, they're utterly foreign to sexuality on almost every level—biological, social, psychological, and spiritual—and they don't have a clue what to do.

The Perfectly Imperfect Couple

Here's an example of how this lack of preparation and abundance of shame can play out in the lives of two people.

At the time of their wedding, Philip and Sue, both 22 years old, were a beautiful, young, glowing couple. They had met each other at church during their senior year of college and were engaged by that following December. They had both grown up in Christian homes that were loving, if a bit rigid, and they had attended Christian grade schools and now a Christian college.

Philip had been an athlete both in high school and in college and had ranked high in his school's student government. By the time he graduated, he had already secured some important job connections in software management. Sue had been one of the popular girls in high school and an outstanding student in her own right. She studied theology and youth ministry in college and had secretly hoped that she would soon marry and have children, rather than pursuing a career in the professional realm.

In childhood, both Philip and Sue had been taught that sexual purity was a priority, and they had experienced a lot of fear and concern from their parents that this be upheld. When they met, both Philip and Sue were still virgins, but they each had significant relationships in the past that had "gone too far." Both of them felt a considerable amount of shame and wondered if God could ever forgive them or bless them with a Christian partner after having engaged in sexual behavior already.

When they started dating, they immediately fell head over heels for each other. Their chemistry was electric, which they saw as a sign that they were meant to be together. In their third month of dating, as it was becoming harder and harder to not be more intimate, Philip proposed to Sue. They set the wedding for June and each chose a mentor in their church who would help them stay accountable to not have sex before marriage. Their "accountability partners" were of great help reminding them that the wait would be worth it. Sue and Philip were able to refrain from intercourse before their wedding night, but each time they were together prior to the big day, they would be overcome with desire and felt ashamed at what they thought was their own weakness. Sue wondered if this was a reflection on Philip's inability to be the spiritual leader in their family. Philip secretly agreed, wondering whether maybe he wasn't as strong as he had thought. The dynamic made them both feel insecure—sexually, spiritually, and emotionally, all at the same time.

The first six months of marriage were bliss. Both had eagerly wanted to begin their life together and they loved every minute of it. Philip landed a great job with an international software firm and was quickly fast-tracked. Sue began working on the youth ministry team at her church and loved the balance of life and work and putting their home together.

Philip and Sue each described their sex life in the first six months as frequent and great. It had started out somewhat rough: not much warm-up, plus there was some pain for Sue and Philip went off too fast. But they eventually figured out how to slow down and learn about each other, which helped them to feel a sense of pride. Occasionally, Sue could reach orgasm during intercourse, which made her and Philip feel great. She said she missed the kissing and touching they did before they were married, but quickly added that "sex is great!"

By the end of the first year of marriage, life had begun to feel routine. Philip often worked late and would stop at the gym before coming home. Sue began to feel like it was time to have a baby. If the message for a good marriage in their church growing up was, "Just don't have sex before you are married," the message for a good marriage after a child was, "It will change your life, but you will love it."

Three years later, Sue was completely overwhelmed. Now the mother of a two-year-old and five months pregnant with twins, she felt like her life was all children, with no personal time, in addition to feeling overweight and depressed.

Meanwhile, Philip was now working long hours and had become emotionally distant. The two of them were rarely sexual, except for a perfunctory "quickie" now and again, and all forms of physical affection seemed to disappear. Philip was constantly frustrated with her and wondered why she had changed, was always irritable, and would deny him sex. He had come to a point where he didn't want anything to do with Sue, including sex.

For her part, Sue felt all alone without support, love, or understanding from Philip—that she was a failure. To her, other women seemed to be happy, and she was living the life that everyone said would be fulfilling. Why was she so miserable? She was scared and had the sensation of having disappeared. She called her best friend and asked how they could have done everything right only to have everything go so wrong. As it happened, Philip came home late that night and said that either they needed to fix the marriage or he was leaving.

Sex-Negativity Was Never Intended

While I know that variants of Philip and Sue's story have played out in the lives of innumerable people of differing backgrounds, what is of significance to me is that it never had to be this way. In my research, I found a treasure trove of ancient Hebrew writing with many sex-positive stories, narratives that bore witness to a God who had been intentional in the gift of sexual desire and sexual pleasure. If these texts were to be believed, then the generations of sexual suffering that Christians had experienced were never intended, and insofar as Christianity has its roots in Judaism, it meant that Christians actually have *within their spiritual DNA* all of the instruction, spiritual discipline, and practices that can prepare a couple for a sexually rewarding relationship, one that can maintain an intimate connection over the long haul. We will discuss the specifics of Judeo-Christian erotic teaching in more detail in Chapter 4, but for now the pivotal point is that the loss of this information in the development of the Western Christian church and much of contemporary culture has come at great and unnecessary cost to the sex lives of many. Knowing this, we can declare that it is time to understand what's going on, embrace the challenge of addressing it, and begin to help people to live into their desire for love, intimacy, and sexual communion the way they were meant to.

In various places throughout this book, I will offer stories of people who grew up in sex-positive, faith-based homes with comprehensive sexuality and gender education—or who did therapy to heal from religious sexual shame. These people grew to craft sexually and relationally satisfying lives. They don't necessarily look the same from person to person, but their relationships are pleasurable, connected, and shame-free.

What to Consider Before Working With Clients With Religious Sexual Shame

It can be a challenge as a therapist to work with someone who has what can appear to be an oppressive faith experience that has affected one's ability to give and receive love well, when you as the therapist may not have experienced the same culture firsthand. But if faith is a thing of value for this person, it is of utmost importance that you as a therapist bring *openness, respect, curiosity,* and *an accountability to how your own beliefs and values* may influence theirs (Grauf-Grounds et al. forthcoming). Our mission as therapists is to support our clients to live fully and abundantly into their integration of sexuality and spirituality, in a way that best serves their value systems and goals. In order to understand our clients' perspectives clearly, we must constantly bring these four qualities. Working with conservative Christians often triggers self-of-the-therapist issues, as their stories of oppression and shame are often evident during key developmental milestones in childhood and adolescence. For many, the healing process can look very similar to someone who has experienced childhood sexual abuse. And in much the same way, working with these clients can trigger countertransference in the therapist (as in, when the therapist, who may have experienced trauma or oppression in their own past, begins to "feel" personally triggered by their client's story). It is critical that the therapist be mindful of his or her own issues as he or she navigates therapy with these clients and seeks supervision and consultation whenever needed.

Looking Ahead

In this chapter, we've taken a look at some of the distinctives of conservative Christian young adults as a demographic group, and how their unique experiences of an overwhelmingly sex-negative culture can manifest in destructive ways in their dating and in their marital and sexual lives. In the next chapter, we'll venture into the actual history that unfolded in the development of Christianity as a formal religion so that we can understand what happened to derail it and turn it from a social justice movement into a religion that has struggled with sex-negativity and sexual oppression for the past 2,000 years. There is so much good around the world that has come from people who have fully embraced the heart and soul of Christianity and who truly live out their faith in the way they love, serve, and live as Jesus lived. In my view, it is largely because of them that God feels alive in our world. My life has been blessed by many Christians. But the story of the cost of sex-negativity and the purity movement has not come from that side of Christianity, but from the more rigid and institutional sides of the religion, the sides more susceptible to blindness and power abuses. It is these aspects of Christian history that we will explore next.

Notes

1. For more information on the hook-up culture, see Bogle (2008) and Stepp (2007).
2. For more information on the purity movement, watch the film *Give Me Sex Jesus* (Barber 2015), and read the book *Damaged Goods: New Perspectives on Christian Purity* (Anderson 2015).
3. See H. A. Paulsen (2007, 49–52).
4. The actual story this person remembers being told is attributed to H. Paulsen (2007).
5. According to the Hebrew Bible, Jezebel incited her husband, King Ahab, to abandon the worship of God. She later became associated with "painted women" or prostitutes. This is the contemporary meaning when used in the conservative church today to degrade women. See 1 Kings 16:29ff., 21:25; 2 Kings 9:30.

References

Anderson, Dianna E. 2015. *Damaged Goods: New Perspectives on Christian Purity*. New York, NY: Jericho.

Anne, Libby. 2012. What I Learned from Joshua Harris. In *Love, Joy, Feminism* (blog), accessed October 25, 2012. www.patheos.com/blogs/lovejoyfeminism/2012/10/what-i-learned-from-joshua-harris.html.

Barber, Matt, director. 2015. *Give Me Sex Jesus*. Film. SideHug Films. http://givemesexjesus.com/.

Bogle, Kathleen A. 2008. *Hooking Up: Sex, Dating and Relationships on Campus*. New York, NY: New York University Press.

Centers for Disease Control and Prevention. 2015. *National Marriage and Divorce Rate Trends*. Last updated November 23, 2015. http://1.usa.gov/1dMPvI2.

Daugherty, Jill, and Casey Copen. 2016. Trends in Attitudes about Marriage, Childbearing, and Sexual Behavior: United States, 2002, 2006–2010, and 2011–2013. *National Health Statistics Reports* 92. www.cdc.gov/nchs/data/nhsr/nhsr092.pdf.

Fisher, Linda L., Gretchen Anderson, Matrika Chapagain, Xenia Montenegro, James Smoot, and Amishi Takalkar. 2010. *Sex, Romance, and Relationships: AARP Survey of Midlife and Older Adults.* Washington, DC: AARP. http://assets.aarp.org/rgcenter/general/srr_09.pdf.

Freitas, Donna. 2008. *Sex and the Soul: Juggling Sexuality, Spirituality, Romance, and Religion on America's College Campuses.* Oxford, UK: Oxford University Press.

Grauf-Grounds, Claudia, Tina Schermer Sellers, Scott Edwards, Hee-Sun Cheon, Donald MacDonald, and Shawn Whitney. Forthcoming. *Attending to the In-Between: How Openness, Respect, Curiosity and Accountability Inform Our Clinical Work and Personal Lives.* New York, NY: Guilford.

Gudorf, Christine E. 1994. *Body, Sex, and Pleasure: Reconstructing Christian Sexual Ethics.* Cleveland, OH: Pilgrim.

Harris, Joshua. 1997. *I Kissed Dating Goodbye: A New Attitude toward Romance and Relationships.* Sisters, OR: Multnomah.

———. 2000. *Boy Meets Girl: Say Hello to Courtship.* Sisters, OR: Multnomah.

———. N.d. *Revisiting* I Kissed Dating Goodbye. Joshua Eugene Harris website, accessed August 31, 2016. http://joshharris.com/kissed-dating-goodbye/.

Kirby, Douglas. 2007. *Emerging Answers 2007: Research Findings on Programs to Reduce Teen Pregnancy and Sexually Transmitted Diseases.* Washington, DC: National Campaign to Prevent Teen and Unplanned Pregnancy. http://thenationalcampaign.org/sites/default/files/resource-primary-download/EA2007_full_0.pdf.

McClintock, Karen A. 2001. *Sexual Shame: An Urgent Call to Healing.* Minneapolis, MN: Fortress.

McKinley Irvin Family Law. 2012. 32 Shocking Divorce Statistics. In *Family Law Blog,* accessed October 30, 2012. www.mckinleyirvin.com/Family-Law-Blog/2012/October/32-Shocking-Divorce-Statistics.aspx.

Nelson, James B. 1992. *Body Theology.* Louisville, KY: Westminster/John Knox.

Paulsen, Heather. 2007. ID060—Emotional Purity. In *Issacharian Daughters* (blog), edited by Genevieve Smith. http://issacharian.com/index.php?mact=News,cntnt01,detail,0&cntnt01articleid=67&cntnt01dateformat=%25d%2F%25m%2F%25Y&cntnt01returnid=48.

Paulsen, Heather Arnel. 2007. *Emotional Purity: An Affair of the Heart.* Wheaton, IL: Crossway.

Powlison, David. 2005. Making All Things New: Restoring Pure Joy to the Sexually Broken. In *Sex and the Supremacy of Christ,* edited by John Piper and Justin Taylor, 65–106. Wheaton, IL: Crossway.

Russell, Cheryl. 2006. Does Religion Influence Sexual Behavior? In *Demo Memo: Demographic Trends with Attitude* (blog). http://demomemo.blogspot.com/2006/09/does-religion-influence-sexual.html.

Schaeffer, Frank. 2011. *Sex, Mom, and God: How the Bible's Strange Take on Sex Led to Crazy Politics, and How I Learned to Love Women (and Jesus) Anyway.* Cambridge, MA: Da Capo.

SIECUS (Sexuality Information and Education Council of the United States). 2005. *"I Swear I Won't!" A Brief Explanation of Virginity Pledges* (fact sheet), accessed August 30, 2016. www.siecus.org/index.cfm?fuseaction=Page.ViewPage&PageID=1202.

Stepp, Laura Sessions. 2007. *Unhooked: How Young Women Pursue Sex, Delay Love, and Lose at Both.* New York, NY: Riverhead.

2 How Did Christian Sexuality Get Derailed?

In 2006, I was asked to write an article for an online journal on the intersection of Christianity and sexuality (Schermer Sellers 2006). The editor had received my name from independent sources as a scholar who was inviting reflection on faith, the body, and sexuality in a unique way. I remember telling him that if I were to write what I had been learning from the sexual autobiographies of graduate students over the previous 17 years—about the vast pain and suffering of people who had been raised in rigid, patriarchal, and authoritarian Christian homes—I would probably make a lot of readers uncomfortable. I had seen far too much unnecessary pain, far too much self-hatred, and far too many unrealistic expectations for sex and marriage, and heard far too many painful stories from decisions and experiences out of this self-loathing and ignorance, to believe that what had been taught in most Christian homes and youth groups had anything to do with sexual, relational, or spiritual health. I found scant evidence of Christ's love and grace, little celebration for these young men and women as God's creation, and sparse awareness that they were beloved just as they were, *in* their bodies, *with* their desires, *with* their foolishness, *with* their hopes and dreams. I found intense ignorance about how their bodies developed, what was normal sexual curiosity at what age, how their bodies functioned and why, and what God's purpose was in giving them their desires and sexual longings in the first place. I heard pervasive stories of how they were punished for innocent body-curiosity play as children, which is a natural way children learn about their bodies. All conversation about touch and sexual curiosity was completely off-limits. They had learned early that if they brought up a sexual topic, they would likely get in trouble, and they would have to sit through feeling how uncomfortable their parents were with the topic. These dynamics weren't the case with *all* of my students or clients, of course—but it was true for the vast majority, probably well over 80 percent of them, from both religious and nonreligious homes.

After agreeing to write the article, I went searching to see if others had been writing about what I was seeing in the lives of my students and clients. What I was stunned to find was that for the preceding three decades, several ethicists and scholars in seminaries and universities across the nation had been calling for the development of a Christian sexual theology that rejects the body-soul dualism and instead represents what Jesus taught and died for: mutuality, justice, grace, and love for all. I found work by many different authors, pioneers in this field, like James Nelson, Beverly Harrison, Christine Gudorf, Merry Wiesner-Hanks, L. William Countryman, Lisa Sowle-Cahill, David Carr, Carey Ellen Walsh, Margaret Farley, and others. These works were intelligently researched and written, and they'd been sitting on library shelves for a generation—and yet for reasons I did not understand, they hadn't made it into the hands of everyday people and church communities.

Christine Gudorf, a professor of philosophy and religion at Florida International University, wrote a stunning book in 1994 called *Body, Sex and Pleasure: Reconstructing Christian Sexual Ethics*, in which she takes a thorough look at the ramifications of building a culture and religious movement on a split of soul and mind from body. "Our society," she writes,

> is in a crisis over sexuality, in part because the churches have been paralyzed by fear of stepping away from the confines of the Christian sexual tradition to develop a responsible sexual ethic which not only fits with our scientific and experiential insights into sexuality, but which better accords with our understanding of the central revelations of the gospel. Society looks to churches to provide moral guidance for public policy in many areas, but especially in sexuality, since the churches have long claimed proprietary interest in sexual behavior. The unwillingness of the churches to risk abandoning a familiar but unworkable sexual ethic has left the broader society without effective moral guidance on sexuality at a time when more and more public policy issues involve sexuality.
>
> (Gudorf 1994, 1)

Gudorf lays the concern out clearly: the church has the history and power to play an important, guiding role in the area of sexual health for society as a whole. Esther Perel, a well-known couples therapist, describes the cost to a couple's intimacy when sex has been socially scandalized. It creates a kind of dissonance, a lack of ease around intimacy. "Taboo-ridden sexuality and excess-driven sexuality converge in a troubling way," Perel writes in *Mating in Captivity*.

> Both lead us to want to dissociate psychically from the physical act of sex. A society that sees sex as soiled does not make sex go away. Instead, this kind of anxious atmosphere breeds guilt and shame in its more extreme version, or a generalized discomfort in its more ubiquitous expression. Sex is divorced from emotional and social continuity.
>
> (Perel 2006, 92)

When sexual expression is separated from emotional, social, and spiritual expression, people are denied intimacy with self, with other, and with their God, and the cost has been profound for our clients and for our culture.

Two Millennia of Sexual Baggage—And What to Do About It

In this chapter I'd like to provide a bit of history so that you can glimpse the evolution of the sex-negative sexual ethics that has continued to inform Christianity even into today. When we are working with clients, it can be helpful to understand the bigger picture and to see the sociopolitical forces at play, hopefully with some measure of objectivity.

Over the last decade as I have been doing this research, I've come to appreciate the impact that culture and politics have in shaping religious discourse, and thus the people we serve. Many of the Christians whom I've served have not known much of the history of Christian sexual ethics, and they may have accepted certain mandates as truth rather than understanding them as constructed beliefs that are situated in a sociopolitical time and place. The experience of most of my clients and students involved being steeped in a particular church family and community that provided a particular religious narrative about bodies and sexuality. This narrative, however, was usually delivered as though it were the absolute truth of God for all time, rather than as having been shaped across time and history or located in a place and an era.

For example, some of my students are surprised when I tell them that I spent my teen years in the middle of the "Jesus movement" in Southern California, going to Christian rock concerts on the weekends with hundreds of other kids from around the region. The central focus of the Jesus movement seemed to be the "rapture" (an end-times belief that Christian believers would suddenly be taken up to be with Jesus) and who had the best Jesus-saved-me-from-drugs testimony. The sociopolitical culture of the 1970s was relatively sex-positive, as was the Christian church at the time. As far as I could tell, the message was essentially this: "Don't have sex until you are married. If you decide to have sex before, make sure you are in a committed, loving relationship and use protection." By the 2000s, however, my clients and students under 35 had grown up in something entirely different, the purity movement (see Chapter 1), an ascetic, abstinence-only movement whose central focus was sex-negative "purity" at all costs.

The Early Centuries—Relegating the Body to the Shadows

Early Christianity spans from the crucifixion and resurrection of Jesus to the First Council of Nicaea (325 CE). These were tumultuous years. The Romans destroyed the Jerusalem temple in 72 CE, and later the once-mighty empire would crumble at about the same time that early Christianity, under extreme persecution, was beginning to form (Brown 1988, 41).

The young Christian movement was centered first in Jerusalem, led by James the Just, who had been considered one of the 12 Apostles and may have been a relative of Jesus. James was martyred around 62 CE, and Jews were banned from the city around 135, all of which weakened the early

Jerusalem church. The Roman Empire from the first and second centuries forward was marked by growing moral strictness to match the corresponding rigidity in society and politics. Christianity, perhaps more influenced by the dramatic social climate and the rampant cultural fear of this time, exalted celibacy and condemned nonprocreative sex.

It was during the reign of Constantine (306–337 CE) that this early strand of Christianity became the favored religion of the Roman Empire. This was the beginning of Western Christianity as we know it. So what kind of "Christian" sexual ethics materialized from the era of Constantine and beyond, and who were its main influencers? How did we come to develop a theology of sexuality that elevated the efforts of spiritual and intellectual growth while simultaneously denouncing, rejecting, and shaming the body and its sensual and sexual desires for touch and intimacy? This is a critical question when we consider that Christianity centers around a deeply embodied event: God's restoration of God's people through the incarnation of Jesus—flesh and bone, skin and hair, walking and talking and breathing and living among the people as God-among-us. If God's ministry is manifested in a human body, God the embodied Son, Jesus of Nazareth, then why has the Christian church maintained a conscience that continually disparages God's chosen avenue for redemption—the human body?

The Spirit/Mind Is Good; the Body Is Bad

Greco-Roman culture at the time of Jesus was patriarchal and hierarchical. Education, money, and power belonged to men, especially men of privilege. Women were an active part of society and may have been advisors in the background, but they weren't visible or prominent in the written and oral history of the time (Farley 2006, 35–6).

Plato (428–348 BCE) and Aristotle (384–322 BCE) were two of the most influential philosophers of ancient Greece. Their influence set the stage in cultural and political influence for 400 years before the birth of Jesus and for centuries following. Central to their philosophy was the belief that the realm of ideas was far superior to the realm of the visible and material world. Plato, in particular, had a fundamental distrust of the observable world, a belief that emphasized that the mind and the soul were trapped in the material body. In this school of thought, the drives of the body were seen as crude distractions from the higher, nobler pursuits of reason and the mind. The soul and mind, not trapped in time and space like the body, were able to access universal truth, and it was these ideas and abstractions that were understood to be the true reality (Farley 2006, 32).

This invisible reality often stood in contrast with the sexual relationships some Greek elite philosophers like Demosthenes and Plato had with their young, adoring male students. Teachers justified the relationships as mutual appreciation: the teacher appreciated the inherent beauty of a young male body (which was understood in that era to be the most beautiful human form), and the students were said to appreciate the ability to pursue the higher

This is missed up. The "teachers" sexually manipulated these young men or boys.

mind and goals with a great teacher. Once the student reached an adult age and of a higher intellectual ability, the relationship became "platonic," or nonsexual. In time, Plato was said to have preferred to transcend sex through self-discipline (Farley 2006, 31). Other Greek philosophers grew to distrust sexual desire, placing an inferior status on sexual pleasure as compared to other human pleasures. It was the realm of ideas, reason, intellect, and knowledge that was the arena of the highest calling (Wiesner-Hanks 2000, 25). Though other philosophers in Western culture hinted at the mind-body split, it was those in the Platonic traditions who were the most responsible for developing this idea, thus laying the foundation for the dualism to become a central thread in Western philosophy from that time forward (Farley 2006, 112). Eventually, many Christian thinkers would adopt and adapt these ideas into theology as well (see Foucault 1978–85, vols. 1–2). St. Augustine, for example, saw the mind and body as separate yet inseparable parts of what it meant to be human. While the soul and mind need the body for its ability to give perceptual data, the body needs to be ruled by the soul and mind (Farley 2006, 32). As religious thought morphed over time, some religions emphasized the distinctions of soul and body, while others emphasized the unity. What we see overall, however, is how many philosophical perspectives were absorbed into developing theologies of the body with striking resemblance. The challenge with theories and beliefs that elevate soul over body is that dualisms breed hierarchies, which in turn often lead to abuses of power, which are fundamentally unjust and would have been antagonistic to Jesus's ministry.

Sealing the Mind/Body Split in Christian Theology

It is important to remember that Christianity did not begin with an established code of sexual ethics. The teaching of Jesus, as recorded in the Gospels, provided the basis of a moral life in the command to love God and to treat one's neighbor with love and grace (Farley 2006, 37–8; Matthew 22:37–39; Mark 12:28–31; Deuteronomy 6:5, Leviticus 19:18). But the entire New Testament was written over the span of about a century, and by the time its latest books were written, the moral and sexual ethics of the Christian movement had morphed into something that provided a lot of room for cultural, philosophical, social, and political influences and upheavals to shape a "Christian" sexual ethic. Judaism brought the theistic approach that said there was one God. Stoicism, the idea that logic, reflection, and self-discipline were of highest value, furthered the mind-body split and deepened suspicions of bodily passion while assuring an emphasis on reason as a moral guide. Patriarchalism, a social principle around which these early societies were organized, impressed upon the early Christian teachers a view of women as inferior to men, despite Christ's demonstrated value of equality between the genders (e.g., see Luke 7:36–50 and John 4:1–42).

The stories of Jesus's relationships with women in the Gospels are in stark contrast to some of what was said about women by early church leaders over the first few centuries of Christianity. Here are some examples.

- Tertullian (the Father of Latin Christianity, 155–245 CE): "Do you not know that you are (each) an Eve? The sentence of God on this sex of yours lives in this age: the guilt must of necessity live too. You are the devil's gateway: you are the unsealer of that (forbidden) tree: you are the first deserter of the divine law: you are she who persuaded him whom the devil was not valiant enough to attack. You destroyed so easily God's image, man. On account of your desert—that is, death—even the Son of God had to die. And do you think about adorning yourself over and above your tunics of skins?" (Tertullian 202 CE, I.1:82–85).

  Origen (theologian and Greek Father, second and third centuries CE): "Men should not sit and listen to a woman . . . even if she says admirable things, or even saintly things, that is of little consequence, since it came from the mouth of a woman" (Origen, quoted in Jenkins 1908, 241–2).

  St. Augustine of Hippo (354–430 CE): "What is the difference whether it is in a wife or a mother; it is still Eve the temptress that we must be aware of in any woman. . . . I fail to see what use woman can be to man, if one excludes the function of bearing children" (Augustine, quoted in Brundage 1987, 85).

There are many more examples to be found throughout the development of church history, but suffice it to say, I believe it is important for us to see how the socio-cultural and political influence of the mind-body split and the patriarchy of this time had a profound influence, blocking the message of the Gospel of Jesus as it pertained to how the body, women, and marginalized people were to be understood.

   This then influenced the church's ability to form a sexual ethic built on how mutuality, grace, mercy, justice, and love could be demonstrated between two committed people. Rather than forming a clear sexual ethic built on these values, what emerged instead was based on rules and behaviors, a series of do's and do-not's that paid no attention to the effect of those behaviors on the people or the relationships involved (Brown 1998, 41–4).

The Intervening Years

The years of the writing and gathering of the Gospels and Epistles of the New Testament Scriptures were chaotic and tense. The Romans had destroyed Jerusalem and the Temple in 72 CE and the whole region was devastated as a result. "In the Gospels we meet, not the world of Jesus, but the very different, more tense world of his disciples," wrote Peter Brown in *The Body and Society*. "The stories in them had been collected in that terrible period to meet the needs and to validate the activities of a group of wandering preachers who claimed to be his true followers" (Brown 1988, 41). Sixty years after the crucifixion of Jesus, the profiles of the Christian communities across Syria

[handwritten margin note:] this reminds me of the greek orthodox nun who attributed male lust to women · nun because days.

and Palestine were vague, and it was still unclear who would most effectively represent the many churches of Christ (Brown 1988, 41–4).

By the end of the second century, Christian communities were scattered to all four corners of the Roman world. Starting from Lyons in the west to Dura Europos near the Euphrates in the east, it would take at least 80 days of travel to reach some of these communities, making it nearly impossible for there to be a complete meeting of the minds on any issue, simply because it would have been impossible to communicate in real-time like we can today (Brown 1988, 64). Asceticism, the high value and struggle against worldly desires and wealth, was a value embraced by many of the followers of Jesus during the first centuries. Property, for example, was held in common as a counterpoint to how the world valued private ownership. Virginity and fasting were common, along with other forms of renouncing the flesh. These early ascetics were a foreshadowing of the monasticism that arose in the third century in Egypt and beyond. "Do not love the world or the things in the world," says the book of 1 John (2:15), an idea that these early ascetics took literally (Brown 1988, 43). You can read of some who, moved by the spirit of God, dedicated their lives to the spread of the Gospel, giving up all their possessions and moving from city to city in voluntary poverty, taking care of the poor or evangelizing (Brown 1988, 43). The apostle Paul, a Greek-speaking Jew, who was the preeminent voice in shaping Christianity after the death of Jesus and author of many of the letters of the New Testament, focused his ministry on the Gentiles and pagans. His message had a kind of urgency, which unfortunately infiltrated his view of the body and sexual desire. Rather than exhibiting the warm faith shown by the Jews and pagans that the sexual urge, although unruly, was capable of loving, ordered expression within marriage, his teaching on sexual ethics focused more on *pornea*, on the potential immortality brought about by sexual frustration (Brown 1988, 55). By allowing the negative to have center stage, Paul left a fatal legacy to future ages, putting an alarmist shadow around sexuality inside Christianity, one that keeps people focused on marrying early, lest they succumb to sexual temptation (e.g., see 1 Corinthians 7:9). The unfortunate reality, according to Peter Brown, is that Paul was not greatly concerned at that time about the avoidance of fornication; he was much more interested in the continuity and validity of social bonds, like the structure of the household (1988, 55).

As we saw with Paul, the cultural ideas and concerns of a particular area would influence other teachers as well. In her book *Just Love: A Framework for a Christian Sexual Ethics*, Margaret Farley describes the confusing and some-times conflicting sexual ethic that appears throughout the New Testament as a result. This is an ethic that

1) Values marriage and procreation on the one hand and singleness and celibacy on the other; 2) Gives as much or more importance to internal

attitudes and thoughts as to external actions and 3) Affirms a sacred symbolic meaning for sexual intercourse, yet both subordinates it as a value to other human values and finds in it a possibility for evil.

(Farley 2006, 38)

This beginning is the backdrop as we enter the more organized formation of the church in the fourth century.

Early church fathers like Origen (185–254 CE) and later Augustine (354–430 CE) became convinced that Plato and Aristotle were teachers whose techniques could be used to draw people to faith in Jesus Christ. Steeped in Platonic thought and without an intention to lead people astray, their reliance on these philosophical underpinnings significantly distracted and diluted the Christian faith.

During this time, the practice of Christian monasticism began to arise as well in various forms. The basic idea at the heart of monasticism is self-abnegation and organized asceticism. The first groups to emerge in the first century were the Essenes and the Therapeutae, who were the precursors to the more formal monastic orders that developed later. These groups took their inspiration from the lives of John the Baptist and Elijah, who both lived in the desert alone, and also from the 40 days in the wilderness when Jesus struggled with Satan (Matthew 4:1–11, Mark 1:12–13, Luke 4:1–13).

Augustine was given tremendous power by Constantine, the emperor, as Christianity became the privileged religious institution in the fourth century and beyond. Some scholars say that between 245 and 529 CE, the gap between what was Christian theology and what was philosophical thought was nearly indistinguishable, thanks to well-meaning Christian writers like Origen, Clement of Alexandria, Augustine, and Pseudo-Dionysius, thus sealing the mind–body split in Christian theology (Viola and Barna 2008, 203). By the fourth century, celibacy, the ultimate expression of the mind's control over the body, had become both a symbol for religious elitism and an instrument of influence. Followers of Christianity, as it had developed to this point, saw this kind of restraint as a form of physical heroism equivalent to a martyr facing down death. By concentrating on sexual restraint and on sexual heroism, Christian leaders could show that they were the bearers of a truly universal religion (Brown 1988, 60). Emperor Constantine, after legalizing Christianity, bestowed upon the Christian bishops more power within their dioceses, and Christian ideas began to shape both imperial law and judicial practice. At this same time, church leaders became even stronger proponents of asceticism (radical practices of self-denial, including sexual behavior, and other rigorous regulations on bodily desires) (Brown 1988, 61–4).

But it is Augustine who is considered the second most influential figure in early Christian theology, next to Paul. While many thinkers influenced the church before Augustine, it is Augustine's intellectual thread that is woven across how Christianity is understood and practiced in much of the world to this day, particularly in the area of sexuality.

Saint Augustine: A Sexually Troubled Soul

Prior to becoming a Christian, Augustine had joined a religious group known as the Manichaeans, a dualistic, ascetic religion that combined Christianity, Platonism, Gnosticism,[1] and several other schools of thought. Among other ideas, Manichaeans believed that sexual desire was innately evil and that procreation imprisoned the soul. "For Augustine the Manichaean *auditor*, sexuality and society were antithetical," writes Peter Brown in *Body and Society*.

> Only in a "true church," composed of the continent Elect, would a true society be found in the form of a light-filled harmony of souls set free from matter. Intercourse, and especially intercourse undertaken to produce children, collaborated with the headlong expansion of the Kingdom of Darkness at the expense of the spiritual purity associated with the Kingdom of Light.
>
> (Brown 1988, 391)

Manichaeans sought to reach the level of the most advanced believers, the Adepts, who could renounce both sexual activity *and* sexual thoughts (Wiesner-Hanks 2000, 31).

Augustine strongly condemned himself for never being able to exercise this level of discipline. After becoming a bishop, Augustine boldly denounced the sect, but it is clear from his writings that the suspicion of both sexual activity and sexual desire continued to influence him. Augustine believed that sexual desire was the one human desire that eclipsed both reason and will. Augustine believed that "desire was the result of human sinfulness and disobedience to God," writes Merry Wiesner-Hanks in *Christianity and Sexuality in the Early Modern World*,

> and hence only God's grace could allow one to overcome it or any other human weakness. Augustine's attitude toward sexuality was thus connected to his very negative view of human nature. In his view, no other after Adam and Eve had free will; original sin was transmitted to all humans through semen emitted in sexual acts motivated by desire, and was thus inescapable.
>
> (Wiesner-Hanks 2000, 31)

At times, Augustine clearly identified sexual pleasure and the desire for it with evil concupiscence (Kelly 1983). As he disparaged the appetites of human nature, he discounted the goodness of the Creator. Wiesner-Hanks goes on to point out that Augustine saw female subordination as intrinsic to God's design in creation, for only men were fully created in the image of God. She quotes Augustine from the *Contra Mendacium* as saying, "The body of a man is as superior to that of a woman as the soul is to the body" (Augustine, quoted in Wiesner-Hanks 2000, 31).

While Augustine offered much that was foundational in the formation of Christian theology, sexual desire and his own desire for women, which he never was able to completely escape, tortured him until the end. His legacy of shame, fear of the body, and suspicion of its desires is with us today. From the sixth century to the eleventh, Augustine's rationale was institutionalized as church documents were written. According to Margaret Farley, a "Christian" sexual ethic was detailed in the *Penitentials*, the manuals for the guidance of confessors. This church doctrine laid out a detailed list of sexual sins and their prescribed penances "with detailed prohibitions against adultery, fornication, oral and anal sex, masturbation, and even certain positions for sexual intercourse if they were thought to be departures from the procreative norm" (Farley 2006, 41). Picking up where the *Penitentials* left off, Gratian, a twelfth-century canon lawyer from Bologna (the center of the study of canon law and civil law), compiled an exhaustive study of canonical law using early scholastic methodology. His compilation, the *Concordia Discordantium Canonum*, later called the *Decretum*, included (in addition to Scripture) Catholic and church council legislation, the writings of church fathers, such as Augustine, and secular law, in an effort to reconcile the canon discrepancies. This collection of canon law "contained regulations based on the persistently held principle that all sexual activity is evil unless it is between husband and wife and for the sake of procreation" (Farley 2006, 41).

The Reformation, 1517–1648

The Reformation is another time in history when Christianity was treated as an intellectual endeavor filled with reason and devoid of "soft" ideas like faith or belief. Rationalistic and theoretical thought was held in the highest esteem, and gaining knowledge in and about one's faith was seen as a way to distinguish oneself. As a result, the mind-body split, already deeply present in Western philosophy and Christian theology, was further cemented into the collective thought of Christianity. Theological pursuits of the mind were highly valued, while emotions, the body, desires, and experiences were seen as untrustworthy, irrelevant, primitive, and dangerous. Sexual desire and women continued to be assigned negative attributes well into the Reformation. By this time, marriage was seen as a kind of necessary remedy for a person's disordered sex drive. Therefore, while marriage was seen as good, as was sex within in it, there was still an Augustinian, pessimistic aura around sexual desire. Martin Luther (sixteenth-century German priest, theologian, and Protestant Reformer) said this about women:

> The woman certainly differs from the man, for she is weaker in body and intellect. Nevertheless Eve was an excellent creature and equal to Adam so far as the divine image, that is, righteousness, wisdom and eternal salvation, is concerned. Still, she was only a woman. As the sun is much more glorious than the moon (though also the moon is glorious), so the woman was inferior to the man both in honor and dignity, though she, too, was a very excellent work of God.
>
> (Luther 1904, 124)

It is interesting to note that it was during this time that René Descartes (1596–1650) was making his mark on the world. Descartes, a French philosopher and early scientist, is credited as one of the major figures in both continental rationalism and the scientific revolution. The heart of rationalism says that truth can be known only through the intellect and deductive reasoning. He had profound influence on the sciences and also on medicine, which has its own long tradition in the mind-body split. Medical science through the centuries has centered on the notion that the body is not connected to the emotions or thoughts of a patient. It has been only in the last 40 years or so that Western medical science has begun to acknowledge that what happens to the body affects and is affected by the mind, soul, and relationships of a patient. Since the de-integration of the body from the heart, mind, and relationships has had a profound effect on our health and well-being in areas other than just our sexuality, I will discuss this in more detail in other areas of this book.

Søren Kierkegaard (1813–1855), the Danish philosopher and theologian, was one of the few voices speaking out against the hierarchy and structure within the church, an arrangement that was replicating the very religious and political structure that Christ admonished. "Christ did not appoint professors, but followers," wrote Kierkegaard. "If Christianity . . . is not reduplicated in the life of the person expounding it, then he does not expound Christianity, for Christianity is a message about living and can only be expounded by being realized in men's lives" (Kierkegaard 1960, 141).

Applications for the Believing Christian

While there are many other significant figures who added their texture to the traditional Christian sexual ethic that we see today, what is important to understand is that throughout history, the gift of our bodies and the gift of sexuality have generally been seen as evil, sinful, and not of God. Bodies, along with their sensations and desires, were not only suspect but also actually thought to be an interference in one's spiritual life and the function of the spirit of God within a believer. In short, while organizing and institutionalizing one of the most valuable faith structures of the human race, those who influenced its formation inadvertently recreated a religious structure that privileged strict, ascetic standards and the denial of the body. According to the research of Peter Brown, the Western church had turned from the contemplation of God to building a society ruled by the iron constraints of the "law of Adam" (Brown 1988, 80–2)—a church that looked surprisingly similar to the one characterized by the religious authorities of Jesus's time. In so doing, they lost sight of Christ's message, which focused on the values of justice, grace, and love, and was demonstrated in and through his incarnated human body. In its most self-serving expressions, this is exactly the kind of abuse of power that Jesus stood against. In failing to understand the body, sexuality, the desire for connection and pleasure, and the lived and embodied experience, Christianity lost what could have been 2,000 years of learning what it means to use the senses to love like Jesus did: loving one's partner, one's children, one's neighbor, those difficult to love, and the created world. Christianity lost the opportunity to understand the image of God within the body and within sexuality. It lost centuries of collective practice in how to love one's partner in a way that expands both parties' capacities for love and grace. Christianity turned away from the rich wisdom of its Hebrew heritage, forgetting crucial, celebratory thought regarding the body, relationality, sexuality, and God's passionate desire for communion with the human race. The church lost 20 centuries of sacred, erotic lovemaking. That's two millennia of valuing, caring for, and celebrating the gift of the body that allows the expression of one's deepest longings, desires, and emotions in the context of love—the desire to be seen, known, loved, and accepted in all ways possible.

"The Christian Scriptures naturally have embodiment at their heart," write Lisa Isherwood and Elizabeth Stuart in their book, *Introducing Body Theology.*

> From the moment when Mary agrees to give birth to a special child, bodies become sites of revelation and redemptive action. Jesus' mission is begun with touch, by water and by a dove. People are touched and healed, they are forgiven and healed. The dead are raised and a woman shows her love through anointing, kissing and massaging Jesus' feet with her tears. The life of Jesus as told by the evangelists is a very physical one; he was not a philosopher simply engaging the minds of people on his wandering through the land. Here was a man who held people, threw things in anger, cursed things making them wither and cherished people back to life. Here was an incarnate/embodied being.
>
> (Isherwood and Stuart 1998, 11)

The Effects Downstream

Inside and outside the church, immense suffering, ignorance, and confusion are playing havoc with people's sexual lives. When Gudorf speaks of what is not working within our churches, what she is saying is that the prevailing message of "don't have sex until you are married" comes with no context, no body-awareness, no integrated teaching of faith, culture, and the body, and no ongoing sex-and-relationship education as children grow into their adult years. To put it simply: children and adolescents do not need *one* 100-minute (awkward and painful) sexual health conversation; they need *100* one-minute conversations. They need sexual and relational education delivered in many, many sound bites, *weekly*, across their entire childhood and teen years. How is a child or an adolescent who has a deep love for God to understand their anatomy, their beliefs, their wants, their desires, or their changing body without a constant series of conversational stepping-stones throughout their formative years? Healthy sexual-emotional development, rooted in God's good intentions for sexuality, takes place with well-integrated, age-appropriate, and ongoing conversations that integrate knowledge about sex, eros, desire, gender, power, relationships, and God's hopes for them, in small segments, over a long period of time, as the subjects naturally emerge in life.

A Primer in Christian Sexual Ethics

Some Christian ethicists use a Wesleyan framework, arguing that there are four interweaving sources of God's revelation: scripture, tradition, reason, and experience (Nelson 1992). "The entire conversation about ethics, sexual or other, needs to be placed in the context of spirituality," warns William Countryman.

> The New Testament discourse about the Fruits of the Spirit (e.g. Galatians 5:22–23; James 3:13–18) suggest that we are not simply concerned about conformity, but about how the living out of sexual ethics serves to encourage growth and a maturing spirituality. The rules are a means to an end, not ultimate truths in their own right. An overemphasis on the rules, as opposed to life in the Spirit, leads to a dry rigidity that is the very opposite of the good news of the Gospel.
>
> (Countryman 2007, 256)

This focus on following the rules also asks people to be passive recipients in their faith development, as though "here are the directions, now follow them" were a comprehensive guide for teaching people how to live as physical beings. For years, people have remained passive participants in their faith and in their church communities. They have followed rules and participated in community. It was as if the church were filling the mind and ignoring the hunger of the body and soul, the messier parts of our human existence. Not surprisingly, in much of the West, we have been seeing two seemingly paradoxical phenomena at the same time: a simultaneous hunger for a spirituality that engages us, along with a significant drop in the mainline Protestant church (Wellman, Jr. 2008, 3). Following rules or living a passive faith is not feeding this hunger. But fortunately, according to the Christian message from the Old Testament and from early church history, this was never what God intended.

As you may hear from your clients, spirituality is about personal engagement, critical thinking, deep "within" listening, and interacting fully and honestly with our community. For your clients who describe a personal faith, they may speak about God wanting them to engage their faith with passion, and to have a desire to grow in relationship with him. As we will learn in our walk through ancient Hebrew teaching later in the book, Yahweh, as Judeo-Christian heritage has understood, is a personal God. Isaiah 30:18 says that Yahweh longs to be gracious, compassionate, and just. God wants an intimate, dynamic relationship with God's people, and God wants people to become intimately acquainted to the movements of the spirit within them. There is something wonderful about letting oneself imagine and feel the desire to live with passionate abandon into the fruit of the spirit ("love, joy, peace, patience, kindness, generosity, faithfulness, gentleness, and self-control," Galatians 5:22–23)—and with this passion to invite God to participate in one's life.

Helping Our Clients to Think It Over

As we will learn in looking at both Judaism and the teachings of Jesus, there exists no dualism: one part of creation is not made good while another part is made bad. In Judaism we find a deep belief in the goodness of all of God's creation *and* celebrations that honor the body, sexual intimacy, and commitment, and the Old Testament is loaded with examples of how the Hebrew people delight in love, desire, and intimacy, all in vivid sensory detail. In their wisdom all people are called to live out loud, to celebrate their gratitude for the gift of the body and its ability to demonstrate the heart that is within it. Jesus and his ministry also gave no hint of dualistic thinking, but instead gave one of the most important endorsements of all: God the Father sent his Son *in the flesh* to be among the people—and to be for all people (see, e.g., Matthew 15:21–28, 18:18–20)—to teach them, to show them, to touch and to love them. In Jesus they were given all the demonstration they needed to know how to live fully *in their bodies* and fully commit *to actions of love and justice*. Christians are invited to embrace all of Jesus's teachings in the example of how he lived, become more aware of history's influence on their perspectives, and work to shed the parts that are contrary to the life to which Jesus invited them.

A Sex-Positive Gospel

This book, like some of the works and authors I mentioned earlier, is part of an effort to set the record straight. We live in a sociopolitical time where there is room for the truth of a sex-positive Jesus and a sex-positive Gospel message built around his body. We are coming out of some of the most extreme asceticism of recent years, as seen in the purity movement, and we need informed clinicians who can gently help to heal people's religious sexual trauma while still holding on to what is core and precious to them about their faith. This may involve teasing apart religious doctrine from core spiritual faith values and beliefs, and it may also involve a roller coaster of emotions like betrayal, anger, grief, and sadness before any feelings of liberation emerge. But they will, and when they do, it's like spreading wings that are wide, colorful, and wildly alive.

Note

1. Gnosticism is a term representing a collection of ancient religions whose core tenant was to shun the material world and embrace the spiritual world. Gnostic ideas influenced many ancient religions, including early Christianity, with their belief that knowledge was obtained through enlightenment, salvation, and practicing poverty and sexual abstinence. On the complexity of Gnosticism, see Hurtado (2005, 519–561).

References

Brown, Peter. 1988. *Body and Society: Men, Women, and Sexual Renunciation in Early Christianity*. New York, NY: Columbia University Press.

Brundage, James A. 1987. *Law, Sex, and Christian Society in Medieval Europe*. Chicago, IL: University of Chicago Press.

Countryman, L. William. 2007. *Dirt, Greed, and Sex: Sexual Ethics in the New Testament and Their Implications for Today*, rev. ed. Minneapolis, MN: Fortress.

Farley, Margaret A. 2006. *Just Love: A Framework for Christian Sexual Ethics*. New York, NY: Continuum.

Foucault, Michel. 1978–85. *The History of Sexuality*, vols. 1–2. Translated by Robert Hurley. New York, NY: Pantheon.

Gudorf, Christine E. 1994. *Body, Sex, and Pleasure: Reconstructing Christian Sexual Ethics*. Cleveland, OH: Pilgrim.

Hurtado, Larry W. 2005. *Lord Jesus Christ: Devotion to Jesus in Earliest Christianity*. Grand Rapids, MI: Eerdmans.

Isherwood, Lisa, and Elizabeth Stuart. 1998. *Introducing Body Theology*. Sheffield, UK: Sheffield Academic Press.

Jenkins, Claude. 1908. Origen on I Corinthians. *Journal of Theological Studies* 9 (34): 231–47.

Kelly, David F. 1983. Sexuality and Concupiscence in Augustine. *Annual of the Society of Christian Ethics* 3: 81–116.

Kierkegaard, Søren. 1960. *The Diary of Søren Kierkegaard*. Edited by Peter P. Rohde. Translated by Gerda M. Anderson. New York, NY: Philosophical Library.

Luther, Martin. 1904. *Luther on the Creation: A Critical and Devotional Commentary on Genesis* [1–3]. Translated by John Nicholas Lenker. Minneapolis, MN: Lutherans In All Lands.

Nelson, James B. 1992. Sources for Body Theology: Homosexuality as a Test Case (Chapter 4). In *Body Theology*, 55–71. Louisville, KY: Westminster/John Knox.

Perel, Esther. 2006. *Mating in Captivity: Reconciling the Erotic and the Domestic*. New York, NY: HarperCollins.

Schermer Sellers, Tina. 2006. Christians Caught between the Sheets—How 'Abstinence Only' Ideology Hurts Us. *The Other Journal* 7. http://theotherjournal.com/2006/04/02/christians-caught-between-the-sheets-how-abstinence-only-ideology-hurts-us/.

Tertullian. Ca. 202 CE. *On the Apparel of Women*. Translated by S. Thelwall. Christian Classics Ethereal Library. www.ccel.org/ccel/schaff/anf04.iii.iii.i.i.html.

Viola, Frank, and George Barna. 2008. *Pagan Christianity?: Exploring the Roots of Our Church Practices*, rev. ed. Carol Stream, IL: Barna.

Wellman, James K., Jr. 2008. *Evangelical vs. Liberal: The Clash of Christian Cultures in the Pacific Northwest*. Oxford, UK: Oxford University Press.

Wiesner-Hanks, Merry. 2000. *Christianity and Sexuality in the Early Modern World: Regulating Desire, Reforming Practice*. New York, NY: Routledge.

3 American Consumerism

I came that they may have life, and have it abundantly.

—John 10:10

Buying and Selling Sex, Religion, and People

I begin this chapter with four quotes from Wendell Berry, the American novelist, activist, and farmer. More than almost anyone else, Berry could sum up everything I could say about how American culture has played into the mind–body split and added a dose of capitalism for good measure. Our culture's act of turning people into objects and then selling them has had a profound effect on sexuality and intimacy, something that we will explore in this chapter.

> Whether we and our politicians know it or not, Nature is party to all our deals and decisions, and she has more votes, a longer memory, and a sterner sense of justice than we do.
>
> (Berry 1995, iv)

> Especially among Christians in positions of wealth and power, the idea of reading the Gospels and keeping Jesus' commandments as stated therein has been replaced by a curious process of logic. According to this process, people first declare themselves to be followers of Christ, and then they assume that whatever they say or do merits the adjective "Christian."
>
> (Berry 2005a, 3)

> A community is the mental and spiritual condition of knowing that the place is shared, and that the people who share the place define and limit the possibilities of each other's lives. It is the knowledge that people have of each other, their concern for each other, their trust in each other, the freedom with which they come and go among themselves.
>
> (Berry 2012, 71)

People use drugs, legal and illegal, because their lives are intolerably painful or dull. They hate their work and find no rest in their leisure. They are estranged from their families and their neighbors. It should tell us something that in healthy societies drug use is celebrative, convivial, and occasional, whereas among us it is lonely, shameful, and addictive. We need drugs, apparently, because we have lost each other.

(Berry 2002, 98)

The Soul-Body Split in American Culture

As I studied the ramifications of the mind-body split, I eventually found myself examining how it was playing out today in our secular culture, and what effect the split was having on our sexual and relational health. What I had come to notice was that while culture was having its own particular effect, *the pace and values of our culture*, including the mind-body dualism, were detracting from people's experience of intimacy.

Constance was a brilliant young executive. She was driven, disciplined, sharp as a tack, and a person for whom life moved at the speed of light. Like the athlete she had always been, she was at the top of her game and had confidence in her ability to stay there. Being well respected in her field, colleagues and firms would seek her out for consulting because of her expertise. She had esteem, power, and prestige, and she was on her way to financial independence.

On an otherwise normal Tuesday afternoon, Constance was running between appointments and munching on a quick lunch when she took a call from her doctor's office. They wanted her to come back for a second scan on her mammogram, they said, because they had detected something. In a flash, she found herself dealing with a possible tumor and a new series of appointments, as well as biopsies, staging, surgeries, and six weeks of radiation. This experience, along with the suddenness of the massive changes in her life, sent her into a tailspin of deeper and deeper despair and depression. She was being confronted with her mortality in a profound way. Desiring some guidance to figure it all out, she came for counseling.

We began by looking at how she was living her life, particularly how it compared with her values and desires. We learned that it was an earlier brush with mortality—the sudden death of her family in a plane crash during her first year of college—that ignited her determination for a successful career. Now 15 years later, Constance was traveling more than she wanted and working for a firm with questionable leadership. Amid it all, buried deep in her recesses was a desire for deep, loving companionship. She had to ask herself whether she wanted to live the next 15 years the way she had lived the last.

For Constance, the prospect of loving someone deeply was terrifying. She'd already had to bury her family, so she knew the devastation of losing those you love. But she also knew that she wanted the richness and complexity that a profound love could bring, even if it came with a risk of loss. It was then that Constance started to be reintroduced to her God-blessed desire for intimate connection.

Smoke and Mirrors

For Constance, part of what played into those 15 years of relational isolation was our popular culture's tendency to place tremendous value on people of power and influence, the kind of people who make lots of money like she did. Culture had also told her that it didn't matter how fast her life became or how much time she devoted to her job. What mattered most was the goal, the numbers, the bonus, the recognition—the climb. As long as she didn't stop long enough to feel her lack of intimate connection, it would all be fine.

But during those years, Constance was experiencing both a fear of being destitute, without a family to lean on, and a fear of the potential pain that comes with emotionally investing in a partner. These family-of-origin influences, along with the intensity of our culture's obsession with power and success, were woven so tightly together inside her that it was hard to differentiate the strands. In the end, it was the cancer scare that opened Constance's heart to the lingering pain of losing of her family, something she had been working so hard to ignore. But right along with her grief was a sense of *possibility* she found deep inside her of what a fulfilling relationship could feel like.

In our sessions, she unpacked all of it, placing it out in the open where it could be examined. She was living without intimacy, but was this what she wanted for her life? Did this way of living match her values? Did she really place a higher premium on climbing the ladder than she did on experiencing relationships, a foundational part of the human condition? She had come from a family that had loved well and talked often, one that was rooted in a quiet, deep Christian faith. She had grown up comforted by seeing her parents mutually love, care for, and respect each other. She remembered being young and knowing that someday, she wanted what her parents had. But it was during her freshman year of college, when she would have been learning to date and figure out how to develop the kind of relationship skills her parents had, that she experienced the devastating loss of her mom, dad, and little brother.

Constance attempted to cope by diving into college and graduate school. The relational aspect of her development came to a halt, a process further exacerbated by the fact that she hadn't dated much in high school due to her demanding athletic schedule. In other words, Constance was still an 18-year-old, even at the age of 33, when it came to relationships. Her dating experience and sexual awareness were still young, vulnerable, and untested. She had missed those crucial years of trying out relationships, talking over the ups and downs with friends and her parents, and learning who she was. Instead, she was essentially starting from scratch and would need a lot of coaching and care around dating, sensuality, and sexuality.

As Constance and I discovered together in session, swirling inside of her was a maelstrom of values, beliefs, pain, fears, culture, time, loss, family, and faith, all playing a part in how she experienced that defining moment of discovering she had cancer. There was a great deal of "sorting out" to do before she could lay out a clear vision for what she desired and what emotional and relational resources she would need in order to craft the next chapter of her life. But amid all the questions, one thing was becoming clear for Constance: it was no longer good enough just to follow what her culture said was what mattered—the nonstop scramble to attain the next level of professional success. She needed something more, something deeper, something that spoke to her whole, undivided, nondualized self. She needed to learn how to experience her humanity in all its fullness and complexity. She needed to relearn how to be *all* of Constance.

What's the Body Got to Do With It?

That's a tall order for those of us who, like Constance, grew up in the West, because the same soul/mind-body dualism that infected Christian faith has made its way into the fabric of our very economy. Whereas Christianity often values soul and mind over body, our consumer economy treats the *body* as a commodity and ignores any impact on the spirit and mind, almost as if they don't exist. "It has been said that a society's organization and value system are reflected in its perception of the human body," writes Joan Ohanneson in her book, *And They Felt No Shame* (1983, 56). In this chapter, we'll see some examples of how our market culture perceives and describes the body, as well as look at how advertising influences how we think, what we value, and how we spend our time. Each of those variables (thoughts, values, and time) is finely woven into how we view sexuality, our bodies, partnership, and the time we have to cultivate our drive for deep connection and intimacy. Lastly, we will also talk about how secular culture influences our clients as they're coming to us for help.

The Three Faces of a Marketing Myth

To put it succinctly, when I say that we objectify the body, I mean that we turn the body into a thing, forgetting that she or he is a person with thoughts, feelings, and desires. We do this all over the place: in retail; with modeling and acting; in collegiate and professional athletics; and in other areas. Much of our economy is driven by the practice of first turning people into objects and then using them to sell something or someone else. By doing so, we communicate three messages to the public observer:

1.   If you do not *have this* or *look like that* or *live like this*, you are inadequate, less than, and undesirable, so you must pursue those ideals.

2. As we chase after those ideals, our lives seem busier, faster, and more distracted. We begin to lose the time we need to cultivate that which makes life most meaningful: loving relationships, a generative passion, and for some, a lived faith.
3. Insofar as the culture emphasizes *disposability*, where the new version is always better than the old, we inevitably adopt consumerist thinking in our relationships themselves.

The logical result of these three influences is a constant sense of inadequacy. There is no time to do what nourishes the heart, soul, and body, and we learn to claim entitlement in our relationships by comparing our partner with others and always seeing what's wrong with them, rather than what's good. The result is a ubiquitous sense that "this isn't all there could be," leading to a feeling of dissatisfaction with one's relationships. The dissonance fills the body with stress and the home with disgruntled relationships. Then, as the weight of discontent grows, the scaffolding of life begins to crumble, sometimes monumentally. The offices of psychotherapists and physicians are filled with mounting physical, emotional, relational, and social damage from our culture's message of inadequacy and disposability of situations and people. Underneath this myth is another one: that romance "happens" to us, rather than our choosing our relationships and the quality of intimacy therein.

The Lost Story in Packaging

I remember many years ago laughing with a girlfriend who had a daughter about the same age as mine. She had been explaining to her three-year-old that they would be going to a pumpkin patch later that day, and that there would be chickens and roosters there. "Mia looked at me with the funniest look—you know that serious look she gets," Julie told me. "Mommy," Mia had asked, "will the chickens be wrapped in plastic like the ones at the grocery store?"

We all laughed! Mia had known only the kind of chicken that was purchased at the grocery store for dinner. She had no idea they were living animals. We couldn't help teasing Julie that there was going to be even more explaining to do when Mia had her first experience with a live, breathing chicken!

In 2013, one study estimated that by 2015 Americans would consume more than 15 hours of media a day on all of their devices (Short 2013). Advertisement agencies supporting this media are happy to help us define ourselves with the products they promote, appealing to our desire and "need" with tempting images and stories. The marketing wizardry of product-packaging also helps us to forget about what it takes to get products to us. Mia's live chicken, for example, was separated in her mind from the packaged version at the supermarket, perhaps similarly to how a beautiful cashmere suit at a department store is separated from the Southeast Asian worker barely making enough to survive. We are usually mesmerized enough with the item not to ask questions like, "Was anyone exploited in the process?" or "Do I really need this?" or "Am I buying this to deal with a sense of inadequacy or unworthiness?"

As I've become more conscious of the tactics involved, I've started to realize that there are very few places where we are *not* being sold things. We find ads in movie theaters, gas stations, websites, teller machines, video games, billboards on the highway, TV, magazines, stores, unsolicited text ads on our phones, and a million other places. Even the ads we see online are now tailor-made just for us, based upon algorithms of our spending and viewing history. To become conscious of the blanketing nature of advertisement is quite a task. How are our clients to hold on to their sense of worth and value when they are constantly told that they are too fat, too skinny, too poor, don't have this or that, can't do this or that, can't go here or there, can't drive this or that, or any of countless other regulations and restrictions? It is impossible for a person to measure up if they are continually looking to our culture to tell them that they do.

"Our society," writes William Fore,

> is today cultivating single vision, and the desensitization and the dehu-
> manization that we feel all around us is a kind of sleep or death of aware-
> ness and conscience. We must revive in people a habit of double vision
> that can identify myths and values underlying society and can evaluate
> them from a perspective that transcends the limitations of that society.
>
> (Fore 1977, 32)

This double vision, I believe, is one of the things a good therapist does best. We are often helping people to slow down and listen to their hopes and dreams, to their inner wisdom, to their desires. We often reflect back the marginalized stories of the preferred possibilities that they cannot quite hear but were waiting for them all along. And we help them to live the authentic life they have been craving, helping them to discover the skills for intimacy and relationship that culture has failed to provide.

The Connection Between Stuff and Quality of Life

One effect of filling our lives with more and more products is the increased amount of time that these new possessions take to manage. We may not notice it at first, but eventually, the additional computer, extra car, boat, or new landscaping will have us spending more time just taking care of them than they had previously—a catch-22 in which we have to *work* more in order to *earn* more, just to keep up with what the work allows us to *buy*. Before we know it, we've worked a 60-hour week, used up the evenings and weekends doing chores, and spent much of our sleeping hours fretting about all that needs to be done. In a lifestyle like that, where is a person's joy? Where is pleasure, the body and soul soaking in loving touch or thoughtful conversation? Where are stillness, leisure, and the time for recreation?

The word *recreation* literally means "re-creation," the act of creating something again. To create something is to engage the desires, the passions, the soul, and the body. It is almost always deeply nourishing. As children at play, we were in a near-constant act of creating. Even as adults, when we play we have our own kind of "zone" that we get into. Think about how often you've given a client the homework of doing some form of self-care or "play." My beloved is a skier, so when he wants to find his "zone" and lose himself for a while, he goes to the slopes, and he always comes home so happy and buoyant. What do you do when you find yourself losing time and space?

In the best lovemaking (when we go beyond making *sex* to really making *love*), we are creating new and more abundant love every time. When we come together with the intention to nourish and be nourished, to love and to be loved with an open heart and an open body, *that's* lovemaking, playing together—recreating together.

Where Is There Peace?

The trouble is that to engage in lovemaking as re-creation, we have to have a sense of contentedness with ourselves and with the person we love. However, this is countercultural in a market-driven economy that depends on keeping us only momentarily satisfied and never quite content. Marketing channels contain embedded messages—some subtle, some not—that we are not okay as we are with what we have. If we were content, we'd have less desire for the products that they try to sell us. We'd realize that we probably don't *need* anything else to make us happy, like a vacation home, a car, or new breasts, or a longer and harder erection. When we absorb the sneaky messaging that surrounds us all day, every day, we can start to feel that somehow, we are not enough just as we are.

Our clients will feel this too. If you are working with a young adult, someone who hasn't yet formed a solid sense of self, this constant inundation can sink them into a deep despair. They start to believe on some level that "I will never, ever be enough. No matter how hard I work, no matter what I do or don't do, something in me will always fail to measure up." No wonder depression, anxiety, and suicide rates are on the rise among young adults (Curtin, Warner, and Hedegaard 2016). How can someone form a sense of self, let alone a sense of self-as-beloved, when this subtle message of "you need this" or "you need that" reminds them of just how not-enough they are at every turn?

In the adult world, the trouble gets even more pronounced. Not only do we feel more inadequate, but also we now have less time, more stuff, more things to manage, and more things to support financially. That's nonsense, of course, because beyond the basics of food, shelter, community, and family, is it necessarily the people with more who are more happy? Or are they often *less* free, *more* enslaved to their lifestyle, and *less* happy with life? Research has consistently shown that there is a weak association between income and happiness once people have sufficient income to afford life's basic necessities and have an adequate measure of control over their lives (Quiñones 2006).

Let's add another layer for consideration. With less time and more responsibility, how does a person of faith find time to sit and meditate in the presence of their loving God, or to make time for God's healing love? How does a person who values silence, stillness, and meditation obtain the minutes and hours it takes to cultivate a relationship with God? Where do we find the time to love those entrusted to our care? In the Christian tradition, God desires nothing more than to commune with his people. Even more than the most loving parent, he enjoys the company of his beloved children—to listen, to reassure, to nourish, to celebrate, to give rest.[1]

Now that my kids are grown and off living their fascinating lives, I find myself relating to this aspect of God so much more than I did when they were young. There is nothing I love more than to have all four of our kids home—laughing, talking, goofing around, whatever. I love their company! When our kids are with us, my husband Gary and I are in a state of absolute chaotic bliss, and it reflects in the joy on our faces. We don't just feel happier when they're around: we actually *look* happier, too. Christians believe that humans are made in God's image (see Genesis 1:27), so if this is how *we* feel when our beloved family is around, how much more must this be true of the Creator?

"A community economy," wrote Wendell Berry, "is not an economy in which well-placed persons can make a 'killing.' It is an economy whose aim is generosity and a well-distributed and safeguarded abundance" (1996, 82). Elsewhere, Berry described the simple, quiet ecstasy of being with those we love. "It is possible, as I have learned again and again, to be in one's place, in such company, wild or domestic, and with such pleasure, that one cannot think of another place that one would prefer to be—or of another place at all" (2002, 357–8). I think of this quote every time I am with our kids.

How American Consumerism Diminishes Our Sexual Vitality

In my office sat Jeff and Shari, a lovely, dual-professional couple whom I had worked with at two other key points in their relationship over the previous decade. This time, they made an appointment in a new stage of their life: raising their beautiful and active two-year-old daughter, named Willow. For years, they had wondered whether they would have children. They both loved their careers and were excited to see the future unfold, but how would they negotiate career advancements and possible relocations? The prospect of adding a child to this mix had seemed a bit risky, but as luck would have it, they got pregnant with a little girl who captured both of their hearts.

Sitting with me in session, they shared that they couldn't imagine their life without her. She was their joy, and they both described how being parents grounded their lives with a much deeper purpose and meaning than they had known before, to such a degree that they were surprised by their own level of transformation. While they had heard things like this from people who advocated for them to have a child, they seriously doubted that they would have the same experience. They were finding that it was every bit as good as they had been told.

But even though Jeff and Shari were absolutely at peace with having a child, they were equally baffled at how to negotiate life. Jeff worked 12-hour days and often had to travel overseas. Shari was vice president of a large real estate firm that was leading a major redevelopment effort in Seattle. Both of them described how they felt always short on time, energy, and patience. So much of their time went toward responsibilities that it diminished their energy for each other. They never had felt at odds with each other before, but now their rope had worn thin and even time together felt strained.

"We have always believed that if we made it to these levels in our careers, we'd have financial leverage to buy ourselves some time and space," Jeff told me. "But that has not turned out to be the case."

"We just seem to be scrambling, without the capacity to enjoy ourselves," Shari agreed.

This scenario is common. Many couples find that they are forfeiting a sense of connection, intimacy, and love in the hopes of reaching that next place that might ease their lacking resources. Like many others at this stage of life, Jeff wondered about the trade-off of keeping his nose to the grindstone for one more season. "If I go full-force for the next couple of years, ignoring all else, trying to make vice president," he asked, "will it end up being worth what it does to our family?"

Cultivating intimacy is like growing a garden: it needs time and attention, and it can only be ignored for so long. As therapists, we see this all the time in our offices, often in the form of beautiful, once-passionate couples who are there because they have ignored their relationship for years and can't find their way back to each other. There is a reason marriages often improve after the kids are gone: time. (That's assuming, of course, that they haven't drifted so far apart they cannot find their way back, as often happens for couples at middle age, or that neither person has already left in some other way and refuses to return.) It is important to help clients to figure out how to maximize time and resources to nourish their relationship, *when they are raising their children*, and how to make their marriage a priority. But in a culture like ours, one that emphasizes the climb, the chase, and going fast, that's not always easy to do. It's as though one's house was on fire but he or she refused to acknowledge the flames. I've met countless couples whose marriages were smoldering and about to break into an all-out firestorm. Some have even been therapists themselves, people who believed in marriage with all of their hearts but couldn't figure out what to do next. Often they would say they were too stressed, too overloaded, or too distracted to get counseling or to go on a couples retreat. "We'll do it next year," they might say, "but not right now. We're just too busy." Almost without fail, "next year" becomes "this year"—and nothing changes.

Priority Discipline

A fast-moving market economy attacks quality of life by demanding our time. The culture we live in has a serious need for critical thinking and the rediscovery of what I call *priority discipline.* Our most precious relationships and our most nourishing stillness require uninterrupted time and attention. We know that to build a good relationship with our kids, our lover, our friends, and our family, we need focused time and the intention to listen and love. We need moments of fun, adventure, and connection. In order to nourish our souls, we often need space, maybe silence, maybe a walk along the ocean or in the woods. We need the discipline to unplug in order to nourish what is most precious to us. The challenge is that most of us no longer have natural time-breaks. Storefronts no longer roll down at 8 p.m. or on Sundays, and technology is perpetually "on" and demanding our attention. And in just about every one of these places, advertisers are there, waiting to pry their way into our time.

Life now requires tenacious mindfulness and discipline to match our daily choices to our priorities. We must decide, ahead of time and regularly if necessary, how much of our time and attention is going to be spent where. Then we must try to honor those decisions to the best of our abilities. We must let go of the myth of "multitasking" and learn to be present to one thing at a time, one person at a time, one moment at a time. We ought to be willing to say "no" to some things and some people in order to say a full "yes" to whatever represents our highest priorities. This becomes a new spiritual discipline.

Even as I am writing this, I realize what an audacious idea it is—or as my friend Bill would say, a "bold, hairy, audacious idea." I recently received an e-mail from Georgia, a client who attended our last couples' intimacy retreat with her husband, Roland. In her pleas, you can hear a sense of powerlessness against the pressure on her time and the effect the strain was having on her marriage.

"I saw what an amazing relationship we could have during the retreat and for a couple of weeks after," she wrote, "but slowly we have gotten back to our normal routine and I am getting very sad. We are trying to implement the things we learned, but we are getting so busy. Sex is turning back into the thing we need to check off the list. How do we get back to doing things as we did them on the retreat—to make *that* our new normal?"

As you secure boundaries, say *no*, and make choices, there will be feelings, concerns, and consequences. Perhaps you have experienced this yourself or seen it in your clients. I hear stories of trying to work alongside a young, single executive who can give 70 hours a week at the office, setting the bar so high that it makes my client feel like a complete underachiever because she has children and is committed to making it home in time for the kids' soccer games. I hear of dads who take reduced-hour jobs in order to parent more equally with their career spouse, yet consequently feel invisible and undervalued both with other men at work and with mom-professionals from other families. One dad told me that he tried to go to his church's group for moms on Wednesday mornings but that he hadn't been welcomed. Where is a dad to get support?

On the couples' intimacy retreats that our institute runs, our clients have shared countless stories about comments from friends confused about why they would go on a retreat like ours in the first place. "Was something wrong?" they might ask. "Is it a sex retreat?" "My husband/wife would *never* go to something like that!"

But why should people feel strange that couples would take time to cultivate some of the most important aspects of the human experience, intimacy, and sexuality? The fact that such an idea is novel for many people is, by itself, evidence that we give very little support for marriages in our culture. Try saying you're leaving work early, or even on time, to spend time with your partner, and see if you get a bewildered reaction from your boss or coworkers, like many of my clients have. The idea of built-in, cultural support for nourishing marriages and families is not only counterintuitive: it is countercultural. We live in a culture that does not offer more than lip service to families or marriages—even while they are the heartbeat of healthy people and healthy communities.

Getting Beat Up and Beat Down

Some time ago, I was working with Christoph and Emile, two physicians who had been married for eight years. Having worked with and taught doctors for a long time, I had gained an understanding of what their training involved and what their clinical life had become since the advent of managed care. In addition to their professional demands, Christoph and Emile also had two kids, a four-year-old and a toddler just under two. The older child had never—not once—slept for more than a few hours at a time. Both parents were beyond exhausted by the time I met them.

Christoph and Emile were lovely people and described a refreshing, mutual, egalitarian relationship. They loved each other deeply and they respected each other as friends, colleagues, parents, and lovers. Their mutuality extended back to its roots in medical school, where they had met, so they had been working to nurture their relationship for a long time. But by the time they came to see me, they were beyond distressed. Like Jeff and Shari, they were worn so thin that their emotions were a frayed wire. Given the demands on their time and energy, it came as no surprise for me to hear that things like nourishing touch, quiet time together, and sex (let alone *good* sex) were nonexistent. They were just too empty. If one wanted sex and the other acquiesced, the fallout and resentment that came afterward were often worse.

We spent a couple of months laying out their values and goals, as well as working through the question of what kinds of memories they wanted from their parenting years. We then laid out potential five-year, incremental life-courses. Through seeing life in chunks that corresponded to their kids' progressing ages, they started to come up with a plan for the next several years that allowed more space for things like parenting, eroticism, improving their marriage, and investing in their home life. It was a brilliant plan, but it came about only after they were lifted out of the muck and mire to figure out what they ultimately desired. This process is an example of priority discipline, the intention to craft on a daily basis the life that we most value.

Marriage Is Not a Product

Consumerism can wreak another kind of havoc on relationships, the sort that creeps in anytime we apply market language to marriage. Advertisers have long been creating an image of what they want us to desire or feel we need. In his book *Take Back Your Marriage*, Bill Doherty points out that advertising executives have begun pursuing our normal, everyday desires as well—the ones they don't have to manufacture because they're already there. People get thirsty, so Sprite's "Obey Your Thirst" is an example of this practice, Doherty writes, along with "Your kids always get what they want—now it's your turn" by Toyota (in this case, the want hasn't been named, only acknowledged). Old Spice had a commercial that showed an attractive man standing just outside a shower and saying, "Look at your man. Now back to me. . . . Sadly, he isn't me. But if he . . . switched to Old Spice, he could smell like he's me." These kinds of ads increase our piling sense of *disordered* needs, a skewed sense of entitlement that basically sounds like "I've been putting off what I want for too long, and so I *deserve* this" (Doherty 2001, 30–1; Old Spice 2010).

The problem is not the advertisers, or even our market-driven economy itself. It is a challenge to us to pay attention to the effects. If our consumer culture is constantly teaching us that the new is better than the old, that we have a right to have what we want, then we risk objectifying others when this kind of thinking is applied to our committed relationships. I have seen parents apply market-driven thinking to how they see their partners and marriages. Since many parents and spouses don't have a keen understanding of how the development of intimacy happens over time, they often become dissatisfied, critical, and disgruntled, chasing after expectations that are unrealistic.

As a buyer, I can switch from Company A to Company B if Company B is providing a better quality at a better price than A. I'm generally not under any burden of loyalty. But when this kind of entitlement and disposability is applied to our intimate relationships, it can send us down a path toward dissatisfaction at best and dissolution at worst. "What happens," Doherty asks, "when we approach marriage and family life as entrepreneurs?" When the honeymoon is over and tough times come, as entrepreneurs we are prepared to cut our losses, to take what we want from our old marriages in order to forge new, supposedly more perfect unions, until they also fail to meet our expectations. Most couples marry with every intention to remain faithful and committed, but without priority discipline, these values are in danger of being eclipsed by consumer values of personal gain, low cost, entitlement, and hedging one's bets. "In consumer culture," Doherty continues,

> the exit door is always accessible. Commitments last as long as the other person is meeting our needs. We still believe in commitment, but powerful voices coming from inside and outside tell us we are suckers if we settle for less than we think we need or deserve in marriage.
>
> (2001, 39)

Doherty isn't talking about relationships that suffer infidelity, abuse, abandonment, or chronic addictions; these situations may necessitate divorce. But what is being seen in the offices of family therapists and clergy are stories of a generalized dissatisfaction and a desire for something different, an embedded assumption that "the right relationship" will make them feel fulfilled and happy 100 percent of the time—or that you can virtually ignore your relationship and it will stay dynamic and deeply connected. Of course, both ideas are foolish, but most of us succumb to this kind of thinking at some point. While seasons of frustration are par for the course in marriage and relationships, what is different now is the way in which the sense of dissatisfaction rips at the very fiber of a couple's commitment. It is as if the fabric of the bond between the two people has holes in it and is actually very fragile. Perhaps we have forgotten how tough we really are, and how difficult life and love can be. Like seasons, life has winters and they can be harsh, but they serve an important purpose in helping to grow our character. Marriage and parenting have always served that purpose in the human experience.

A Frail Connection

Joe and Marilyn, a 20-year couple with two teenage children, were classic examples of a pair who had *resisted* consumerist thinking in their relationship, in spite of everything they had seen around them.

"We have friends all over who are splitting up over being unhappy, or where one of them is already in an affair," said Marilyn in my office. "We have been under a ton of stress for a couple of years, and I know it has been hard on both of us. But frankly I don't think we can wait. For a long time, I have wanted more intimacy in our relationship. I want more touching and more time for just us. I can tell within me that I have a growing sense of detachment with Joe. I'm afraid it could lead to me wanting out. But I don't want out. I really do want to grow old with this man. But I want to feel wanted by him, too."

Joe was clearly connected to her; I could see it in the way he watched her talk. When she had finished, he looked at me and said, "I am here because I want things to be better, too. I don't know what to do, and we are so busy that I can't find my way through the chaos. But I want what she wants and I want help to figure it out."

Marilyn and Joe could see the frailty in their commitment, and they wanted to strengthen it. Marilyn was struggling, wondering if her dissatisfaction warranted coming to a therapist or even a separation. Like all of us, she was being affected by consumer culture. But rather than simply buying it, she made the decision to say, "Let's get help"—and he said, "Okay." They were able to resist the siren-call of our cultural obsession with the new-and-improved, and they decided to do the hard work of sorting through what was required to make their relationship all that it could be.

Sadly, Joe and Marilyn aren't typical. The vast majority of couples don't come into therapy until one has decided to leave or has already left through an affair. But while these situations are much more difficult, many are still salvageable. Doherty developed questions for checking to see whether a relationship is suffering under a cloud of consumer thinking. I frequently review these questions with my clients.

Is Your Marriage Becoming a Consumer Marriage?[2]

1. I regularly compare my spouse unfavorably with other men or women.
2. I think mostly about my spouse's contributions to our problems, not my own.
3. I think much more often about how my spouse is not meeting my needs than about how I am not meeting my spouse's needs.
4. I find myself adding up my contributions to my marriage.
5. I find myself thinking that my spouse is getting a better deal in this marriage than I am.
6. It is much easier for me to focus on my spouse's defects than on his or her strengths.
7. I wonder from time to time if I should have had higher standards when I chose a mate.
8. When we are having hard time, I often ask myself whether the effort I am putting into this marriage is worth it.

I hope this list, and the invitation to think through this lens, will help you with your clients. When we focus our thoughts on the negative aspects of our partners, fixating on their weaknesses, comparing them to someone else or to another person's marriage, then we will inevitably have a more pessimistic view of the relationship. We notice and feel more of what we pay attention to. Likewise, negative thinking begets negative thoughts and negative thoughts beget negative feelings. Negative feelings beget negative actions—which can bring you and your partner down, get you both discouraged, and tempt you to look elsewhere when what you want is probably right in front of you. I often say to my couples, if you have something to say about what you want *for the relationship* or *for yourself*, then say so. (I caution against telling their partner how they want *them* to change. This usually leads nowhere except to more negative thinking *focused on the other*.) While they don't have the power to change another, their relationship is a separate entity all its own. If they have a hope for their relationship that they'd like to work toward, then as a therapist, you can help them to begin the conversation. I try to remind people that marriage is a relationship that invites growth through challenge, not through ease, which is why vows are written the way they are. There will be disappointment, and your partner will not be exactly what you had hoped for in a mate. But if there is openness, respect, justice, and love then you can build a deeply satisfying relationship through focus, intention, and patience.

Grow Up, Show Up, and Shape Up

"The best way to keep the consumer culture from dominating your marriage," writes Doherty,

> is to see yourself as a citizen of your marriage, which is another way to say be intentional, committed and part of a community. Being a citizen of a marriage means taking responsibility to make things better and not just be passive, to value the marriage itself and not just your own interest in it, to struggle to make it better by naming problems and changing yourself first, to take the long view that values your history together as a couple over short-term pain and struggle, to accept the inevitable limitations and problems, to see how your marriage affects many other people in your world, and to hold onto the dream, never fully fulfilled, of a more perfect union.
>
> (Doherty 2001, 47)

Marriage is not a product. It is a process, a lifestyle that seeks to grow you into a better person. I often tell couples that marriage wants to help you to *grow up, show up, and shape up!* Like with a potter who spends months crafting a single, unique piece, marriage is a kiln that can solidify the clay of our selfhood into a vessel for carrying fresh, overflowing love. In difficult times, marriage will ask you to put on courage in the face of fire, and to be your clearest and best self in the face of risk and vulnerability. It is this kind of challenge that hones and refines you, that helps you become who you were meant to be. Marriage is your personal kiln, a place where you learn the art of loving, something that is not always easy or comfortable. That's why marriage is a spiritual discipline. It teaches you about love *and your vows* as you live into them on purpose.

So what does the soul-body split in a market-driven economy have to do with experiencing a more sacred sexuality for our Christian clients and for ourselves? Everything. Just as the church has been damaged by the soul-body split, our economic structure has been damaged, too. In order to focus on the material and the physical, marketers depend on the idea that people won't listen to what their souls and consciences are saying.

But what might happen if Christians and non-Christians alike were to decide to explore the beauty and gift of their personhood, their soul-body, their partner, their children, their neighbor, their community, and their environment? What if we were to slow down and observe what is going on within our soul/body, within our home, within our relationships, with more passion and intent to be present? What if people were to get clear about what is enough, what is meaningful, what is success, what is significant, what they want their life-legacy to be? What if, rather than looking outside of themselves and their relationships for affirmation or comfort or esteem, they began to try to absorb more of God's purposeful love, acceptance, and grace—in their bodies, in their souls, and between and around them? What if we all began to be responsible for the effect that manufacturing, market-ing, and purchasing have on us and on those around us? What if we began to believe that the abundant life we were meant to have, we already have? What if we were to *really try* to believe in our belovedness?

Mind–Body Recursive Cycles: How Messages Affect Us

At the end of this chapter you will see two models in the form of two recursive cycles. Figure 3.1 is a cycle built on the unhelpful mind-body *split* message of Judeo-Christian history and American culture; it reveals more of the impact of consumerism. The other model, Figure 3.2, is on a more helpful, *unified* mind-body message from Judeo-Christian history and American culture; this model reveals the potential impact of justice and community thinking. The models are there for you to use to help your clients reflect on how messages can shape our lives and our decisions.

"To the offer of a more abundant life," writes Wendell Berry,

> we have chosen to respond with the economics of extinction. If we take the Gospels seriously, we are left, in our dire predicament, facing an utterly humbling question: How must we live and work so as not to be estranged from God's presence in His work and in all His creatures? The answer, we may say, is given in Jesus' teaching about love. But that answer raises another question that plunges us into the abyss of our ignorance, which is both human and peculiarly modern: How are we to make of that love an economic practice?
>
> (Berry 2005b, 137)

As therapists who serve people locked in a vault of unworthiness and shame, part of our job is to help them figure out how to break free and remove themselves from that dark, confining place. True success comes for people when they are able to live fully into their passions and believe in their infinite value. In the next chapter, we will see that the God whom they learned about as a child is actually much more loving and sex-positive than their wildest imaginations ever could have foreseen.

Mind-Body Recursive Cycles

Split Mind-Body Cycle

Family of Origin Beliefs about Your Mind, Heart, Soul, and Body

1. How were you taught to value your mind, heart, soul, and body?

2. How were you taught to value others' minds, hearts, souls, and bodies?

3. What was most important to your family?

4. How do the answers to these questions interact with any of your experiences of unhelpful cultural and/or religious beliefs?

Unhelpful American Cultural Beliefs

1. Market-driven consumerism = Want more, buy more, use more.

2. Those who have more money and beauty have more power, influence, and value.

3. Your only responsibility is to yourself; what you want is the most important.

4. Gender: Men are providers, aggressors, and influencers: women are nurturers, passive co-contributors.

Unhelpful Historical Religious Beliefs Born from Patriarchy

1. Rules **must** be followed and were "ordained by God."

2. God **requires** obedience.

3. The body's desires will lead you astray and are to be tamed.

4. Sexual behaviors before marriage are damaging to you and your future partner.

5. Men are head of the household, and the leaders of the church.

Figure 3.1 Mind-Body Split Cycle

Unified Mind-Body Cycle

Helpful Cultural Beliefs

1. Market-driven consumerism: I will consume and own what is necessary while paying attention to the effect on others and my community.

2. All creatures have innate value.

3. I am responsible to myself, others, my community, all of creation, and any core faith values.

4. Gender: All people (women, men, children) were created equal and are to be treated with the utmost respect.

5. I have a responsibility to myself and others to be all I was created to be and to leave this world a better place.

My Beliefs about Health of Mind, Heart, Soul, Body, and Community

1. How do I want to value my mind, heart, soul, body, and community?

2. How do I want to value others' minds, hearts, souls, bodies, and communities?

3. What do I want the legacy of my life to be?

4. What do I want my role to be in cultivating love, justice, humility, compassion, and healing in my life and in the world?

Helpful Historical Judeo-Christian Beliefs

1. God created all people in His/Her image (Elohim).

2. It is through accepting and absorbing God's relentless love for us that a desire to live in mutual respect and love is manifest in our choices and words (John 4:24).

3. The body's sexual desires are a gift from God to bless me, bless another (if I partner), and make us all conduits of God's love into the world (e.g., Song of Songs).

4. Jesus was revolutionary in how he honored women and people who were otherwise ignored or marginalized. He stood against patriarchy and the misuse of power given to the rich and privileged (e.g., John. 8:3ff.).

Figure 3.2 Unified Mind-Body Cycle

Notes

1. See, for example, Psalm 32:8; Isaiah 55:1–3; Matthew 11:28–30; Mark 10:14–16; John 5:40, 6:37, 7:37–38; Revelation 22:17.
2. This list is adapted from Doherty (2001, 43).

References

Berry, Wendell. 1995. Endorsement Statement. In *The Dying of the Trees: The Pandemic in America's Forests*, written by Charles E. Little, iv. New York, NY: Penguin.

———. 1996. Conserving Communities. In *Rooted in the Land: Essays on Community and Place*, edited by William Vitek and Wes Jackson, 76–84. New Haven, CT: Yale University Press.

———. 2002. *The Art of the Commonplace: The Agrarian Essays of Wendell Berry*. Edited by Norman Wirzba. Berkeley, CA: Counterpoint.

———. 2005a. *Blessed Are the Peacemakers: Christ's Teachings about Love, Compassion and Forgiveness*. Berkeley, CA: Shoemaker & Hoard.

———. 2005b. *The Way of Ignorance and Other Essays*. Emeryville, CA: Avalon.

———. 2012. *The Long-Legged House*. Berkeley, CA: Counterpoint.

Curtin, Sally C., Margaret Warner, and Holly Hedegaard. 2016. Increase in Suicide in the United States, 1999–2014. *NCHS Data Brief* 241 (April). Atlanta, GA: Centers for Disease Control and Prevention. Last updated April 22, 2016. www.cdc.gov/nchs/products/databriefs/db241.htm.

Doherty, William J. 2001. *Take Back Your Marriage: Sticking Together in a World that Pulls Us Apart*. New York, NY: Guilford.

Fore, William. 1977. Mass Media's Mythic World: At Odds with Christian Values. *Christian Century*, January 19, 1977, 32–8.

Ohanneson, Joan. 1983. *And They Felt No Shame: Christians Reclaiming Their Sexuality*. Minneapolis, MN: Winston.

Old Spice. 2010. *Old Spice | The Man Your Man Could Smell Like*. YouTube video, 00:32. Advertisement, posted February 4, 2010. www.youtube.com/watch?v=owGykVbfgUE.

Quiñones, Eric. 2006. *Link between Income and Happiness Is Mainly an Illusion*. *News at Princeton*. Princeton, NJ: Princeton University. Published June 29. www.princeton.edu/main/news/archive/S15/15/09S18/index.xml?section=topstories.

Short, James E. 2013. *How Much Media? 2015: Report on American Consumers*. Executive Summary. Los Angeles, CA: Institute for Communication Technology Management, University of Southern California. www.marshall.usc.edu/faculty/centers/ctm/research/how-much-media, accessed August 31, 2016.

4 Hope for Clients
The Lost Message of a Sex-Positive God

Body and spirit marry in the chapel of the soul. They marry every minute of every day, in all activities and in all inactivity, in all thoughts and in all actions, or they marry not at all. If they don't marry, we do not know sexuality with soul, and therefore our sexuality remains incomplete and insufficiently human. We do not find the soul of sex by spiritual-izing the body but by coming to appreciate its mysteries and by daring to enter into its sensuousness.

—Thomas Moore, *The Soul of Sex* (1998, 24)

It was Sunday evening and my beloved and I were just finishing the closing reception on our latest couples retreat when Simon, one of the husbands, cornered us.

"Hey, you guys," he said, "I need you to know how important this week-end was for me. It turned my world upside down. I never knew sex could be so amazing, so spiritual, so erotic." Tears began to fill his eyes. "I honestly never expected to feel that way about my wife again. If I had any idea that sex could be this fulfilling, I don't think I would ever have wanted to look at porn. It doesn't hold a candle to what I have experienced this weekend. I just had no idea that sex could be like this. Thank you for putting this together and for holding our hands through it."

Core Sexual Values in Jewish and Christian Culture and Spirituality

I begin with Simon's story because a big part of what we try to do at our Passion for Life™ Couples Intimacy Retreats centers around highlighting ancient, sex-positive ideas and practices that have been largely forgotten, often for centuries. In this chapter I will uncover ancient Hebrew stories that dem-onstrate a celebratory understanding of sexuality, one that was neglected in the formation of the Christian church. I will provide examples of narratives that can help Christian clients to believe that not only is their sexual desire good but also it's actually an intended gift of the living God. These narratives will also point toward how to be in relationship with one's sexuality, and with one's beloved, in a way that is nourishing, fulfilling, and sacred, all at the same time. I will also demonstrate that while the wider Christian church essentially failed to develop a liberative, grace-filled sexual ethic, Jesus's ministry itself provided more than enough information about love, justice, and how to be in relationships with others, to give the scaffolding necessary to build a sex-positive ethic of eros. Throughout this chapter, I will provide a faith rationale that can support any therapist working with a conservative Christian client who feels mired in religious sexual shame and doubt.

Lost Mystic Jewish Wisdom About Sexuality

Let's go back in time and space to Jerusalem around 500 BCE (about two centuries before Plato and Aristotle) to hear a story from Jewish mysticism.

> *The masters of the day were distressed. Adultery was spreading rampant as plague among the people. The authorities were at a loss as to how to curb this powerful drive. Finally, driven to desperation, they began to pray. For three days they fasted, weeping and pleading with God, "Let us slay the sexual drive before it slays us."*
>
> *Finally God acquiesced. The masters then witnessed a lion of fire leap out from within the Temple's Holy of Holies. A prophet among them identified the lion as the personification of the primal sexual drive.*
>
> *They sought to slay the lion of fire. But the result was that for three days thereafter the entire society ground to a standstill. Hens did not lay eggs, artists ceased creating, businesses faltered, and all spiritual activity came to a halt.*
>
> *Realizing that the sexual drive was about more than sex, that it somehow echoed with the Divine, the masters relented.*
>
> *They prayed that only its destructive shadow be removed while retaining its creative force. Their request was denied on high with the insightful response: "You cannot have only half a drive." The greater the sacred power of a quality, the greater its shadow; the two are inseparable. So they prayed that the lion at least be weakened, and their prayer was granted. The lion, less potent but no less present, reentered the Holy of Holies.*
>
> (Talmud—Mas. Yoma 69b, quoted in Gafni 2003, 7)

In this story we see the power, the paradox, and the dilemma in sexual desire. The Jewish teachers could see that while the drive is forceful and needs management, the core impulse in sexual desire is at the heart of all creative endeavors. Our drive to create relationships, to make love, to create ways of serving others, to discover beauty and divine revelation—these are all part of the core human desire to live meaningfully, to be fully alive. In fact, the Bible itself offers evidence that by acknowledging their desire, Christians actually resemble an important part of God's character.

When we let our core desires find expression in ways that are loving and just, we participate in the creative process that is part of the image of God within us, spoken about in the very first chapters of the Bible. Genesis 1:27 says, "God created humankind in his image, in the image of God he created them; male and female he created them." The word used for God here is *Elohim*. ALH (Eloh) is a feminine singular Hebrew word for God and *-im* is a masculine plural ending. In Hebrew, when masculine and feminine elements of a word are united, they represent that within the word the female, male, and creative potencies are all united. This form suggests the image of God as having masculine and feminine qualities *and* the creative force within. God *is* the creative life force of love and of desire. Therefore, if humans are a reflection of the image of God, then humans are the only creatures with drives to create complex relationships with deep, intimate bonds.[1]

Human desire, having its root in God's character, was said to be powerful— so powerful that people needed God's guidance and wisdom to discern and decipher how to use it, how to enjoy it, and how to tame it when they needed to.

Desires Find Their Freedom in Boundaries

A key paradox of the human condition, as understood in early Christian and ancient Hebrew thinking, is that boundaries, discretion, and discipline are actually requirements of freedom. Psalm 119 talks about how living *without* boundaries and discipline paradoxically enslaves us to the hunger of greed—a hunger that promises to satisfy but never does and never actually will. Freedom of expression in all human desire is found *inside* the boundaries that liberate the desire to serve, nourish, love, express, and create. Our bodies in their most free state are intimately serving the desires of the heart *with love* to bring more love and justice to us, our lover, and ultimately to the world. According to these Jewish values, our sexuality is not fully experienced without love for self, God, and other.

According to one study of almost 1,000 emerging adults, "63% of college-aged men and 83% of college-aged women preferred, at their current stage of life or development, a traditional romantic relationship as opposed to an uncommitted sexual relationship" (Garcia et al. 2010, referenced in Garcia et al. 2012, 12). In urban America, single people often find that unattached, unboundaried sex is in high demand and great supply, yet many singles find that somehow it's not enough. Thanks to the law of diminishing returns, the "high" doesn't stay, and over time, young adults learn that casual sex doesn't satisfy the core human desires of being seen, known, loved, and accepted. In the end, sex without love leaves people wanting. But sexual expression that manifests and magnifies love—love for self, love for other, *and* love for God—has the capacity to leave the soul and body resonating in spiritual and sexual satiation. Desire that is expressed in self-serving or hurtful ways, like running from partner to partner in casual hookups, can become a form of oppression. It can oppress not only one's partners, who become an object of sexual gratification, but also the one with the desire, by ignoring the needs to be seen and known. Sex devoid of love can be empty and hurtful, but sex with love of self, other, and God can bring wholeness, satisfaction, and healing to both persons.

The Image of God in Sexual Desire

For Christians who grew up hearing the message that their sexual desires were not to be trusted, the idea that desires can be good, even sexual ones, often comes as a very new idea. Even Justin, our client at the beginning of this book, wouldn't dare to listen to his experience with Marta. What if he was wrong? Clients may find themselves feeling like they need to protect themselves from this idea, that this idea is somehow dangerous, because after all, if they're wrong, there is often a deep fear of making God unhappy.

I have clients who remember being told throughout childhood that their heart was deceitful and wicked, a reference to Jeremiah 17:9, and who cannot remember being delighted in or feeling beloved. Yet we know from Psalm 37:4 that when a person fully seeks God, they can know that their heart's longings are actually *from* God. "Take delight in the Lord," the psalmist wrote, "and he will give you the desires of your heart." Sometimes, the best evidence of the voice of God within is simply *the desires* that a person feels. I often invite clients to begin to listen deeply to their heart and to their body—to breathe deeply and to take a body-felt inventory of the senses. "What is your body telling you?" I'll ask. "What do you feel? What do you smell? What is aching? What feels just right? And what does it all suggest to you about what God might be trying to say?" (Some of your most religiously abused clients might be so closed off from their bodies that they're not able to answer any of these questions. You may need to begin with much more concrete questions pertaining to the body in order not to further shame them.)

In their book *The Sacred Romance*, Brent Curtis and John Eldredge say it this way:

> The inner life, the story of our heart, is the life of the deep places within us, our passions and dreams, our fears and our deepest wounds. It is the unseen life, the mystery within—what Buechner calls our "shimmering self." It cannot be managed like a corporation. The heart does not respond to principles and programs; it seeks not efficiency, but passion. Art, poetry, beauty, mystery, ecstasy; these are what rouse the heart. Indeed, they are the language that must be spoken if one wishes to communicate with the heart. It is why Jesus so often taught and related to people by telling stories and asking questions. His desire was not to engage their intellects but to capture their hearts.
>
> (Curtis and Eldredge 1997, 6).

Like Simon, the participant who talked with Gary and me at the end of our couples retreat, the longings of the heart can be expressed only through the vehicle or "voice" that is the body. We cannot express our hopes and desires or act on our loves or express any inner motivation without the body coming along to bring image and expression to what is inside. A man cannot express love to the one he loves without using his mouth to speak, or his thumbs to send a text message, or his hands to caress, or his lips to kiss. Sometimes the body is the most expressive instrument to transmit our love. A woman cannot give all the passionate feeling in her heart to the man she's loved for 30 years without her hands to cradle his face, or her arms to pull his naked body close at night. Our body is the pen with which we write our life story, beginning with our first breath and ending at death. The body gives a physical representation of the things that happen in the "inner chambers" of thought, desire, reason, and emotion.

It's not that we have no control over what the body does. As we mature, we develop ways of disciplining the body so as to decide and direct *which* inner desires get expression and how. Everyone, at one time or another, has had to suppress the expression of one desire or emotion in pursuit of a higher goal or purpose. I may desire nothing more than to go for a hike on a beautiful, clear day, but if I have a higher calling that day to my work, my children, or a prior commitment, I choose to defer the desire to hike, putting it aside for a later time when I can live into it fully and without reservation. But even though we can't gratify every desire all the time, the point is that desire itself is an essential component of God's character in a Judeo-Christian understanding of the universe. Christians who have grown up suspecting their desires to be primarily problems (instead of primarily expressions of God's good creativity) can learn over time to see them as evidence not of their fallen nature but of their identity as creatures made in the image of God. As we'll see later, there are ways to invite Christian clients into embracing their desires, seeing them as a gift, and even using them as worship. It may take time and persistence to learn how, but it will be worth the effort.

We Are Body, Mind, and Spirit

Richard Selzer, the surgeon who wrote the book *Letters to a Young Doctor*, described the body as "our spirit thickened" ([1982] 1996, 10). This was the way he came to understand the sacred, unexplainable experiences he witnessed with some of his patients. Despite his training as a physician and scientist, his clinical work taught him that the experience of the body could not be separated from the experience of the spirit. For example, a person's will to live, or passion for life, could have everything to do with how they recovered from their surgery. Recent brain and biochemical studies suggest that we have nerve cells in the stomach and around the heart that communicate feelings in the same way that mood chemicals do. We are learning that the mind and body are so connected that Dr. Candace Pert of Georgetown University Medical Center uses the term "body/mind" to describe these aspects of who we are. Her research shows that we store memory on all of our senses through the molecules of emotions, mostly neuropeptides and their receptors. "The chemicals that are running our body and our brain are the same chemicals that are involved in emotion," Pert says. "And that says to me that we'd better pay more attention to emotions with respect to health" (Pert, quoted in Chatfield n.d.; see also Pert 1986). This also reinforces how central our ability to create satisfying, intimate relationships is to our overall health and well-being. More and more, we're learning that the physical body and the emotional or spiritual body cannot be separated—which seems to imply that the emotional body is also entwined with our relational lives in an emotional feedback loop.

If this does not feel clear to you, ask yourself the following questions. How is your emotional contentment affected with regard to life, your work, your overall outlook, when your relationship with your partner is falling apart? Or, how is your emotional contentment affected with regard to life, your work, your overall outlook, when you are extremely worried or distraught about something happening with one of your children?

To love deeply is to see the image of God. When we give expression to the love we feel, by using the body to show it, we participate in the nature (2 Peter 1:4) of the God who "*is* love" (1 John 4:8, emphasis added) and took on a physical body to show us his love by example (see Philippians 2:7). For Christians, who believe that Jesus *is* God-in-the-flesh, it's not difficult to see that God has a body, a mind, and a spirit: the physical body of Jesus the God-Man, the mind of the Father who created the universe in the first place, and the Spirit of God who has been present and active since creation. So because we also have body, mind, and heart, just like God does, then we're allowing (mind) ourselves to express (body) the love we feel (spirit), and we're actually participating in God's nature and becoming more like God.

For therapists, our task is often to help our Christian clients to understand the interconnections and integrations of all that they are—that their desires, and the expression of love, have their roots in God's character itself, a phenomenon that includes their bodies and their sexuality.

Hidden Treasure

After doing some biblical research to find answers for my clients, I've come to believe that God has given us everything we need in the stories, studies, and sacred writings of the Old and New Testaments for understanding the profound purposes of sexuality. I found that there is a wealth of erotic and sexual wisdom contained in the pages of Scripture—but oddly, for all the abundance of the treasure, it wasn't easy to find.

My first step had been to look within Christian *history*, to see if there had ever been a time when there had been a sex-positive Gospel rooted in the Good News of Jesus and his "new covenant" of forgiveness, restoration, justice, and profound union with God.[2] But time after time, as I waded into the development of the Christian church from the first centuries forward to modern times, I hit concrete walls, typically having to do with harsh, patriarchal mandates, doctrinal rules, and trite, fear-based, sex-negative explanations. As a Christian, I believed that God had given us the spiritual intimacy instruction that we needed, but where was it hiding?

So out of my Swedish stubbornness, I set out to explore *Jewish* history, writing, and wisdom. I reasoned that the sexual pain, shame, and naïveté that I had witnessed in the stories of hundreds of faithful young Christian men and women in my clinical work and in my students could not have come from a sexual ethic built on the life and ministry of a God of love. If it had, people would have been coming into my office with a greater sense of the *purpose* of sexuality, a deeper sense of being at home with their sexual feelings and curiosities, and better teaching to help them to imagine and desire what was possible for them in committed partnership. Most of all, they would have reported a greater sense of familiarity with God's deep love, acceptance, and grace in their sexual desire. They would have been growing in fullness, knowledge, and love, and a sense of play and delight in the blossoming of their sexual desire. More often, though, that's not what I saw. Instead, the vast majority of Christians who came to my office or my classroom showed deep-seated shame for experiencing or acting on sexual desire, or naïveté about the realities of being a sexual creature in the first place.

None of that sat well with me. I couldn't believe that the God of the Hebrew people, the same God whom Christians claimed as well, would impart this kind of repression into the lives of people God loved. God *must* have offered more than the suffocating sexual ethics passed on to the Christian people after 300 CE. Plus, I had also seen that so many of the world's other leading religions (e.g., Hinduism and Buddhism) had centuries of sacred writing on how the sexual relationship could be a form of worship. Why didn't *Christian* tradition and teaching seem to have anything other than the message of "don't have sex before marriage?" What was I missing?

So I set out to study the Hebraic roots of the Christian church, and what I found were magnificent stories of how God had used sexuality and sexual imagery to communicate God's love—stories that became starting points for showing my Christian clients the depth of God's love and devotion to them. Let me share a few of the stories here with you.

The Story of the Mirrors

As the children of Israel traveled toward the Promised Land, they needed to build a tabernacle, a portable temple that would serve them until they could build a permanent one. Gold and copper were necessary for the effort, but while there was plenty of gold, the copper was harder to come by. The artisans needed copper in order to build the laver, the washing station that would sanctify the priests before they entered the Holy of Holies, the sacred space where the Ark of the Covenant resided and where the *Shekinah*, the presence of God, was believed to dwell (Blum 2007).

The people understood how important the washing ritual was; they had already witnessed the instant incineration of Aaron's two sons, Nadab and Abihu, when they hadn't taken care to enter this space correctly—and so the copper laver was an essential part of the preparation (Leviticus 10:1–2; Idel 2005, 28). Regarding the tabernacle, Exodus 30:21 says that "they shall wash their hands and their feet, so that they may not die."

As the tent was being prepared, the women who had contributed their gold for the tabernacle had also brought their copper mirrors. But it is said that Moshe (Moses) knew that these mirrors had been used by these women to prepare themselves for sex with their husbands during the time of slavery in Egypt (Blum 2007).

In those days, the story goes, when the men had been exhausted and unable to make it home from work, the wives had traveled to meet them and stopped along the way to cleanse and prepare themselves using their mirrors. For this reason, Moses at first didn't find the use of these mirrors appropriate for something as important as the laver, and he sought Yahweh's counsel as to what to do (Blum 2007).

But God surprised Moses by telling him that the mirrors, in assisting sexual union, were part of the reflective imagery of God's desire to sanctify and join with his people. For these reasons, God corrected Moses, saying that it was his desire for the copper from the mirrors to be used in the making of the laver—and that in fact, these mirrors were "more precious to me than anything else" (Blum 2007).

The Hebrew people came to see the connection between God's love and desire to commune with them as a symbol of the communion between husband and wife. They began to see a link between the careful cleansing ritual that the rabbis went through to prepare their hearts, bodies, and minds to enter the Holy of Holies and the mindfulness with which they needed to enter sacred lovemaking. They came to believe that sexuality devoid of God can become a demeaning and degrading part of creation, just like the fate of Aaron's sons. Sex could be cavalier—mindless, careless, selfish, maybe even obsessive—but it didn't have to be. It could instead be a mindful, caring, loving, intentional moment in which both persons took each other's body, mind, and soul into account, and the living God as well.

It was within this intentional, mindful union that a couple would find a most holy of spaces, a "Holy of Holies" where they would also encounter God. Yahweh's love for his people was said to be a holy eros—a divine longing, like a lover's, for union with his people and for their flourishing and well-being—and he gave the gift of that blessed union of deeply intimate, loving sex as a way to demonstrate just how powerful his love for his people was.

The Story of Desire and Ash

In biblical Hebrew, man is called an "Iysh" and woman is called an "Ishah." The difference in these two words comes down to just two letters, *Y* and *H*—letters that also happen to be the shortest unpronounceable name for God: Y(yud) and H(hay). As we'll see, many Jewish scholars believe that this holy name is precisely what a man and woman embody when they join together in a carefully prepared time of union. Essentially, they become partners in creating a tabernacle of love, a dwelling place for God. By creating a sacred space through intentional, open awareness of heart and body in their approach to intimate touch, a couple frees the masculine and feminine energies of the Divine in each other; this simultaneously ignites the creative force that is unleashed when the masculine and feminine energies of God are present. The couple is literally making or creating love through their mindful, intimate touch. In the Christian tradition, God is seen as love (see 1 John 4:8, 4:16) and thus is at the center of it all. The symbolism of the universal creative force of love and of the powerful presence of God in intentional lovemaking is breathtaking.

The Kabbalists (scholars of Jewish mysticism) believe that the "tabernacle" created in mindful, intentional lovemaking was another way that God demonstrated his desire to make a home in the material world, just as the Holy of Holies was a dwelling place for the Divine in the Temple. This image of God's desire is so physical, in fact, that the same Jewish preparation practices for priests to ready themselves to enter the Holy of Holies *also* applied to partners in preparation for entering their tabernacle of lovemaking. Each spouse was expected to know that they were entering into a place where no one was allowed to go without God's invitation—or in other words, the act of lovemaking was considered as holy as the act of entering into the innermost chamber of the temple.

There's another bit of linguistics to notice here, too. If we remove the letters of God (Y and H) from the man's name (Iysh) and the woman's name (Ishah), we are left with *aish*, a word literally meaning all-consuming fire or ash (Blum 2007). We've seen that when lovemaking is entered into with mindfulness and intention, a fiery passion can burn, with God's presence and love filling the very core of the union. Many people naturally experience this at an intense time in their relationship, like in its early days, when intention and mindfulness come easy, or when a couple commits to a season of deliberate focus on each other and the relationship itself (like a couples retreat). But the word *aish* suggests that when lovemaking is entered into lightly or dismissively, sexual desire eventually burns the would-be lovers to dust. Perhaps this is what the Song of Songs means when it says (in 2:7 and echoed elsewhere), "I adjure you, O daughters of Jerusalem, by the gazelles or the wild does: do not stir up or awaken love until it is ready!"

We see the same concept playing out in our current culture every day. When handled incorrectly, sex can become an insatiable drive that threatens to extinguish all other creative pursuits that a person may have. Or as we often see in marriages where intimacy and erotic playfulness haven't been nurtured well, desire burns itself out, leaving the couple withdrawn from each other and alone, perhaps unable to connect at all, and certainly not in sex. Between the two extremes is the phenomenon of "making sex," which is the loveless sexuality we discussed a moment ago, as opposed to making love. "Making sex" tends either to burn itself out over time or to burn out the people involved. Sex alone, detached from love and a sacred sense of awe or mystery, is unsustainable and unsatisfying in the long run. When people are unsatisfied with their sex lives, they become lonely and isolated and often feel deeply rejected by their partners. Even though they are "having sex," and maybe even having orgasms, they are not feeling seen, known, loved, and accepted. They are not feeling wanted or chosen, key elements for igniting the flames of our sexual passion. This is what separates making love from making sex. It is the intention and mindfulness of the love–energy behind the intimate touch that make all the difference.

It's not hard to tell when the lovemaking element of eros is missing. Clients, Christian or not, whose sex lives feel detached, dead, transactional, or filled with obligation, are often ill-equipped to know how to make things better, so they do unhelpful things: they complain, blame, cheat, withdraw, lose themselves in work or alcohol, or distract themselves some other way. These adaptations often make the problem worse, not better, even though they all make sense when we consider that most of us grew up in a culture that failed to teach any skills in emotional, relationship, or intimacy intelligence.

If a couple is mindless with their sex life, they cannot expect their intimacy and pleasure to grow any more than a gardener can expect a garden to weed itself. The Hebrew people believed that lovemaking required *preparation* of the space, the heart, and the body. The couple had to approach each other with the *intention* to enter into love, careful *attention* to giving and receiving during the encounter, complete *presence* to self, the other, and the Divine, and an *awake* body, fully animated in breath and in eyes (Blum 2007). The rest was up to the creativity and energy of the couple, and whatever appetite they had in that moment. Chances are it would be a little bit different every time.

Cherubim

According to many Jewish scholars, another critical conceptualization of the divine-human relationship in Jewish literature was the celestial presence that indwelled the two cherubim over the Ark of the Covenant in the Holy of Holies. According to one school of thought, the cherubim were the most important feature of the whole temple. "It was due to them [the cherubim] and due to their maker [or makers] that the Temple stood," wrote Rabbi Pinhas ben Yair, a second-century CE Palestinian teacher. "They were the head of everything that was in the Temple, for the Shekhina [presence of God] rested on them and on the Ark and from there He [God] spoke to Moses" (quoted in Patai 1990, 83). The cherubim were said to be the vehicle through which Moses was able to hear the divine voice.

The cherubim were thought to have an amount of life in them and were said to turn toward each other when Israel followed God's commandments, turning away from each other when Israel sinned. While there were gold cherubim in each rebuilding of the Temple Tabernacle, the dimensions, depictions, and positions of the cherubim varied. Some were open-winged, in mutual protection of the Ark; some were seated in sexual embrace over-top of it. The explanations of this appear in many places across Hebrew literature, though they are often vague. That was on purpose, because it was feared that explicit descriptions would be too easily misinterpreted in the wider culture. For example, it would have been difficult to explain to the pagan culture of that day that the cherubim were sacred symbols, not idols, and that they physically expressed certain *attributes* of God without actually *depicting* God.

"When Israel used to make the pilgrimage," reads another Talmud passage from the third century, the priests "would roll up for [the people] the parokhet [or the curtains separating the Holy of Holies], and show them the cherubim which were intertwined with one another, and say to them: 'Behold! Your love [hibbah] before God is like the love of male and of female'" (Patai 1990, 84).

An eleventh-century commentator explains this passage this way: "The Cherubim were joined together, and were clinging to and embracing each other like a male who embraces a female" (Patai 1990, 85). Moshe Idel, a leading Jewish scholar, has written that the nature of the intertwining cherubs functions as a metaphor of the divine eros that God has for his people. When the last temple was destroyed in 72 CE, the role of the cherubs as a dwelling place for the presence of God was believed to be preserved through the sexual union of a husband and wife when the couple prepared to enter their sacred space with the same kind of intention and preparation as a priest entering the Holy of Holies (Idel 2005, 33–4).

The Song of Songs

My beloved speaks and says to me:
"Arise, my love, my fair one,
   and come away;
for now the winter is past,
   the rain is over and gone.
The flowers appear on the earth;
   the time of singing has come,
and the voice of the turtledove
   is heard in our land.
The fig tree puts forth its figs,
   and the vines are in blossom;
   they give forth fragrance.
Arise, my love, my fair one,
   and come away.
O my dove, in the clefts of the rock,
   in the covert of the cliff,

> let me see your face,
>   let me hear your voice;
> for your voice is sweet,
>   and your face is lovely". . . .
> My beloved is mine and I am his;
>   he pastures his flock among the lilies.
>   (Song of Songs 2:10–14, 16)

Rabbi Akiva (50–135 CE), whom the Talmud calls the head of all sages, said that "all the Scriptures are holy, but The Song of Songs is the Holy of Holies!" (*Mishnah Yadayim* 3:5).[3] Yet again we see an early Jewish teacher, around the time of Jesus, telling us that the central and primary text of Jewish living involved the highly evolved, erotic love and sensual awareness of God's presence and love of his people. If the Song of Songs is the Holy of Holies of Old Testament scripture, then all of the other texts and Jewish teaching must serve the purpose of the Song of Songs.

This text is about experiencing God's presence and essence through a passionate, awe-inspiring, and boundless love. It is an erotic message of union in which a merging of love—God's love and human love—melts into an experience of the God of Love. This is a new idea for many Christians, particularly those who have not been exposed to a Jewish understanding of the Song of Songs and who have been taught to fear sexuality, sensuality, desire, and eros. Therapists shouldn't be surprised if conservative Christian clients can't remember having heard much teaching from the Song of Songs. Christians I have spoken to refer to it as one of the most ignored books in the Bible.

Could that be because the Song feels risky? Perhaps so, considering that the Holy of Holies, the inner sanctum of the Temple, was difficult to enter and was full of danger. Only the high priest entered in, and only once a year, on the Day of Atonement. On this day, he had to follow the ritual of preparation with the utmost care, or he would die. Preparations involved readiness of heart and mind, cleansing of the body, wearing sacred clothes, and bringing incense and blood for the atonement of sins (see Leviticus 16). Here again, we see the parallel process between God's love for his people, his desire to be in intimate relationship with them, and the reciprocal devotion given and desired, just like committed partners preparing for a lovemaking session with each other. Yahweh wanted a mindful, essential relationship with his people, and he wanted the same thing for lovers when they made love.

Long after the tabernacle became obsolete, the curtain (or parochet) in the Jerusalem Temple, which separated God in the Holy of Holies from the everyday people, was said to be 60 feet in height, 30 feet in width, and four inches thick. On the day of Jesus's crucifixion, the Bible says there was a sudden earthquake and darkening of the sky. At that moment the curtain was ripped from top to bottom (Matthew 27:51, Mark 15:38, Luke 23:45), a feat that was not humanly possible. Jesus, according to Christian doctrine, is understood as the ultimate and eternal atonement, and the tearing of the curtain designated that from that moment forward, God's dwelling presence was no longer held exclusively behind the parochet within the Holy of Holies. Christians believe that through Christ's atoning death and resurrection, direct relationship with God was now possible for all people—the price was paid, and God's presence could now dwell within and between us at all times and in all places, as the Shekhina had done previously. One might even say that humanity's relationship with God was even *more* erotic than before, because one no longer had to be a priest, and it no longer needed to be a specific day of the year. God's intimate presence was available to anyone, anytime, anywhere; that's how much God craved a loving union with humanity.

For conservative Christians, an important takeaway from this discussion of Judeo-Christian heritage is this: to experience intimacy with the Creator, a person must come with a prepared heart, body, and mind; and likewise, if they hope to experience the fullest capacities of intimacy with God and their partner in their sexuality, they must come prepared in body, mind, and heart to every encounter.

The Vow of 'Onah and Other Jewish Attitudes About Sex

I often complain about how American culture and the church largely fail to provide guidelines to direct the development of sexual health—a sexual ethic, if you will. However, Jewish culture has long had a series of directives that have guided the development of loving and just sexual relationships. The following is a type of Jewish sexual ethic from the vow of 'Onah and from Jewish fertility guidelines. Rather than focusing on what *not* to do, like the traditional sex-negative Christian ethic has done, these guidelines provide a framework for building a dynamic, expressive sexual relationship that can last an entire lifetime. As you will see, these guidelines take gender differences, power differences, and situational differences into account while remaining stunningly elegant.

Sex Is Considered a Woman's Right, Not a Man's

The husband is given the vow of 'Onah, which is one of the religious obligations he assumes at marriage. 'Onah is the commandment to supply all forms of well-being and pleasure to his wife. According to Moshe Idel, the term 'Onah as a religious obligation is not connected to the sexual satisfaction of the husband, but to the special sexual needs of the wife (Idel 2005, 18, 147). The husband has a duty to ensure that all forms of sexual touch are pleasurable for her. He is also expected to watch for signs that his wife *wants* intimate touch, and to offer it without her asking for it (Pitchon 1995, 209). In her essay, *Sexual Behaviour among Ultra-Orthodox Jews*, Hannah Rockman expounds on the requirements of the husband and shows that there was an insistence that all sexual touch be accompanied by closeness (*kiruv*) and joy (*simchah*) (Rockman 1995, 193). This level of attentiveness and intimacy raises lovemaking onto a higher, more emotional and spiritual plane. It also changes the sexual exchange from one that is more masculine to one that is more feminine—that is, it's collaborative, non-goal-oriented, pleasure-focused, experience-rich, and whole-body-oriented. Sex becomes, as my husband would say, something that exists "for *play*" instead of "for *ejaculation*." As a sex therapist, this is a game changer for many heterosexual relationships where women and men have been allowing themselves to be passive participants of transactional and obligatory sexual exchanges driven by an idea that sex is "for men" instead of for pleasure and connection.

Sex and Sexuality Are Not Seen as Primarily About Genital Intercourse

Under 'Onah, all forms of sexual enjoyment are recognized, from the simplicity of holding hands up to and including sexual intercourse. This vast sexual enjoyment is seen as a vital component of pleasure and an act of immense significance, something that requires commitment and responsibility toward each other and to any offspring that might result. In fact, two weeks of every month for Orthodox Jews were devoted to other forms of intimacy *outside* of intercourse. This introduction of the forbidden, and the recognition of all loving touch, helped to keep the sexual relationship fresh and varied, allowing couples to add something to their sexual repertoire, instead of dancing the same old dance, time after time (Rich n.d.).

The Purpose in All Sexual Touch Is to Reinforce the Loving Bond Across the Lifespan Together

Sexual touch is expected to evolve and change over time as life stages are traversed together. The idea that the elderly do not have sex is a foreign concept in the Torah. Here again, we see the focus to be not on intercourse or how the penis performs but on loving touch. It is expected that loving, sexual touch will continue even as bodies change, babies are born, illness occurs, life happens, and the flesh begins to deteriorate (Rich n.d.).

Sexual Touch and Intercourse Were Meant to Be Celebrated in Joy

Sex is not to be experienced in anger, disinterest, when drunk, or in self-interest. Sex for selfish, personal satisfaction without regard for the partner's pleasure is wrong and considered evil. A man may never force his wife to have sex or use sex as a weapon against a spouse, whether by depriving the spouse of sex or by compelling it. It is considered a serious offense to use sex (or its absence) to punish or manipulate a spouse. Here we have several statements that remind us that we are to enter the sexual relationship mindfully and with the intention to honor ourselves, our partner, and our God (Rich n.d.).

Jews also understood that these were serious offenses if broken. The word "evil" is rare in the Torah, and when it does appear, it is considered very strong language. Here it is understood that people had the capacity to hurt each other deeply in and through their sexuality if it was used in a selfish or mindless way (Rich n.d.).

In Jewish Law, Sex Is Not Considered Shameful, Sinful, or Obscene

Sex is not a necessary evil for the sole purpose of procreation. Some familiar with Hebrew scripture might point out that sexual desire comes from the *Yetzer hara*; the so-called evil impulse is no more evil an impulse than the desire for food and water, cravings that also originate from the *Yetzer hara*. Because of this, sexual desire was not seen as sinful or obscene. Instead, it was seen as a gift to be nurtured and cared for, so much so that to this day, a Jewish couple considers it a "double blessing" if they make love on the Sabbath (Rich n.d.).

Sexual Enjoyment Is Recommended for Times When Procreation Is Impossible

Permissible sexual touch is not limited to behaviors that would lead to procreation. The realm of acceptable contact is extended to allow other activities, too, such as playing out a fantasy together or making love in a tub. Safe forms of bondage (consensual, light, and with an agreed-upon "safe word") were considered, too. In any event, "the duty of a man to engage his wife sexually is not contingent upon whether or not there is the possibility of pregnancy," wrote Rabbi Moshe Feinstein, a twentieth-century Lithuanian Orthodox rabbi, "for it is mandated in the responsibilities of marriage that she should receive pleasure and not suffer, no different than the mandate that she be clothed and sheltered" (Feinstein, quoted in Winkler 1998, 51).

Making Love Involves Being Mindful of the Body, Mind, Soul, and Spirit of Your Partner

The Torah uses the root word Yod-Dalet-Ayin, meaning "to know," to describe sexual union as a knowing of your spouse in mind, soul, and body. This word illustrates that all sexuality, the act of knowing another in Yod-Dalet-Ayin, is meant to involve the whole of a person, including the heart and mind, and not just the body (Rich n.d.). The Jewish understanding of sexual knowing and sexual sharing between a husband and wife took the whole person into consideration—heart desires, body desires, thoughts, and feelings. The body was not separated from the mind or heart.

This accountability to heart and mind in sexual intimacy seemed lost in the message I heard from many Christians who were told that if you "knew" someone before marriage, it meant you had been sexually active. It had a very punitive connotation. The focus was on the physical boundary that was crossed. They had been taught that the translation of "to know" was sex-negative and used as a form of judgment. But this negative connotation was not in the original Hebrew meaning. The focus was a reminder of each partner's accountability to the heart, soul, and body pleasure of their partner in the sexual exchange. It was about intention, mindfulness, mutuality, and connection.

Hebrew Elegance

When you examine the vow of 'Onah and the fertility guidelines highlighted earlier in light of other developmental and relational tendencies especially evident in many heterosexual relationships, we see a kind of ancient wisdom emerge. Let's see what we can glean from the Jewish tradition and teaching in this chapter.

In the story of the copper mirrors, we learn that God sees committed, loving, and conscious lovemaking as symbolic of an aspect of God's great love and desire for his people. The Tabernacle story teaches that when a committed couple wants to share intimate sexual touch, they are to see it as sanctified, sacred, and holy, just as if they were priests preparing to enter the Holy of Holies to commune directly with the presence of God. Eros has the capacity to be dangerous and unpredictable when not taken seriously, but ecstatic and mysterious when entered into with preparation, intention, mindfulness, and reverence. The story of the cherubim, together with the Song of Songs, shows that God longs for his creation the way lovers long for each other. This longing for his people to be lost in him, and he in them, seems woven throughout these Hebrew stories. Like two lovers filled with love and trust, God desires for there to be no walls between him and his people, just as in lovemaking partners become lost in each other. The human image used to remind us of God's deep love is that of two lovers, fully embodied, fully in love, and filled with passion and desire, together making and creating love. All sexual embrace is about the deepest connection to the one we have chosen for the rest of our lives. These Hebrew traditions show us that God wants the same with and for his people.

The vow of 'Onah and other Jewish guidelines in committed partnership remind us of a few important aspects of sexual fulfillment that might be valuable to some of our clients. In fulfilling the vow of 'Onah, the responsibility is given to a *male partner* to become the lover of a woman—to study how to pleasure and love her. This request, especially in heterosexual relationships, invites both men and women to grow in areas that often do not develop until midlife—but they are areas that *need to grow* for a marriage to stand the test of time.

Men can tend to lead from their place of drive, purpose, accomplishment, and competition—a fact not only of social conditioning but also of the biology of the male brain (Brizendine 2010, 18–19). In Eastern philosophy, this is known as the second chakra. Symbolically, men lead from their pelvis; we see this in young boys who turn sticks into swords and in teenage boys who see sexual expression as a conquest. A young man's growing edge in marriage is to learn to see, hear, learn, and study *another* in order to meet the other's needs. To love well relies less on competition, conquests, or goals, and more on learning the nuances of one's beloved. Husbands are not competing with other men; they are learning to grow their skills in relating and loving. The discipline of truly *learning* their wives helps men to connect their pelvis to their heart. The sooner men learn the value of their relationships to ground their life-purposes, the fewer mistakes they make in low–return investments (e.g., too much time spent traveling), the less pain they inadvertently cause, and the more quality time they gain with kids and spouses (high–return investments).

Women, by contrast, tend to lead with the heart. In Eastern philosophy, this is the fourth chakra. The female brain structure and hormonal fluctuations reveal a diversity in gender expression (Brizendine 2006, 7–8). This is supported in cultural conditioning as well, and is revealed when we see little girls who turn two sticks into a mommy stick and a daddy stick, or when we see adolescent girls who are all about getting a boyfriend and being "in charge" of their friendships. In this 'Onah command, a woman must learn to communicate what she wants. But first she must learn to value her body, learn her body, her pleasures, and her desires. She must learn to communicate these things in clear, overt ways, as an essential form of caring for herself and finding well-being and purpose in life and in her relationships. She must let go of being the sole "driver" of a relationship and let herself fully receive and be fully known. She must develop a voice and a "drive" for *herself* and for her sexuality—in essence, connecting her heart to her pelvis. This is a significant skill if a woman can learn this early in life.

The Jewish law of 'Onah sets up the arrangement so that marriage, and particularly the connection and pleasure within the heterosexual relationship, helps both the man and the woman to grow in their natural areas of weakness while learning interdependence with each other. This helps to balance the growth between the two partners, so that the relationship can be more in tune and more mutual from the outset.

In American society, whether from the church or culture, men (and women) are taught that sex is about intercourse (how the penis functions, centering around ejaculation) and that they (men) are entitled to sex once they're married. How much sex, and how often it happens, is based on *their* wants, which only reinforces the tendency to lead from the pelvis and to reduce the need to learn the skills necessary to be a great lover (to a woman). Women, on the other hand, culturally learn that it is all about intercourse and about the man's sexual drive. They learn that they do not have to know or communicate what brings *them* pleasure. The focus on intercourse and a man's pleasure tacitly teaches women to ignore their sexual pleasure while focusing on the rest of the relationship. When women try to drive the relationship alone and men try to drive the couple's sexual life alone, desire will burn out—for her, for him, or for both. At best, it leads to a lifeless form of eroticism.

However, according to Jewish tradition, the sexual relationship is seen as a wonderful gift and an invitation into a kind of sacred sanctuary. It is to be entered into mutually, thoughtfully, carefully, and only when both parties seek to be fully present to give and receive. It is not to be entered into lightly, selfishly, or when angry, distracted, or chemically influenced, and it is never to be used as a tool to hurt, manipulate, or coerce one's partner. To enter the Holy of Holies at the heart of each person and at the heart of the relationship where each will be fully open, exposed, and ready to meet each other and their Creator—that is the goal of eroticism. What happens next is entirely up to them and is their mystery to unfold.

Core Christian Teaching That Was Not Incorporated Into a Christian Sexual Ethic

Sexuality is not a central focus of Jesus's ministry, as recorded in the four Gospel books of the New Testament (Matthew, Mark, Luke, and John). But learning how to love and treat each other was a major focus of his teaching. Jesus made it clear that justice, grace, love, forgiveness, and equality were to be granted to all people regardless of status, gender, ability, or ethnicity. Jesus told his followers that they were to love each other like he loved them, and that it would be through this example of love that others would see that they were his followers. The last night Jesus was with his disciples, he said to them, "Love one another. Just as I have loved you, you also should love one another. By this everyone will know that you are my disciples, if you have love for one another" (John 13:34–35).

Back in Chapter 1, I mentioned the stories of the woman at the well in John 4 and the woman brought for stoning in John 8. These are two of my favorite stories of Jesus, because they are powerful examples of how Jesus defied the religious, social, and political norms of the times, which tried to dictate who was worthy of love and respect and who was not. Jesus demonstrated that these women of marginalized status were of utmost importance and value. These values were of such importance to Jesus's ministry that we see story after story where he decisively and blatantly stood against abuses of power—government to the people, men to women, rich to poor, able-bodied to disabled, and the "righteous" toward those considered sinners (see Matthew 9:11–13 and 12:1–14; Mark 5; Luke 4, 9, and 13; John 5).

When we combine the core values of Jesus's ministry with the wisdom of the Hebrew people, we see how possible it is to construct a solid, sex-positive, Judeo-Christian sexual ethic. We see a God who sought to teach about love and justice, who earnestly sought an intimate relationship with his people, and who utilized images and symbols of erotic love to demonstrate the depth of his love. Human sexuality finds its most erotic, dynamic, and satisfying experience inside the context of love, trust, safety, commitment, and desire. People come alive in the context of safety and love. We all crave to be seen, known, loved, and accepted, just as the woman at the well and the woman brought for stoning did. When our lover provides this for us, we are often much more able to provide this for ourselves and to ask for it from our lover. Combined with the Hebrew beliefs about the sanctity and erotic beauty of sexuality, Jesus provided a great deal of insight about how to be a fabulous lover.

Core Values in Action

Think about these core values in the context of an erotic, God-honoring sexuality, like what we've distilled from Hebrew teaching in this chapter. I'd like to ask a few questions and examine this dilemma with Justin and Marta, our couple from Chapter 1. Here is what I did with them.

Justin needed to feel that his faith tradition was honored, but in a way that also honored his evolution as an adult in his relationship with Marta. His faith was important to him, but he described it as contextual and relevant. He did not see God as a God of rules, but as a God of freedom and love. He believed that boundaries served the purpose of ultimately providing freedom to experience abundance of the best of what God had in store. He also echoed what others have said, that he had a responsibility to identify and engage in activities that ultimately challenged exploitive and oppressive institutions and relationships (see Cahill 1996, 125–30). After we talked in session about all the Hebrew stories and the nature of Jesus's ministry, and the values that Justin felt informed what Jesus did and how he taught, we began to process through these questions that I believe failed to be integrated into what emerged as the prevailing Christian sexual ethic.

- Love, grace, and justice are constant New Testament themes, punctuated as a set of values reflecting the nature of God through the life, ministry, death, and resurrection of Jesus. How do committed love and sexual expression look when centered in love, grace, and justice? In Justin and Marta's relationship, we explored the ways by which each of them expressed love, grace, and justice, and how these themes played out emotionally, intellectually, in conflict, socially, with touch and affection, in communication, and spiritually. I asked them questions like "How had they developed these themes over time?" and "How did they want to grow and change?" and "How did they manage these changes together?"
- Christ's ministry centered around his compassionate offer to join with the Divine, to join him, to leave everything else and follow him. How do romantic love and sexual expression look if they invite you into communion with God's presence? I asked Justin and Marta to think about the times when their relationship felt most connected, when it felt most spiritually bonded, and how they might heighten their sense of presence, attention, and intention through intimacy practices that could be done daily and weekly.

- Jesus vigorously opposed the misuse of power practiced by those in political and religious authority. His many forms of confrontation were more than acts of subversion; he demonstrated a new religious code of ethics, involving positive practices of invitation and inclusion toward all people—rich, poor, Jew, Gentile, weak, sinful, man, woman, or minority or dismissed status. He left no room for the abuse of power by the religious or political elite and demonstrated that all people were of equal standing with God. How does committed sexual expression look when lovers realize that each is as precious as the other in God's eyes? In Justin and Marta's relationship, I asked them to think about the times when power felt imbalanced in their relationship or when feelings got hurt. What were the circumstances that surrounded this? Together, we deconstructed gender, culture, and family-of-origin issues that were getting the best of them, sometimes without their awareness. For example, Marta had a bossy side that came from being a firstborn in a loud, northern European family. At times, this aggression could shut Justin down, leaving Marta feeling ignored and unvalued and therefore completely infuriated. The cycle wasn't pretty. Once they both had a chance to see how the dance activated both of their family-of-origin "hot buttons," they were able to own their own reactivity and speak from their feelings, rather than attacking or withdrawing. It completely changed their dynamic.

- Jesus demonstrated a fervent intention to love and draw others into the face and love of his Father. How is committed love demonstrated through sexuality when lovemaking is seen as a holy communing in God's love? What is shared when every part of oneself seeks both to see and to reflect the image of God with and within one's beloved? With Justin and Marta, as we moved our conversation away from which sexual behaviors they had or had not done and moved toward discussing how they demonstrated their love for and with each other, both Justin and Marta began to see how their values were so much more aligned with each other even in a way that coconstructed a kind of core spirituality that was at the very heart of their bond. I remember one very sweet session when Justin turned to Marta and said, "I think one of the things that I have always loved about Marta is the same thing I love about my faith in Jesus. She is fierce in her fight for justice and her belief that all people deserve to be loved well regardless of where they come from." He was gazing into her eyes as he said this. Her face had a kind of glow to it, as though she could see for the first time how much his faith meant to him. It was about love, deep love—his love for her, his love for humanity, and his love for God. It felt like an important turning point in our time together. Their lovemaking, whenever and however it was to happen, in all its diverse expressions of wild, tender, quick, and slow ways over the course of their lifetime, would involve a recognition of their deep love of self, other, and God, demonstrated in countless sexual and nonsexual ways through touch.

Each of these core concepts in Jesus's ministry gives us the essential ingredients to build a deeply intimate, erotic, fun, and spiritual connection with our partner through all forms of intimacy. They also highlight relational and emotional skills that take years to understand and to practice. In many ways, that's what makes them so rich and powerful. They are not mandates: they are *qualities* to be developed in oneself and within one's relationship.

Here are some questions you might consider posing to a Christian client struggling with religious sexual shame:

1. How would you approach your lover (intimately, sexually) if you wanted him or her to feel God's presence, love, and justice in every way you touch? How would you want your lover to approach you in order to help you to experience God's presence, love, and justice and to help you know that you are chosen by God?

2. How would you (physically) approach your partner if you wanted him or her to experience the image of God within them? How would you want your partner to approach *you*, bearing in mind the same wish to experience God's image within you, to know of his desire to love you?

3. How would you (physically) approach your lover to show your desire to share and to serve one another, versus expecting your needs or their needs to trump or silence the desires of the other?

4. How could you express to your partner that you wish to open your heart and receive and give love with your fullest attention, presence, and sensual awareness? How could you open your heart to receive the loving intention of your partner?

Healing Sexual Shame

Many Christians struggle to let go of the mandates that have wounded them. But the process of writing a new, sex-positive story that honors their faith while also having their story heard by an empathic and compassionate person is the beginning of the process. When I am working with clients, I often conceptualize the healing of religious sexual shame as a four-step process: frame, name, claim, and aim. I will talk about this in much more detail in Chapter 6, but here's a primer. *Frame* involves a client receiving the framework of sex education that they have never had before. *Name* is the process of getting their story heard and accepted by someone who cares for them. *Claim* has to do with claiming one's body in all of its wonderful, unique aspects, undoing any harmful messages inherited from religion and culture. *Aim* is the process of beginning to write a new story of where they are going, what they now believe, and what their legacy is going to become. These four processes may need to be visited over and over, and walking through them can be like untangling a tightly wound knot. But in time, with patience and love, the body and heart will free themselves from all of the shame and hurt that have kept a client from experiencing joy.

For many Christians, it can feel overwhelming to learn of all that they hadn't been taught, to hear these stories for the first time and realize the rich and beautiful history that was intended to nourish them sexually. It can be a challenge for them to begin joining their love for God with their experience of human erotic love. But your ability as a therapist to walk with them patiently and lovingly as all of their feelings and questions emerge, swirl, rise, and fall will be a remarkable gift not only of healing but also of claiming their birthright of freedom, creativity, and sexual passion, all rooted in the example of a God who loves us more deeply and intimately than we know. For most people, it is a wild concept to go from believing that all pleasure is bad and suspect to believing that God wants them to live a life of abundance: "I came that they may have life, and have it abundantly" (John 10:10). It takes time.

Notes

1. I think it is important to note here that this creation account does not exclude LGBT persons. The "Adam" in this Jewish interpretation was masculine and feminine. See Ephilei (n.d.).
2. The "new covenant" refers to the promise Jesus made, as a representative of God, with all people regardless of background, gender, lineage, status, or affiliation, that they were chosen by God, called by name, beloved children, redeemed and forgiven. He called people through his ministry and example to a life of service to those who are disenfranchised, to stand up against injustice, and to love, forgive, and extend grace just as they had been given these things by God and others in the name of God. See Jeremiah 31:31; Luke 22:20; 1 Corinthians 11:25; 2 Corinthians 3:6; Hebrews 8:8, 13, 9:15, 12:24.
3. Accessed through Sefaria, an online library of Jewish literature: www.sefaria.org/Mishnah_Yadayim.4?lang=en, accessed August 31, 2016.

References

Blum, Rick. 2007. The Most Sacred of Places. *Parabola*, Summer, 14–17.

Brizendine, Louann. 2006. *The Female Brain*. New York, NY: Morgan Road.

———. 2010. *The Male Brain: A Breakthrough Understanding of How Men and Boys Think*. New York, NY: Broadway.

Cahill, Lisa Sowle. 1996. *Sex, Gender and Christian Ethics*. Cambridge, UK: Cambridge University Press.

Chatfield, Cynthia. N.d. Your Body Is Your Subconscious Mind: Mind-Body Medicine Becomes the Science of Psychoneuroimmunology (PNI) (Chapter 6). In *A Formula for Healing Cancer: The Latest Research in Mind-Body Medicine*. E-book. www.healingcancer.info/ebook/candace-pert, accessed August 31, 2016.

Curtis, Brent, and John Eldredge. 1997. *The Sacred Romance: Drawing Closer to the Heart of God*. Nashville, TN: Thomas Nelson.

Ephilei [pseud.] N.d. Androgyne Adam. Component of *Transcendent Christ Transgender Christians* by the same author. Posted on *Transgender Christians* (blog), accessed August 31, 2016. www.transchristians.org/book/hijra-to-christ/adam.

Gafni, Marc. 2003. *The Mystery of Love*. New York, NY: Atria.

Garcia, Justin R., Chris Reiber, Ann M. Merriwether, Leslie L. Heywood, and Helen E. Fisher. 2010. *Touch Me in the Morning: Intimately Affiliative Gestures in Uncommitted and Romantic Relationships.* Paper presented at the Fourth Annual Conference of the NorthEastern Evolutionary Psychology Society, State University of New York at New Paltz, NY, March 27.

Garcia, Justin R., Chris Reiber, Sean G. Massey, and Ann M. Merriwether. 2012. Sexual Hookup Culture: A Review. *Review of General Psychology* 16 (2): 161–76. Obtained via NIH Public Access. www.ncbi.nlm.nih.gov/pmc/articles/PMC3613286/pdf/nihms443788.pdf, accessed September 1, 2016. doi:10.1037/a0027911.

Idel, Moshe. 2005. *Kabbalah and Eros.* New Haven, CT: Yale University Press.

Moore, Thomas. 1998. *The Soul of Sex: Cultivating Life as an Act of Love.* New York, NY: HarperCollins.

Patai, Raphael. 1990. *The Hebrew Goddess*, 3rd ed. Detroit, MI: Wayne State University Press.

Pert, Candace. 1986. Wisdom of the Receptors: Neuropeptides, the Emotions, and Body-mind. *Advances, Institute for the Advancement of Health* 3 (8): 8–16.

Pitchon, Eduardo. 1995. Hasidic Attitudes towards Sexuality. In *Jewish Explorations of Sexuality*, edited by Jonathan Magonet, 205–12. Providence, RI: Berghahn.

Rich, Tracey R. N.d. Kosher Sex. Posted to *Judaism 101*, curated by Tracey R. Rich. www.jewfaq.org/sex.htm, accessed August 23, 2016.

Rockman, Hannah. 1995. Sexual Behaviour among Ultra-Orthodox Jews: A Review of Laws and Guidelines. In *Jewish Explorations of Sexuality*, edited by Jonathan Magonet, 191–204. Providence, RI: Berghahn.

Selzer, Richard. (1982) 1996. *Letters to a Young Doctor.* San Diego, CA: Harvest.

Winkler, Gershon. 1998. *Sacred Secrets: The Sanctity of Sex in Jewish Law and Lore.* Northvale, NJ: Jason Aronson.

5 In Pursuit of a Sex-Positive Gospel

Strategies for a New Sexual Ethic

In your world the value of the individual is constantly weighed against the survival of the system, whether political, economic, social or religious—any system actually. First one person, and then a few and finally even many are easily sacrificed for the good and ongoing existence of that system. In one form or another, this lies behind every struggle for power, every prejudice, every war, and every abuse of relationship. The 'will to power and independence' has become so ubiquitous that it is now considered normal . . .

As a crowning glory of creation, you were made in our image [God's image], unencumbered by structure and free to simply 'be' in relationship with me and one another. If you had truly learned to regard each other's concerns as significant as your own, there would be no need for hierarchy.

—William P. Young, *The Shack* (2007, 123–4)

Fiona was confused and hurt, and she wanted to leave her relationship.

I met the beautiful 20-year-old, a conservative Christian and a friend of my daughter's, while visiting Chloë in New Zealand on her study-abroad experience some years ago. Fiona had asked me out for coffee and advice after she found out what I do for a living.

As she opened up about her life, she told me about Brandon, her boyfriend back home with whom she had become sexually intimate, but who, I was learning, had been abusing her. They had been together all through high school and had gone off to college together. Brandon had been the star athlete in school, and other than a temper, he had been a pretty good guy throughout most of their early dating years in high school. But as soon as they got to college, he pledged a fraternity and quickly fell into a lifestyle of drinking and hard-core partying. As his alcohol intake increased, so did his demands for sex, his angry outbursts, and his public criticisms. Before Fiona had left for New Zealand, Brandon had forced her to have sex and later had left a party with another woman.

By the time I met her, two years into her relationship with Brandon and shortly after the rape, Fiona was feeling like her life was spinning out of control. She knew that she wanted to be finished with him, but she was very confused about what she *ought* to do. Should she stay with him because they had become sexual? Or did she somehow deserve his treatment because she had not "waited" for sex with him until marriage?

There was a religious element to the way Fiona described her feelings of guilt and confusion. Was this God's punishment? Was the Lord angry with her for being sexually active before marriage, and was his anger coming out in the form of her boyfriend's abuse? Or perhaps, was God simply letting her experience some kind of consequence for her choices?

Fiona was from a tight-knit faith community back home, but no one seemed to have any inkling of what had been going on behind closed doors, including how intimate Fiona and Brandon had become and how abusive and controlling he was toward her. No one knew about his pattern of blaming her for all his hurtful actions and choices, like when he would berate her for his bad grades because she had been too busy to help him study, or how he would blame her for their sex life because of how she dressed or because she didn't try harder to stop him. But even if Fiona's family *had* known, even if she had opened up to them, she feared that she would only be judged for having allowed herself to become so "weak" and "sinful" with Brandon. She had watched how others in her church and youth group had been treated when they had not lived up to the exacting standards that were set. She heard the gossiping that was done by other kids and by the parents about who was having sex or smoking pot or coming home late. She remembered the time that Pablo and Nancy, two kids in the college group, had gotten pregnant and had come in front of the church to tell the congregation that they were getting married because of the pregnancy. She remembered how humiliated they seemed and how embarrassed she felt for them, and now she felt as though there was no one safe to talk to.

For Fiona, the toxic mix of influences—the acid of the verbal and physical abuse from her boyfriend, the shame she feared from her church, and the pain of her resulting sense of isolation (let alone being an ocean and half a continent away from her home in Ohio)—had left her with barely an ounce of self-worth.

Studying abroad had had at least one positive effect, though: the extra distance had given her the space she needed to think and reflect. By the time I talked to her, she knew that she desperately wanted to break up with Brandon, and what she needed was support and compassion to walk away—not condemnation and blame.

The Irony of Shame

Pause for a moment and think of all the people you have served in your practice who have felt deep shame, or try to think of a time when you have felt the weight of shame in your own life. In your experience, how have these emotions manifested and affected relationships? How have they affected your clients' sense of value, or your own?

I've encountered shame countless times in my own practice and classroom. "Ashamed" and "not valuable" are terms that I've heard students and clients use to describe how they felt as a result of their Christian upbringing, along with words like "rejected," "dirty," "damaged goods," "all wrong," "perverted," "guilty," "bad," "confused," "angry," "worthless," "hopeless," and—perhaps most tellingly—"dead inside."

Research has shown that shame and condemnation can have a profound effect on the development of persons and their relationships; they've been described as insidious, covert, and mentally painful (Rahm, Renck, and Ringsberg 2006, 109). The experience of shame develops interpersonally; for a child, shame is usually rooted in a relationship between the child and someone or something they are attached to or care about. It involves the child's increasing awareness of how the perceived defective self may appear to others, combined with a simultaneous sense of self as worthless and rejected by others, particularly the person the child cares about (Murray, Waller, and Legg 2000, 85). For example, one study revealed that little girls at age five were more likely to show shame if they had experienced authoritarian parenting when they were three (see Mills 2003, 329). Plus, parents who perceive their children as angry, especially girls, are more likely to report authoritarian practices at age five—thus further feeding the development of shame (see Mills 2003). In one study on parental attitudes, a higher level of shame was found among 5- to 12-year-olds whose parents perceived them as falling short of their ideals (Wei et al. 2005).

Many theorists consider shame to be an experience or attribution about the whole self—an intense, negative feeling about the self *in its entirety* (Mills 2003). Shame theorists suggest that this emotion is likely to be promoted by a parenting style or family system that reflects a negative attitude to the child and consistently points out what the child is doing wrong. A sense of shame is then credited to the whole self. As one study defined it in 2003, authoritarian parents are demanding and directive, place a high value on obedience and conformity, and are unresponsive or outright rejecting when a child fails to meet their expectations. They provide an orderly environment, a clear set of rules and regulations, and careful monitoring of their child, but they expect unquestioning obedience and will use force and punishment to assure it. In short, in families where children experience shame, the marks are essentially threefold: the child is held to high standards and expectations, given little control and autonomy, and punished for failure (Mills 2003).

Here's how it plays out in many conservative Christian circles. I have seen that *exact* parenting style—the unreachable standards, mixed with judgment—wielded by youth group leaders on their students, particularly around issues of sexual desire and expression. These harsh and punitive attitudes create the atmospheric conditions for shame and a globally negative sense of self. Low self-esteem is often the result, the exact opposite of the belovedness that the Christian story says God wants them to know and feel. The sense of being unacceptable often plagues a person for years and interrupts possibilities and relationships. The fact that Fiona, my young friend from the New Zealand coffee shop, felt this way after being steeped in a conservative Christian environment throughout her development is just one example of how this phenomenon can play out later in a person's life. Fiona believed it was her actions and the actions of her boyfriend that made her unworthy, and that she had failed everyone she loved. She felt unworthy of compassion and grace, and she had been suffering this shame in silence.

Love in Action: The Core of Jesus's Ministry

It makes no sense that the prevailing sexual shame of conservative Christian young adults should be the norm. Not only is there *incredible* sex-positivity in Christianity's Hebraic roots (as we saw in Chapter 4), but also the example of Jesus himself from the New Testament shows that shame was the last thing on his mind. Take the famous story of the Samaritan woman at the well in John 4:4–42, or the woman brought for stoning in John 8:2–11. Jesus was downright scandalous. He defied every rule that marginalized the poor and disenfranchised of society, listening to the voiceless and giving power to the powerless in both episodes. People who had been convinced of their worthlessness were the people he was most drawn to, because to him, all people were of infinite value. But the ones who were most grateful were those who felt abused and devalued by the culture and the elite. Jesus humbled those who were abusing their power, both in political office and in the church. In John 4, he accepted water from an outcast woman and gave her such an attentive, grace-filled hearing that the shame of her life washed away before his eyes. Then in John 8, he reminded a whole host of men ready to stone a woman caught in adultery that they were no different, and then he treated her with love as well.

In one of the wildest of Jesus's stories (Luke 7:36ff.), set at an elite dinner engagement, he allowed a street woman to break a flask of expensive perfume over his feet and to rub the oil into his flesh with her hair, using her tears to express her deep gratitude. On the occasion of this act of love, he admonished all the others that their gratitude paled in comparison to hers. Then, after his resurrection, Jesus did not appear to his male disciples first, but to female (hence, socially marginalized) followers (see Matthew 28:9ff., Mark 16:1ff., Luke 23:55ff., John 20:11ff.). Jesus was, in light of the sociopolitical rules in place at that time, a rebel, a renegade, a feminist, a representative of love and justice for all (see Luke 7:36–50, Luke 24, John 20:11–16).

The Gospels don't reveal everything about Jesus and aren't complete enough for us to know all of what he said or did (John 21:25). But the themes of his ministry are consistent and provide the guidance we need to know about what *love in action* looks like.

Some Things Haven't Changed

Both the Samaritan woman at the well and the woman caught in adultery show the prevailing religious leadership's thinking in that time and place: a tendency toward condemnation, criticism, and judgment if someone didn't measure up. This is exactly what we see in conservative Christianity today and why the word "Christian" is so often synonymous in the public eye with condemnation, judgment, and ignorance. The guiding values of the prevailing religious leadership of Jesus's time were power and a gender and ethnic double standard. This was opposite to the justice, mercy, and faithfulness that Jesus taught (e.g., Matthew 23:23). I've seen time and again, in my practice and classroom, and in conversations like the one with Fiona in New Zealand, how this kind of "leadership" can crush the spirit while also failing to motivate a change of heart. High-handedness, like with the religious leaders of Jesus's day, may produce momentary compliance, but there's nothing life-giving about it. Quite the opposite, in fact: its byproduct is heart-piercing shame. The great irony of conservative Christian sexual ethics is that the person whose teachings are the foundation of the faith stand in stark contrast to the condemnation and judgment that so many people have experienced in their religious upbringing.

The Radical Responses of Jesus

Let's go back to the two stories in the book of John and examine Jesus's response and its effect on these two women. We know from the text that Jesus engaged these women in respectful, loving, nonjudgmental dialogue (John 4:7–29, 8:2–11). We know from cultural history that his attending to these women in *any* way, let alone an *equal* way, was taboo. In fact, we know that since the Samaritan woman was drawing water in the hottest time of the day (4:6), she was dishonored in her community. We also know that a "respectable" Jewish man like Jesus would never have talked to a woman. Then we see that he chose to reveal *for the very first time to anyone* that he was the Messiah, the Chosen One of God—to a Samaritan woman, of all people!

I am equally struck by her response to him. At first, she is apprehensive, then stunned, and then overcome with joy and gratitude (see John 4:9–29). Isn't this transformation stunning, especially from the standpoint of a therapist? I wish I could see transformations like hers in my office during every session. This episode in the Gospel, in fact, is where I find my greatest admiration of Jesus, and the story of his power that captivates me more than any other in the entire narrative. How could *one brief encounter*, with a woman who had previously been convinced that she was worthless, elicit this set of emotions? What kind of presence, attention, kindness, and love was emanating from Jesus? How does a Samaritan woman, scorned and hated by Jewish culture, a person who probably had no remaining hint of self-worth or value, become overwhelmed with a sense of value and hope after a single conversation like this?

The Power of Being Seen, Known, Loved, and Accepted

It is my belief that Jesus's example gives us everything we need to know, study, and practice in order to be *lovers* in the fullest sense of the word. I imagine that in order for the woman at the well or the woman brought for stoning to have responded to Jesus in the way they did, he must have been incredibly attentive: piercing, loving eyes, gazing deeply into theirs, a bodily presence clearly intent on sharing affection, a peaceful and forgiving aura about him, and a visible intent to serve. I imagine him fully inhabiting his body—that is, with deep, solid breath, perhaps leaning forward, all of his body still and attentive. I imagine him being fully present: his thoughts staying with the conversation, not drifting off elsewhere, his intent to hear, accept, love, and heal. I imagine his kindness to have emanated from him in a way that these women couldn't mistake, filling them with a sense of being cared for. Then, as Jesus revealed his knowledge of them while remaining loving and compassionate in his full presence, they could begin to believe they *were* in fact seen and known—and yet still powerfully loved, without pretense and without condition. They were beloved; they were chosen, just as they were right then and there, *without changing*, Jesus's healing love capturing their hearts so that in that moment, their shame dissolved and they were transformed.

As we see through Jesus's example, when people are seen, known, loved, and accepted, when they are treated with justice and taken seriously, they often become filled with love and grace. The heart softens and healing begins. Leadership doesn't have to be humiliating, disrespectful, or dismissive. It can be clear, direct, loving, and grace-filled, all at the same time. The response of the human heart to this kind of leadership is to grow toward love, compassion, and justice.

Go and "Sin" No More

The story of the woman brought for stoning (in John 8:2–11) ends with her standing all alone in the town square with Jesus as he asks her, "Where are they? Has no one condemned you?" As she states the obvious—that her accusers have all dispersed, unable to accuse her in the face of Jesus's challenge—he gently says, "Neither do I condemn you. Go your way, and from now on do not sin again" (John 8:10–11).

I have heard many conservative Christians use this later phrase as a reminder of how they (Christians) are charged with monitoring each other's sin. They use this verse to justify judging and condemning each other's behavior, even though all people share the trait of imperfection. I can even remember as a college student listening to a pastor use this verse to justify how we needed to "confront our brothers and sisters" when we saw sin in their lives. But this story clearly demonstrates how *all the people* were sent away. *All people are imperfect.* None of us have the right to condemn one another. We are only given the mandate to love like Jesus, period. And that, in and of itself, is a very tall order. This is an important aspect of this story to share with clients who have been convinced that others have the right to judge and condemn them. It's not true. *All of them* were sent away. And even Jesus, the one "perfect one," did not condemn: he only loved. It is love, not judgment, that inspires change.

A Sexual Ethic Driven by Christian Values and Accountability

When we see how Jesus interacted with people, we see how we are called to treat others and ourselves. We also see how grace, love, compassion, and justice are the change agents of the human spirit and the human community. When we are treated with dignity, we strive to be our best selves and we strive to help others to be their best selves. Acting with grace, love, compassion, and justice takes self-discipline because we cannot think only about ourselves. We must consider the context, the Other (if an Other exists), and the consequences of our actions. While we celebrate and honor our desires, we also modulate them depending on the larger context of how our desires will serve our values of grace, love, compassion, and justice to all concerned. This is what a sexual ethic looks like when it is driven by Christian values. It has Jesus's values at the heart (grace, love, compassion, and justice) and it honors relationships— with self, with God, and with Other (if there is one). This accountability is always at work. It is the simple and difficult paradox of learning to apply loving like Christ in and with our sexuality, but rather than being behavior- and rules-driven, it is values- and relationship-driven. Therefore, rather than asking questions like "how far is too far?" the conversation tends toward questions dealing with what a person desires and hopes for in relationships as part of their personal development. This happens over bits and pieces as a child grows up—day by day, week by week, month by month.

As someone begins to think about exploring dating, the conversation broadens out to include the many ways of discussing a romantic "Other." At first, the question centers around what love, grace, compassion, and justice mean in a relationship emotionally, spiritually, intellectually, socially, and sexually. Then, as a relationship evolves, the question shifts to center around how the person sees each of these elements evolving over time.

One Hundred One-Minute Conversations

Jesus was a storyteller, using stories and metaphor ("parable") to demonstrate the nature and values of God. Sex wasn't at the top of the list of his metaphors, but love, justice, compassion, and grace were. What can these values teach us about how to be a good lover?

It turns out that a great deal of those principles can be applied to sex education and the building of intimacy. While there is a fair amount of knowledge to acquire as we grow, along with social, emotional, relational, and sexual intelligence for navigating the complex world of intimate relationships, we can use the lenses of justice and love to guide us like a rudder guides a boat. How often do parents help their children understand if they are acting lovingly or justly? How often do they ask them if they feel they are being *treated* lovingly or fairly? How often do they help them examine whether something happening on TV is loving or just? How do we help our children learn to forgive or offer grace to someone who has hurt their feelings, or teach them to manage conflicts in their lives by asking for compassion or grace from someone else?

All of these skills are part of the art of growing intimacy, relational tools that can help a person build a securely attached, loving relationship someday if they choose, when combined with good sex education along the way. A sexual ethic built on the values of love and justice, combined with the 100 one-minute conversations of a comprehensive sex education over a child's developing years, can help an adolescent to feel confident about themselves. Research shows that these kids make safer choices, become involved in sex later in their development than other kids, and describe themselves as closer to their parents overall (Martino et al. 2008).

"I grew up with four sisters," wrote Carly, a Christian who was 35 when I had her as a student. "Each night, my mom would come and tuck us in, one by one. This was the coveted 'all-mine mommy time.' It was the only time we got her each to ourselves for a few minutes.

"I remember asking her a question about my breasts one night when I was about eight years old, because they seemed to be growing oddly and one had a bigger bump than the other. This particular night, she stayed a little longer and told me about the changes going on in my body. She told me I could let her know if I had any more questions, and that we could find our own quiet 'mommy time' to talk.

"Over the next few years, I asked her every question that I could conceive of, sometimes because I wanted to know, and sometimes just because it meant that she would sit on the edge of my bed for a few extra minutes. Over the years, we talked about everything—sex and sexuality, marriage, relationships, health, safety, pregnancy, bodies, boys, and other things. It was only later, much later, that I learned that my mother's lively conversations were maverick—that not all moms were having this kind of conversation about bodies, sexuality, marriage, relationships, pregnancy, health, and safety.

"But at the time, I thought that all kids learned about life and sexuality from their mother and that everyone felt special about it like I did. Since it was an open and ongoing conversation between Mom and me, the ideas of sexuality integrated into the story of my little self at each juncture as I grew. As a result, as I entered junior high school I knew about sexuality and that it was important and special—and that I was special, too. But aside from scheming up more questions to ask my mom, by the time I got to the eighth grade, I was much too busy with things far more interesting, like athletics and friends, to be too concerned with boys or sexuality.

"It wasn't until adolescence and my church's youth group that I got all the classic conservative Christian stuff. I remember one of our youth leaders, a kind of know-it-all guy, saying that 'the questions should not be, "how far can I go?" but "how pure can I be?"' Other things were emphasized too, like 'no masturbation,' 'no pornography,' 'abstinence only,' and wearing purity rings. Without the years of open conversations with my mom, I might have adopted black-and-white thoughts, like, 'if you have premarital sex, then you are a bad person,' or 'if you wait until you get married, then you will have awesome sex.'

"But none of that actually proved true for me. Sexuality, life, and relationships were never reduced to black-and-white proscriptions. They were given life and flesh through conversations with my mom and how we lived as a family. In early adolescence, I began to study Latin dances. Doing so not only influenced my sexuality but also instilled in me a deep sense of responsibility *for* my body and *to* my body. I developed a sense of power over my body and an intimate knowledge of my own physicality. I grew in my ownership and pride, and I demanded that my body be treated with respect, chiefly by myself but also by others. Respect meant taking care of it whenever and however I felt I needed to. Dancing was an extremely sensuous experience. It taught me to inhabit my body with my soul and heart.

"Much later, when I met my husband, Steven, it was the first time I had met someone who captivated me, and he was the first person I had cared about enough to find myself desiring to be intimate. We were both very open to physicality, and our relationship became intimate quickly. We decided together to keep intercourse set aside and to use our developing relationship to guide us in becoming increasingly more familiar with our bodies and our senses. We talked about everything first, and anything we felt ready for was fair game. We viewed our lack of intercourse as a discipline for both of us, figuring that marriage was going to require extraordinary discipline all its own. We also figured that since intercourse had been given so much weight in our culture and in our church, by taking the time to get to know all the other ways we liked to touch and be touched we'd have a more erotic and sensuous sex life when we *did* get married than most other couples we knew.

"Since intercourse as the 'main event' was out of the way, we were free to be creative with each other. There was no particular, expected end-event. We weren't focused on ejaculation or orgasm: we were just focused on loving and pleasing each other.

"What's interesting is that I knew that the church wasn't involved in weddings or marriages until the twelfth century.[1] This meant that ideas of what we are to do before and after marriage were decided in the formation of religious tradition, instead of being mandates from Scripture. So even though we stood within tradition by waiting to have intercourse, it was for reasons that served our faith and belief in what would help us ready our relationship and sexual lives for marriage that guided us to set the parameters we did. We never felt guilty, shameful, or bad about what we did, nor self-righteous about what we didn't do. We were true to ourselves, each other, and our forming couple. It's hard to imagine feeling bad about that."

Helping Our Christian Clients Respect Their Decision Making

Let's debrief Carly's story. If you have a Christian client who grew up amid rigid sexual ethics that not only focused on behaviors—no sex (intercourse and other sexual behaviors) before marriage—but also then went further to ask them to not commit any sexual impurity in body, mind, or spirit or any action or thought that might lead to temptation, this story might sound very shocking to them. There is much more than a hint of what Paul in the New Testament might refer to as "sexual immorality," and there is a fearful chorus of loud preachers who will say, "But what about how Scripture says there is to be 'not even a hint of sexual immorality'?" (see Ephesians 5:3 NIV).

But let's play with this a little. If Jesus is the incarnated God, in the flesh, who came among the people to teach them love and justice, can't we reasonably say that God actually *likes* the flesh, that God has *good* intentions for when two committed people get together and experience intimacy? Carly and Steven might actually be a *good* example of what can happen when two people, children of God and committed disciples of Jesus who were also fortunate enough to grow up with lots of love and guidance, decide to live out of their God-sanctioned embodiedness. Wouldn't the Lord want this incarnated love to be experienced by all of God's children, including Carly and Steven? Isn't that part of why Jesus came in the first place—to redeem the human body?

At each place that sexual curiosity arose, Carly was lovingly invited into a conversation to help her to understand her curiosity, the gift of her body, and the hope that she would always treat her body as a special gift from God. Her mother gave her incremental bits of information over a long period of time, presenting them with love, grace, and safety all the while in a conversation that unfolded naturally across Carly's early life cycle. All the conversations Carly was having with her mom seemed to provide sound sexual health information inside a Christian sexual ethic. In their conversations, Carly and her mom looked at love, grace, compassion, and justice in the areas of her emotional, spiritual, intellectual, social, and sexual development.

We know from research that this parenting style is correlated with the development of self-esteem, body image, talents, and desires among the children who receive it (Richardson and Schuster 2003, 30). We also know from research that when a child's sexual curiosities are handled in grace and truth, whether in a secular or a religious home, it is these youth who become sexually involved the latest and have the least number of hurtful sexual experiences, body issues, or shame burdens (Richardson and Schuster 2003, 30). When kids are raised with an integration of sexuality and spirituality, they are more likely to have a satisfying sex life as an adult. One study revealed that those who saw sex as sanctified (holy, blessed, spiritual) had higher rates of sexual frequency, satisfaction, and variability, while those who had high degrees of global religiousness (religious service attendance, Bible reading, prayer) and low degrees of understanding around how their faith and their sex life went together had lower sexual frequency and sexual satisfaction (Murray-Swank, Pargament, and Mahoney 2005).

Carly was an example of how someone can develop in a healthy way. Over time, through all of those talks with her mother, she had become clear about the kind of person she'd be attracted to. Like her, he had to have a loving and trustworthy heart and be a person of integrity. He would need to be able to listen well and take her seriously, just like her mother had done. Through her dancing, she had developed a love of the body and an appreciation of sensual expression. She looked forward to being in the right relationship in due time. She had grown an inner confidence in her ability to find a man who would want touch of all kinds, and who would be driven not by his sexual drives alone but by what it means to love through all parts of the body. He would want touch to be mutual, loving, and considerate of her.

This was exactly the kind of relationship that Carly and Steve developed. Since conversation had been a big part of the relationship from the beginning, all of the touching and expression of love that took place between Carly and Steve were done mutually, without guilt, and with lots of care and consideration.

Breaking Old Rules: Following a Road Map

For many Christians, it's difficult to understand how a relationship like the one Carly and Steven developed even before they were married could honor the core values of Jesus's ministry. That kind of ethics is very different from one focused on rules of do's and don'ts. You will encounter this reaction in your counseling practice, given enough time. But I hope you've started to see that Jesus cared about virtues like respect, grace, compassion, and justice, that we learn to love each other in ways that demonstrate those qualities, and that we honor each other, ourselves, and God. His goal was for us to flourish in his abundant love and then go on to overflow that love to others. He understood that this love was fully expressed when embodied. He didn't shy away from embodiment; I don't believe he wanted us to shy away from it, either, but rather to be responsible to it. Jesus cared about keeping the *spirit* of the law over the *letter*, especially when the spirit revealed grace, mercy, and love. The road map to intimacy works the same way.

While many Christian parents and youth leaders might not want kids to have any romantic or sexual expression prior to marriage, I think we fail to ask the more important questions when we make proscription our focus. We fail to ask questions like these: "What parenting and faith-based practices help adolescents and young adults to develop a strong sense of self?" "What conversations and activities can we engage kids in that help them develop a protective appreciation for their bodies, minds, hearts, and relationships?" "What experiences can we invite our kids to have that give them a vision and desire for the healthiest, most flourishing eroticism as adults?" We know that so much of what Carly's mom quite naturally did—her 100 one-minute conversations of sexuality, sexual health, relationships, gender, safety, and growing up—did this for Carly, just like the research has shown.

Fifteen years and two kids later, Carly and Steven are enjoying a well-developed relationship. They are deeply attached and committed, they enjoy each other's company the best, and Carly tells me that they have a wonderfully exciting, sacred, and varied sex life.

Stories like theirs allow us to wonder with our clients if sexual expression might be a place to look for communion with God, grateful for all the ways God loves them. We can wonder if this is the kind of confidence, safety, love, justice, self-awareness, and relationship savvy that God would want for them. Are they being equipped to live into a long, committed relationship with the kind of strength of character and generosity of heart needed to navigate all the varied terrain of a long relationship if that is what they choose? To do so is possible only through thousands of short moments of teaching, of exactly the sort that Carly's mother gave her in her growing-up years.

When an adolescent or young adult begins to build on this sexual and relational health foundation, making their own decisions, unfolding their own story of loving relationships, they will be writing the first pages of a sexual story they'll want to pass down to their own children. Carly's mom knew something about this, and Carly gets to live an exciting, fulfilling erotic life with her husband as a result.

Out With the Old, in With the New

In a Jesus-centered, sex-positive sexuality, the body is seen to be integrated with the spirit, mind, and soul of a person. Interaction of any kind, sexual or otherwise, is recognized to be part of the mind-soul-body relationship experience. There is an intrinsic accountability to the effect of words, behaviors, and motives (sexual and otherwise) on self, Other, and one's communion with God. There is a commitment to value and love the Other—all Others—like Jesus loved. In such an atmosphere where sexual conversations take place in small soundbites over the span of childhood and adolescence, elements of conversation about God's creation, what it means to grow, and the ups and downs of life and relationships all take place naturally. The pace is unhurried and the conversational environment feels safe to both parties. God's love and purposes in sexual desire, in granting a sensual body, and the conditions and purposes of a deeper communion are given the time and thought that they deserve—where children are invited to examine and reflect in age-appropriate ways on the body, relationships, and sexual curiosities. There are books all around the house on anatomy, ecology, sociology, different cultures, different religions, different family types, the life cycle of animals, plants, and people, and the reproductive cycles of different forms of life. As kids get older, parents help their children to connect the dots by wondering aloud about the impact of certain words or behaviors on other areas of life. There are many questions offered so children have an opportunity to think for themselves. Discussions of justice are frequent, as children learn to notice how others are being treated and how power is being used to help or to hurt. All of these discussions help children to filter love, grace, compassion, and justice through the lens of their emotional, social, spiritual, intellectual, and sexual health, which simultaneously gives them more advanced critical thinking skills.

Reflect again on the split mind-body and the unified mind-body cycle from the end of Chapter 3 to see how these cycles have played out in your own life. Invite your clients to do the same.

Learning in Action

Let me give an example of how a parent who desires to raise his son inside a sex-positive, Gospel sexual ethic might manage a situation like porn use. Let's say that one evening, a father notices that his 13-year-old son has called up porn with his friend on Dad's laptop after school, accidentally leaving it open afterward. In this situation, the father might wait for a quiet time when he can speak openly and say something like this: "Hey John, I noticed that you pulled up a porn site this afternoon on the computer. Do you want to tell me about that?"

"Not really," John might reply awkwardly, turning a little red. "Isn't that kind of weird, Dad?"

"Well," his dad might say, "I'm curious. It's not uncommon for boys your age to be curious about erotic websites, and I'd be willing to guess that your friends talk about this kind of stuff. Why don't you tell me some of what you saw?"

John looks at his dad as though his father has lost his mind. He's not about to tell what he saw! So his dad continues, calmly and lovingly.

"How did your body respond?" he asks. "Your body is created to respond to sexual stimulation. That's normal and good; you were created this way. I'm created this way too." He pauses a moment, then goes on to ask, "Was there any part of you that wondered if this was a good thing to do? I believe that God guides us in a still, small voice inside of us, helping us to know what is life-giving to us and others, and what might be hurtful."

At this point, John is ready to open up, at least a little. "Well, I don't know. Tyler really wanted to see this stuff and I kind of went along. I was curious, I guess. But it also felt funny."

"That makes a lot of sense," his dad replies. "One of the ways to decipher if something is good for your heart and life is to ask yourself other kinds of questions. For example: the people you saw in the pictures or videos are real people, people like you and me, created by God. Ask yourself, are they someone's daughter or son, someone's mother or father, brother or sister, grandchild? What might it be like for you if your sister or cousin was involved in something like what you're seeing? Would it be okay with you? Why or why not?"

At this point, John looks mortified. "No way!" he says. "That would *not* be okay if it were my sister!"

Calmly as ever, his dad continues, gently listing off some guiding questions for John to consider next time. "Looking back on what you saw, how you felt, and what you believe, where did you see people being treated with kindness, love, grace, compassion, justice? Did you see a willingness to be seen, known, loved, and accepted—no games, no acting, no pretending? Or were people using each other in any way? If they were, who was using whom? What do you think this is like for the user? For the one being used? Do you think this sexual activity helped them to feel more loved and valued, and helped them to feel God's love for them? Why or why not? I'm not telling you what to believe; these are just the kinds of questions I want you to be able to ask yourself when you engage your sexuality, your mind, and your heart. All of you, each of those parts, is so fabulous, such a gift from God, that I would never want you to feel badly about them. I would never want you to treat them in any way that was not ultimately okay with you. I offer you these questions about love, grace, compassion, and justice to help you make the best decisions for you. Does that make sense?"

"Yeah, Dad, that does," John says.

His dad goes on. "I had to figure all this stuff out for myself, too, when I was growing up," he says. "And I'd be happy to tell you a bit about how I figured things out for myself, if you want to hear. But I guess it's important to know that there are some sites that exploit people and can be violent and there are others that are not. My preference would be that you would protect your mind and heart from images that might be exploitative or violent to people, and keep your mind focused on the kind of sexuality you hope to have someday with someone you love.

"Lots of your friends will likely be involved with treating women and others in exploitive ways," his dad continues. "There is an attitude right now in masculine culture that says, 'That's cool.' But it really isn't, and it doesn't feel good in our hearts, even when we pretend it does. I know it, and you will know it too. There will always be pressure to go the way of emptiness. Sometimes we make good decisions, and other times we have really good lessons that come from making less-than-good decisions. But remember, there is no such thing as a mistake if you turn it into a lesson."

By now, John is listening attentively, and his father is moving toward wrapping up the chat.

"Son," his dad says, "I want you to know that your sexuality is one of the most wonderful, powerful things that make up who you are. I believe it was given to us to bless us and bless anyone we share it with. I want you to see it as a great gift, not to be taken lightly—something that can be used to heal and nourish you and, one day, the person you love. My hope for you is that even though we live in a world that can often use sex to hurt others, you will choose to use it to make the world *better* in some small way. You are writing your own sexual story now, just like I wrote mine when I was a young man like you. I want yours to be a story you love, and a story you will someday enjoy telling your own partner and kids. Just try to be mindful about what you want your sexual story to say."

John had still been listening. His dad wasn't quite sure he understood, but he hoped that John had taken something in. Mostly, he just wanted John not to feel shame, but instead to feel informed of the value of his sexuality and empowered to be in charge of his decisions. He knew it would be years until this conversation would truly make a difference, if ever—but he was willing to let it be one more little chat in a long series of other ones along the way. He thought fondly back on his years fishing with his uncle Sam and all the conversations they'd had about growing up, about sexuality, about his role in protecting those weaker and less fortunate than him, about what guys had been like when Sam was in college, and what Sam wished he could do differently. He was so grateful for Sam's trust and forgiveness over the years and for being a safe person to talk with when he was in college, and how he had been a model for the kind of dad he now wanted to be for his son. He knew how lucky he was to have had even one safe person in his life.

No Such Thing as a Mistake

It is in these nonreactive, nonshaming conversations that we can guide parents in helping their children to connect a sexual act to the effect the act has on relationships, on family members, on themselves—and invite them to begin articulating the elements that align with their core beliefs. In a similar way, when we model this kind of nonreactive conversation with our clients around the integration of faith and sexuality, we give them a safe place to examine what aligns with the still, small voice within them. We teach them to trust themselves, and in so doing we demonstrate that we trust them as well.

A Sexuality of Honor and Love Is Like Great Jazz

The greatest jazz artists in history, people like Miles Davis, John Coltrane, and Wes Montgomery, became great through many years of commitment, study, practice, intention, and attention to every nuance of their art. The same is true of the great lover, who seeks to love his or her beloved *into* the fullness of their potential. Our clients who have been marinated in years of shame and condemnation, who have been fed decades of misinformation, have lots of diligent practice ahead of them if they are to master the art of loving, and to shed the influences of fear and the poison of judgment and condemnation. But the freedom, joy, and delight that await them is worth *all* of the patience and practice: take it from me, or take it from Carly. Our work with our Christian clients who are suffering under religious sexual shame is to help them to see their belovedness and begin to live into a sex-positive Gospel ethic, one in which they feel seen, known, loved, and accepted while they seek to see, know, love, and accept another. Sexuality is our most potent, renewable resource for pleasure, vitality, juiciness, playfulness, connection, creativity, relaxation, and spiritual experience. It is the breath of life, and we have the honor of helping our clients discover it.

Two years after meeting Fiona in New Zealand, and a little over a year after she returned to her home college in the States, she e-mailed me to say she had found a way to leave her boyfriend. She had joined a women's studies group on campus, an organization that was drawing attention to the rise in sexual assault on college campuses, and she had also been seeing a therapist. She thanked me for being the first person to hear her story and give her a sense of being loved and valued, and she talked about how it had given her the courage to find a counselor when she got back home and to start taking her life back. She had even found ways to start taking back her faith from all the judgment she'd been believing.

She said she wasn't currently dating anyone, at least not then. But she felt much better about herself and about the whole prospect of being in another relationship someday. She was a whole lot clearer about the kind of person she wanted to be with. Right now, she just enjoyed helping other women to stand up for their rights as she went around speaking at sororities about dating violence. Her "voice" in the e-mail sounded stronger and more determined than it had at the coffee shop in New Zealand. I could feel her sense of peace and liberation, and I could only imagine that as she lived out her new freedom, other young women around her were catching the aroma of her Gospel ethics as well, and imagining what it would be like to live their sexuality like the Good News was good news.

Note

1. See Fiorenza and Galvin (1991, 320).

References

Fiorenza, Francis Schüssler, and John P. Galvin, eds. 1991. *Systematic Theology: Roman Catholic Perspectives*, vol. 2. Minneapolis, MN: Fortress Press.

Martino, Steven C., Marc N. Elliott, Rosalie Corona, David E. Kanouse, and Mark A. Schuster. 2008. Beyond the "Big Talk": The Roles of Breadth and Repetition in Parent-Adolescent Communication about Sexual Topics. *Pediatrics* 121 (3): 612–18.

Mills, Rosemary S.L. 2003. Possible Antecedents and Developmental Implications of Shame in Young Girls. *Infant and Child Development* 12 (4): 329–49.

Murray, Clare, Glenn Waller, and Charles Legg. 2000. Family Dysfunction and Bulimic Psychopathology: The Mediating Role of Shame. *International Journal of Eating Disorders* 28 (1): 84–9. doi:10.1002/(SICI)1098-108X(200007)28:1<84::AID-EAT10>3.0.CO;2-R.

Murray-Swank, Nichole A., Kenneth I. Pargament, and Annette Mahoney. 2005. At the Crossroads of Sexuality and Spirituality: The Sanctification of Sex by College Students. *International Journal for the Psychology of Religion* 15 (3): 199–219.

Rahm, G.B., B. Renck, and K.C. Ringsberg. 2006. "Disgust, Disgust beyond Description"—Shame Cues to Detect Shame in Disguise, in Interviews with Women Who Were Sexually Abused during Childhood. *Journal of Psychiatric and Mental Health Nursing* 13 (1): 100–9.

Richardson, Justin, and Mark A. Schuster. 2003. *Everything You Never Wanted Your Kids to Know about Sex (But Were Afraid They'd Ask): The Secrets to Surviving Your Child's Sexual Development from Birth to the Teens*. New York, NY: Crown.

Wei, Meifen, Philip A. Shaffer, Shannon K. Young, and Robyn A. Zakalik. 2005. Adult Attachment, Shame, Depression, and Loneliness: The Mediation Role of Basic Psychological Needs Satisfaction. *Journal of Counseling Psychology* 52 (4): 591–601.

Young, William P. 2007. *The Shack*. Newbury Park, CA: Windblown Media.

6   Clinical Applications

Four Steps to Healing Religious Sexual Shame

When the heart is flooded with love there is no room in it for fear, for doubt, for hesitation. And it is this lack of fear that makes for the dance. When each partner loves so completely that he has forgotten to ask himself whether he is loved in return; when he only knows that he loves and is moving to music—then, and then only, are two people able to dance perfectly in tune to the same rhythm.

—Anne Morrow Lindbergh, *Gift from the Sea* (1955, 97)

How Life Experience Shapes Our Sexual and Spiritual Understanding

Shame and "Should-ing" on Yourself

Susan was crying as she told me that something must be wrong with her. She was 28, newly engaged to a man she had been dating for several years, and feeling miserable.

Since she was now engaged, Susan thought that these were supposed to be the happiest days of her life. Instead, she felt drained, consumed by all there was to do to get ready for the wedding. The two of them were hardly ever sexual anymore, but since they were now engaged, shouldn't they want to have "lots of sex"?

I gently explored with her where these ideals of bliss and endless sex came from. Together, we unpacked the "shoulds" she had absorbed about engaged women from her cultural and family background, such as "I will feel so excited and 'in love' when I get engaged," or "we will be so in love that we will not be able to keep our hands off each other," or "I will feel absolutely certain about my upcoming marriage."

Susan had been so anxious about not feeling like she thought she "should" that she hardly knew what she actually *felt* anymore. I diverted and asked her to tell me about George, her fiancé, like how long they had been together, how she would describe their relationship, and what she loved about him. I also asked about her family, George's family, and her friends. I asked her to describe how they "do family," such as whether the parents were supportive of their relationship. Without hesitation, Susan described a loving family, along with a playful and respectful relationship between her and George over those four years. She adored his family and how the families got along, and she described a wide, nurturing friendship network that was very supportive of the relationship the two of them shared.

When I heard Susan talk about all the things that were *right* about their relationship, it became clear to me that "what was wrong" was simply the unhelpful, unexamined female cultural discourses about getting married that had shaped her beliefs and, in turn, her current suffering. As we named and teased out the cultural "shoulds" from her actual lived experience and beliefs about her relationship and upcoming wedding, she was able to let them go and feel her excitement and gratefulness again. But it only came through stopping long enough to examine why she felt certain things *must* be true in her relationship with George and how she and he really were on solid ground after all.

Susan's story is a common example of how unexamined "shoulds," norms, and assumptions can wreak havoc in our love lives. In this chapter, we will explore what is learned and absorbed about intimacy, spirituality, sexuality, gender, and power during our developing years from influences like family, friends, and culture. As you and your clients tease apart what is learned, you'll be better able to hold it in front of you and examine how it fits with core values, beliefs, desires, and experience. From there, we can help our clients to make decisions about what they will gratefully keep as an integral part of who they are, and what they will place aside to make room for *different* beliefs, ideas, and experiences, ones that better fit the person they are and the priorities they embrace.

The Hidden Influence

Janis and Paul came to my office to discuss their sex life—or, rather, their lack of it. Janis described how as much as a month or two were routinely passing without sex (what she clarified as intercourse). Paul agreed, citing how their lives were so busy that it seemed like they only passed each other in the night. Even when they were home together, he said, they tended to "recharge" in different rooms—him on the computer and she with a book or a TV show. "All of my girlfriends say that their husbands always want sex and are hassling them all the time," Janis continued. "Paul never hassles me or even complains. I am beginning to think that he doesn't even desire me."

Can you identify the cultural discourses embedded in Janis and Paul's dilemma? They're subtle, but they're powerful in how they shape their meaning in the situation. For starters, there's the assumption that the frequency of their sexual intercourse should be higher than it is. Second, there's the assumption that intercourse is the only sexually intimate behavior that counts. Furthermore, there's an assumption that a woman can tell whether a man desires her by whether he is the sexual pursuer or aggressor.

Like Susan, it was important for Janis and Paul to unpack the cultural narratives that were not serving them or their relationship and set them aside. Only then could they examine what they wanted and believed—and create something new between them that was aligned with what they wanted for their relationship.

The American Cultural/Religious Sexual Narrative

The vast majority of the people I've interviewed or counseled during my career tell stories of being yelled at, humiliated, or embarrassed when "caught" playing doctor with a same-age neighbor, cousin, sibling, or friend when they were five or six. Many other stories describe "being caught" when engaged in developmentally normal sexual curiosities and behaviors in childhood and adolescence. When this is coupled with an otherwise silent conversation about sexuality and an authoritarian or controlling parenting style, like the ones we've seen in previous chapters, children learn to implant shame and a sense of worthlessness somewhere deep inside them, and it stays rooted there into adulthood.

In my research, I have found that at least 80 percent of people raised in the United States have grown up in homes that were silent, ignorant, or reactive about sexuality and sexual development. When kids do not feel safe asking questions about their body and pleasure, and when they don't feel safe exhibiting normal curiosities about their genitals and pleasure, they learn shame, a feeling that says, "Something must be wrong with *me*. Something must be wrong with who I *am*, and not just with what I *do*."

What Children Teach Us, and Why We Need to Listen

I remember a day many years ago when my daughter and goddaughter, both about four years old at the time, were playing in my daughter's bedroom, which was just off the kitchen in our house. My friend Karen and I were in the kitchen making dinner and sharing a glass of wine when one of us looked at the other, then suspiciously over at the doorway, and said, "It's been a little too quiet in there."

As we approached the door, trying hard to be stealthy, we could hear the girls whispering and giggling on the other side. Then, opening the door, we were presented with a living, breathing, 3-D version of a Rembrandt in full color.

Both of the girls were stark naked. Using their bodies as a canvas, they had taken markers and colored *all over* each other—the whole body, not just parts. To this day, I regret not thinking to grab the camera before I said, "Oops! Markers are for paper, and you girls need a bath!" Karen and I had a good laugh, in part because we knew that this was normal curiosity at their age (I had already been through it with my son), but also because one of our favorite kids' books was *Purple, Green and Yellow* by Robert Munsch (1992), the story of a little girl who colors over her whole family with magic, colored markers.

What Is Childhood Sexuality?

Even though we are born sexual—our sexual functioning begins before we are born (Haffner 1999, 26)—childhood sexuality in our culture is as ignored, and as poorly understood, as adult sexuality. Throughout infancy and childhood, it is a normal developmental step to be playful and sensual, to explore by doing what feels good, whether we're alone or with playmates. This process is as natural and normal a phase as learning to walk, but unlike stories of learning to walk, most people remember their sexual development with stories of being shamed or otherwise injured in childhood by those around them unaware of what was normal and healthy.

"Silence suggests that eroticism is dirty, inherently embarrassing, dangerous, inappropriate, or vulgar," writes David Schnarch in his landmark book, *Constructing the Sexual Crucible* (1991, 318). "Silence is an education in sexual attitudes and gender roles. Like it or not, the family is always the predominant purveyor of the child's sexual map and attitudes toward eroticism." I would add that this is also true for a child's map of self-worth, and his or her core *spiritual* values, relevant to questions like "Does God love me, or condemn me?" or "Is my sexuality good or bad?" or "Are my desires for pleasure from God, or do they separate me from God?"

Schnarch goes on to say that

> the sex-affirming Hebraic roots of Western civilization have been masked by Augustine's legacy of eroticism-hating sexual dualism, perpetuated by authoritarian-rooted Christian dogma, which negated the basic worthiness of human beings. The evolution of Western culture is a history of theologically based sexual oppression.
>
> (Schnarch 1991, 548)

These aren't small concerns. A culture that shames children for normal sexual expression plants seeds that manifest themselves in *adult* life in the form of disturbances in relationship, intimacy, libido, and sexuality. Sexual shame can sever the experience of sensual pleasure in deep, loving attachment because it eclipses a person's ability to feel seen, known, loved, and accepted with and through their sensual body. The impact of this on intimate relationships and family stability is profound and far-reaching.

The One Thing I Tell Young Parents

The most important thing young parents can do to help their child to develop a secure sense of sexual health, beyond obvious things like love and protection, is to understand the developmental tasks of their child, including their sexual, sensual, and physical curiosities. This requires preparing for their curiosities ahead of time, and seizing opportune moments to comment about what is good and right in a given situation (like exploring bodies with a same-age friend, putting their hands down their pants in the grocery store, or peeing on the park lawn). Being prepared buys parents time to decide *how* to respond to such an event, instead of to react. This also includes the ongoing plan to have 100 one-minute conversations about sexuality along the way as children develop.

Think of this ongoing life-education conversation (which includes sexuality) as a chat that happens in pieces at least weekly. Encourage parents to look for opportunities to say something short and sweet, *frequently*. It helps to be one step ahead of children developmentally, aware of what is coming next, so that they can make a reasonable guess as to the kinds of topics that are emerging in the child's life. The more often parents talk about the normalcy of sexuality and intimacy in the human condition, the easier it becomes for everyone. Research shows that parents who do this raise children more likely to delay sexual activity, to use contraception, to talk to their partners about sex, and to see their parents as a resource to them (Guilamo-Ramos, Lee, and Jaccard 2016). Most fascinating of all, research has shown that kids who grow up with ongoing sexual health conversations with their parents describe themselves as closer to their parents overall (Martino et al. 2008). The key reason why it is critical for parents to become sexually literate is, of course, for their children's sexual health and safety. But secondarily, keeping the conversation open with one's kids increases the likelihood that parent and child will remain well bonded, the parent remaining a trusted resource through adolescence.

Clinical Applications for Adults With Religious Sexual Shame and Trauma

When I work with clients, I often use a four-step process to deconstruct the destructive messages they may have absorbed from cultural influences, including the conservative religious experiences they may have had, along with our culture's objectification of sexuality and the body and the underavailability of good sex education in many families. The four stages in this treatment process are not linear but circular. If we think of the narrative of shame as a tightly woven canvas wrapped around the heart and mind, it's easier to understand that it can be unraveled only thread-by-thread, in a circular fashion. Sometimes, to free a thread, you must set it down and pick up another, working with that one for a while before going back to the first one. That's normal, but it's best just to follow the threads patiently, one by one, and unravel the canvas slowly. As we walk through these four steps together, remember that the *order* is not nearly as important as that you follow *all* of them.

The Four Elements of Healing Religious Sexual Shame

1. Frame—Build a Framework of Sexual Knowledge

Sometimes, the best thing we can do for our clients is to build a framework for accurate education about sex and the body. In sex therapy, we often use a model known as "PLISSIT" to guide the therapeutic process, an acronym standing for "permission, limited information, specific suggestions, and intensive therapy." The PLISSIT model highlights the fact that for the vast majority of people who come for sex therapy, they first need permission to talk about sex and sexuality—reassurance that awkwardness is a normal feeling in a culture like ours that silences this conversation, but that the desire to know and understand is good. It is also important for clients to know that they are not alone in their desire to be heard with compassion, and to be given permission to get accurate information about human sexual functioning or the wide range of normal sexual behavior. Permission is the first structural element of our framework.

Beyond being given permission to talk about sexuality, the second element is basic information about human sexual functioning (remember that family and culture often haven't given this to them). Many will want help separating myth from fact. Most of my clients are relieved to have someone walk through anatomy and arousal cycles with them.[1] They may want to know trends or statistics, about safe sex and STIs, or to know ranges of "normal." They will likely have many fears and questions, like "Is my desire for this or that behavior or fantasy normal?" I have learned over the years to offer information by saying, "Would you like to learn the latest about such-and-such?" I find that many people think they should already know and thus won't ask. They may also want help figuring out what is right for them. For some, that will be all they want or need. Once they figure this out, they will be content to figure out the integration of their sexuality into the other domains of their life on their own or with their significant other.

Next, there will be many who also desire specific, action-oriented suggestions on what they can *do* to deepen their understanding or expand their sexual behavior. They may want tasks they can try, books they can read, exercises they can do at home, or example narratives from other people who have found what works.

The Frame process provides both permission to explore and access to information. In this process, clients have learned about arousal cycles, safe sex, and STIs, along with how to deepen connection through spiritual intimacy or other forms of sexual exploration. I like to encourage my clients to learn about their own pleasure—to learn how, where, and in what way their own body likes to be touched, and to notice how their feelings, thoughts, and desires respond to different kinds of physical contact. I invite clients to see their whole, integrated body as a miracle—unique unto itself, utterly unlike anyone else's—and to see themselves as the expert of this unique and special body.

Another aspect of framing is to help clients to learn about gender and power messages in our culture. Encourage them to gather with friends to watch documentaries like *Miss Representation* (Newsom and Acquaro 2011) and *The Mask You Live In* (Newsom 2015) by the Representation Project, and perhaps to follow the viewing by discussing social and cultural pressures and how to protect and support each other. If your client is a woman, you might frame by role-playing how to stand up for oneself. Or if your client is a man, you might role-play how he can best be protective with the women he cares for or how to get support in accessing and expressing his emotional wisdom. In framing, you might explore intimate relationships by inviting your clients to read books like Resnick's *The Heart of Desire* (2012), McCarthy and McCarthy's *Sexual Awareness* (2012), or Johnson's *Love Sense* (2013), or to listen to *Men, Women & Worthiness* by Brown (2012).

2. Claim—Claim and Celebrate Your Body

So much of marketing culture is aimed at inviting people to disapprove of their bodies or appearances so that they'll spend more money in search of being good enough. But part of our job as therapists is to help our clients to see that life is too short *not* to appreciate the deep beauty of their own uniqueness, and the legitimacy of their human desire to be seen, known, loved, and accepted. This is theirs to *claim*, and to live boldly and loudly every day.

As therapists, we can encourage clients to make "gratitude lists" or to write affirmations of themselves on paper. As you work with couples, invite them to locate the places in their bodies where they feel joy, gratitude, or love—and to live "from" these places. I often invite women to go to an all-women's spa for a day and to observe how women of all shapes and sizes let themselves be pampered. Another place women and men can do this is at clothing-optional beaches, where they can experience not being objectified, often for the very first time in their lives. If neither of these experiences sounds comfortable, I may recommend that they find someone over 60 who feels especially comfortable in his or her skin, and to interview them about how they got to that level of peace about their physical self.

As a therapist, you can also invite couples to explore sensual pleasure and play, to seek out their inner child and to discover their body again and the joy it can bring. Help them to befriend and inhabit the *power* in sexual arousal—a power we're often conditioned to fear. In this kind of sensual play, there is no goal other than fun and pleasure.

If clients have places in their bodies that feel tight or hurt, help them learn to listen deep to the "story" within that might be triggering those feelings. If they feel guilt or shame when they experience pleasure, help them to learn to sit *with* those feelings and to identify the message that invited the original shame. Help them to claim a new story around the gift of pleasure, one that says, "This is okay, this is beautiful, this is the way God created me—this is *me*." This may best be done through discussing a book like Emily Nagoski's *Come as You Are* (2015), or some other book that guides your client in discovering pleasure. Help them learn to give to themselves whatever amount of love and grace is needed for any hardship or pain they have suffered. Always give them permission to heal and to find whatever help and support they need for this part of their journey, remembering that many people, including many conservative Christians, will have to be *invited* to the idea that they're allowed to explore these things in the first place. With many of my clients, I have found it helpful to counsel in a group setting so that support and stories can be shared between clients and couples—to help them to see that they're not alone. Regardless of how you proceed with claiming, the goal is to help your clients to own that their bodies are good gifts, along with the powerful sensations that they experience.

3. Name—Name and Share Your Story

If your client's sexual story has been shrouded in secrecy, ignorance, trauma, fear, or shame, you'll need to help them find a safe tribe of compassionate, loving, and empathetic people who can bear witness as they name, identify, and bring image to their story. This is a type of walk-about; naming takes time. Shame, however, cannot live in the presence of love and begins to fade in the absence of judgment. It is difficult for a person to grow up in a culture as sexually silent, ignorant, and confused as ours and not absorb heaps of shame, unless someone changes this reality for them. It is important for your client to know that nothing is wrong with them—that they are, in the words of the Bible, "fearfully and wonderfully made" (Psalm 139:14). They deserve to have their story heard and grace and knowledge granted to them.

If your client has an inner circle of friends they trust to begin this process of sharing, help them to begin a practice of storytelling with each other. Help them to set some initial parameters and boundaries—confidentiality, for example—so that the group can talk together in safety. Groups can talk in person if they are close, or virtually if they live far away—whatever works. As long as loving and compassionate witnesses are able to hear a client's story and share their own in an atmosphere of acceptance and grace, you will have guided your clients into an environment where they can practice the Naming process. You may want to run a group or do a weekend retreat focused on story-healing.

4. Aim—Aim to Live Your Sexual Legacy

For most of my clients shrouded in religious sexual shame, their sexual stories, prior to their work in therapy, have been constructed for them by others. Often, it's been done without their permission or awareness, and certainly without a sense of self-ownership. In the Aim step, I want to hand the "pen and paper" back to my client, and invite them to begin the process of actively writing their story of sexuality and intimacy in any way that will bring *them* joy and nourishment. Framing deals with the present—what the human body *does*. Claiming and naming deal with the past—where we've been, the good and bad. In aiming, we look toward the future, helping clients to see that from this point forward, it'll be *their* story and no one else's. We invite them to consider what their values, their hopes, and their desires are, and we help them aim to write their sexual story.

Here are some of the questions I might ask:

- What is the legacy you want to live into?
- What is the story you want to share with the children in your life?
- When has sexual touch been most spiritual, satisfying, and meaningful for you, and how can this be cultivated?
- What resources are available that can expand your integration of body, mind, soul, and spirit as you expand your sexual repertoire?
- When will you know you are ready for varying degrees of vulnerability with another person?

Above all, focus in on this question: "What story do you want to write that will honor the beautiful, unique gift that is the sensual, powerful *you*?"

Naked Antics and Cameras

As your clients weave these four healing threads—Frame, Claim, Name, and Aim—they will gain more sexual, emotional, relational, and spiritual intelligence with each pass of the four-part cycle. They'll also strengthen a community of loving, compassionate, like-minded others, each discovering the power and beauty in the gift of pleasure and the exquisite liberation that comes from crafting their own authentic sexual legacy. As their therapist, you will see a profound transformation occur right before your eyes. As more people live boldly and unapologetically into the gift of their sexuality in ways that allow them to feel seen, known, loved, and accepted, throwing off generations of ignorance and shame along the way, you'll notice parents reacting to their four-year-old children's naked antics with *laughter* and *delight*, rather than reaction—remembering to capture the moment before hoisting them off to the bath!

One Woman's Story of Weaving Through the Threads

Lily described her relationship with her parents as very close, affirming, and supportive throughout her development. But she also recalled a certain silence around the topic of sexuality. As it happened, Lily was 11 years old before she learned about even the existence of sex. In her opinion, speaking with me as an adult many years later, it was fairly old *not* to have had "the talk."

Still, while sexuality wasn't a topic of conversation in her family, Lily's parents did give her agency regarding making decisions about her relationships with boys, which indirectly empowered her to make decisions about her sexuality. As a young adolescent, Lily said, she was quite open and curious about sex and sexuality, and she recalled trying to gather information about the topic from encyclopedias and magazines.

While she was still quite young, her family moved to a Christian commune that focused on "fleeing evil" and "leaving the world." There was "lots of discipline," she said, in an effort to be "perfect in Christ," and the commune was characterized by extreme rules that all its inhabitants were expected to follow. These included not having any physical contact with the opposite sex prior to marriage.

While Lily said her parents were "a little bit countercultural," providing much space for Lily to think differently and challenge the rules, the oppressive environment of the commune took a toll on the way Lily experienced herself, and she constantly doubted her value. She remembers feeling judged and "dirty" for how she dressed, or how her clothes fit her, even though she was doing what she was told. So when Lily was 11 years old, and a boy who was at least three years older than her "took things farther" without Lily's consent, Lily felt ashamed, like she was somehow complicit in their interaction. The unwanted sexual experience resulted in an experience of not wanting anything to do with male attention or sex for a number of years.

When Lily started to experience natural sexual responses as an adolescent, she felt confused about what to do with her feelings. "I remember watching *First Knight* with Richard Gere when I was about 15," she recalled, "and totally having a physical response to a kissing scene. I remember that it was such a shock, like, 'what is this?'" Around the same time, she went through what she later called a "bad girl phase," which was really no more than holding hands with a guy, or hanging out with a boy one-on-one, which were both against the commune's rules. Lily recalled feeling shame about this, though as an adult, she recognizes that she was quite "safe and careful" in those times. Still, because Lily was exposed to extreme, black-and-white messaging, she said that what was very innocent and natural felt very forbidden.

Today, Lily believes that as a result of the commune's oppressive environment, she developed an eating disorder as an adolescent. When she was a college student, Lily began a powerful healing process through counseling, along with positive, affirming relationships with women. These relationships began the long process of naming her story and taking her life back from shame. It was through these experiences that Lily began to claim her body, to appreciate its strength and health. She grew to a place of really believing that she was beautiful, and out of this newfound love for her body, a "new confidence" in her sexual self emerged as well. This, she said, started to impact her relationship and sexual experiences with guys, as she began to think, "Yeah, I look great. Others should enjoy this."

But while Lily found tons of sexual liberation and freedom in this healing journey, she shared that it also created more shame. Lily's sexual behavior did not fit with the "black-and-white rules" she was given at her commune or at the Christian university she attended later. In response to the shame, Lily described shame-rooted responses like compartmentalization (pretending she was one person in one situation and another in a different situation), withdrawing from her faith life, and emotional self-flagellating. Because Lily was actively involved in her church and in a nonprofit agency, she felt like a fraud in some ways. "Everyone thought I had everything together," she said, "but I felt so miserable in a lot of ways."

As she journeyed, however, Lily spoke about her profound and meaningful connection with her spirituality and with God, elements of her life that transformed the way she saw her sexuality. She described an experience of standing in her parents' kitchen making tea, and hearing God respond to her withdrawing by saying, "Don't stay away. I'm still here. I'm always going to make this better. Don't pull away—it doesn't matter what just happened." Then, she says, "I remember feeling that God was saying to me, 'What if you never felt like you left, even when the sexual shame was going on?'"

For Lily, this powerful experience testified to God's love and the way that God saw her. She began to recognize that she was craving intimacy and connection, and that she was able to open herself up to receive it more freely from God. In the span of about a year, Lily wrestled with the meaning of sexuality. "I'd pray about it a lot," she said, "and I'd cry about it, journal about it, and try to think about different strategies" for approaching her sexuality. Eventually, she was able to let go and hear God speak to her clearly. This was an important time of healing—of claiming, naming, and aiming with God at her side. She remembers hearing God saying things like, "It's about you being safe, and it's about you being free in this beautiful thing I created." After a gradual shift, Lily was able to come to a place where she felt "completely free in the love of God."

When Lily first began dating Thomas, her now-husband, she was worried that she would "mess it up" by bringing her "old patterns" into the relationship. Thomas had previously been in a marriage in which there was "a lot of brokenness" around sexuality, Lily said, and he himself had engaged in a tremendous amount of healing.

"I felt that he was so free and light," she said, "and I had never been with anyone like that. He just knew that sex was beautiful, and awesome, and he was so vocal about how great I was, and so careful and respectful of what I wanted. So I think we were able to start having conversations early on that were really open about sexuality."

As a result of their openness and love for each other, during their dating years and engagement they both felt tremendous peace, freedom, and intimacy in their sexuality together. Their sexual relationship was (and still is) very grounded in their dialogue with themselves and with God. As a result of this openness and love between her and Thomas, Lily has continued to experience healing in dating and married life. She has been intentional in confronting the "old shame responses" and has had to "deal with them one at a time, to actively reverse the cycle."

Community has played a significant role in Lily's story, and she often spoke about how the voices of women were very important in her journey. Lily, the middle of five girls, shared about one particular sister, who had a very free sexual life and empowered her to have agency in her body and her sexuality. She also spoke about transformative conversations with a female friend who met with her with "zero judgment" and mutual vulnerability, and encouraged her to have meaningful conversations with her new boyfriend about healthy sexual boundaries. In addition, she describes her current pastor and her church, in general, as very nonjudgmental, open, affirming, and encouraging of sexual intimacy.

Now, Lily speaks confidently about her sex life "being in the light," about "God's smile" on her sexuality, and God's prompting toward sex. As a result of the mutuality in her marriage, she shared that her whole self feels deeply bonded to Thomas.

"Sex is such a big part of my life," she says now, "and a huge part of what I think makes me have a really happy marriage. And my marriage is a big part of my life. So, yeah, there's this dimension that I feel so lucky when I think about, like, 'Man, I can just go home and have sex tonight.'" She laughs. "It gets better all the time. It's really an awesome gift."

Frame, Claim, Name, and Aim in Lily's Story

You can see in Lily's story how she circled through the four steps of healing religious sexual shame in her process of healing. Over the years, she learned about the body and sexuality, found ways to claim her body, learned how to tell her story, and became intentional about living her new legacy in such a way that she was "writing" a new story for those who came after her. For Lily, intentionality has become an ongoing process, not a one-time fix-all, but it's a journey that she's committed to walking in her life and in her marriage for the long haul.

In the next chapter we will explore practices that allow us to experience a sexuality that is integrated, one that involves our mind, soul, and spirit, while erotically activating our body and senses all the while. These practices involve full presence—attention, intention, eyes, breath, heart, and body—and will provide a foundation of practical experiences on which clients can start building a sex life that involves their whole selves, not just their genitals. Through these exercises, your clients can start to claim God's good gift of sexuality for all it's worth.

Note

1. Resources at the Northwest Institute on Intimacy website (nwioi.com) will provide ideas.

References

Brown, Brené. 2012. *Men, Women & Worthiness: The Experience of Shame and the Power of Being Good Enough.* Audiobook. Boulder, CO: Sounds True.

Guilamo-Ramos, Vincent, Jane J. Lee, and James Jaccard. 2016. Parent-Adolescent Communication about Contraception and Condom Use. *JAMA Pediatrics* 170 (1): 14–16.

Haffner, Debra W. 1999. *From Diapers to Dating: A Parent's Guide to Raising Sexually Healthy Children.* New York, NY: Newmarket.

Johnson, Sue. 2013. *Love Sense: The Revolutionary New Science of Romantic Relationships.* New York, NY: Little, Brown.

Lindbergh, Anne Morrow. 1955. *Gift from the Sea.* New York, NY: Pantheon.

Martino, Steven C., Marc N. Elliott, Rosalie Corona, David E. Kanouse, and Mark A. Schuster. 2008. Beyond the "Big Talk": The Roles of Breadth and Repetition in Parent-Adolescent Communication about Sexual Topics. *Pediatrics* 121 (3): 612–18.

McCarthy, Barry, and Emily McCarthy. 2012. *Sexual Awareness: Your Guide to Healthy Couple Sexuality*, 5th ed. New York, NY: Routledge.

Munsch, Robert. 1992. *Purple, Green and Yellow.* Illustrations by Hélène Desputeaux. Toronto, ON: Annick.

Nagoski, Emily. 2015. *Come as You Are: The Surprising New Science that Will Transform Your Sex Life.* New York, NY: Simon & Schuster.

Newsom, Jennifer Siebel, director. 2015. *The Mask You Live In.* Documentary. Ross, CA: The Representation Project. http://therepresentationproject.org/film/the-mask-you-live-in.

Newsom, Jennifer Siebel, and Kimberlee Acquaro, directors. 2011. *Miss Representation.* Documentary. Ross, CA: The Representation Project. http://therepresentationproject.org/film/miss-representation/.

Resnick, Stella. 2012. *The Heart of Desire: Keys to the Pleasures of Love.* Hoboken, NJ: Wiley.

Schnarch, David M. 1991. *Constructing the Sexual Crucible: An Integration of Sexual and Marital Therapy.* New York, NY: Norton.

7 Sex Therapy Interventions

The Anatomy of Intimacy

If any thing is sacred the human body is sacred;
And the glory and sweet of a man is the token of manhood untainted,
And in man or woman a clean, strong, firm-fibred body, is more beautiful than the most
beautiful face.

—Walt Whitman, *I Sing the Body Electric* (1855–56, 130)

"O that his left hand were under my head,
and that his right hand embraced me! . . .
My beloved thrust his hand into the opening,
and my inmost being yearned for him.
I arose to open to my beloved,
and my hands dripped with myrrh,
my fingers with liquid myrrh,
upon the handles of the bolt."

—Song of Songs 2:6, 5:4–5

So far, we've been examining a lot of the *whys* behind the reality that our culture, and conservative Christian culture in particular, became a source of such emotional pain and sexual dysfunction. Before we talk about the *hows*, exploring specific treatments and exercises that you can assign to your clients for helping them discover the fullness of their sexual selves, we have one more stop to make: exploring what makes intimacy *intimacy*. In this chapter, we'll talk about how you can guide your clients in connecting their sexuality with their body, with their sense of spirituality, and with their partner if they have one.

I should note a few things before we get started. First, I'll be using Judeo-Christian imagery and language, since that's the orientation of this text and where the specific sexual wounding I'm addressing in America originates. But if your clients' orientation to sacred language is different, try to use whatever paradigm and language will best serve to open their heart to divine love as they understand it. Also, I will offer some ideas for the integration of spirituality and intimacy that are thousands of years old, adapted and borrowed from other traditions. But as I do, please understand that I am not suggesting that these are the only ways to engage one's sexuality. For your clients, there are no embedded "shoulds" in what I am saying. As the vow of 'Onah suggests, people are free to craft the sexual relationship, life, and moments that work for them. I'll be offering one set of ideas for those people who are feeling disconnected, superficially informed, stuck, and in search of options for the misinformation offered by conservative religion.

Also, even though most of what I'll describe in this chapter will be written about couples, many of the ideas and exercises can be adapted for single persons, too. I should also say that while the examples in this section are predominantly heterosexual, the concepts here can easily be adapted for other sexual orientations. The key, throughout everything we'll discuss, is to pursue an integrated, honoring spirit, because that is what is at the core of all relationships at their very best, regardless of who the individuals are. The sacred sexual practices are included here to help clients embrace the gift of their body, their sexuality, and their desire for a deeper knowledge of God's love through sexual touch. Your clients will each be different, but it's the underlying pursuit of deep love, communion with each other and with God, and mutual giving and receiving that will be at the core of every suggestion given.

Understanding the Anatomy of Intimacy

Many couples who have discovered that sense of mutuality and authenticity are easy to recognize just by watching the way they move through their day-to-day lives. People who are at peace with the sexual integration of their body, mind, soul, and faith tend to have a kind of electricity in their countenance, a spring in their step as they approach the people and situations they encounter. They don't show signs of being conflicted within, and in conversation they seem to be at peace with their strengths and their growing edges. They are present to those around them and to life itself. People are drawn to how alive they are: they tend to love well and to attend to others well, and people who interact with them are able to feel seen, known, loved, and accepted in their presence, finding hope in their company. Their choices reflect this appreciation of being, and gratefulness to God. Our two friends Sam and Cris are like this. Gary and I have known them for over 25 years and raised our kids together. Everyone I know who has been in their presence comes away feeling seen and loved. We have been through many fun times and several excruciating times together, so I have seen their many sides. While they are human, they are at peace within themselves and they love well.

Helping Married Clients Out of the Doldrums

But with other people, it's not hard to tell when things *aren't* in balance. As a therapist, you can usually see when something is amiss or underdeveloped in a person's relationships.

Here's a classic example. For many couples who stay together for a long time, sex can become trapped in a routine, focusing on a particular "dance" of sexual behaviors. It won't be hard to recognize couples who are experiencing this, what we might call sexual boredom. As they talk, they will describe how sex happens in basically the same way each time the couple comes together. What started as novel and exciting at first has become predictable, unexciting, and lacking pizzazz over time, and it tends to increase feelings of ho-hum rather than the experience of having made love.

Through recent developments in brain science, we know that "routine" sex, like any other repetitive behavior, tends to be self-reinforcing over time: whatever behaviors, physical responses, thoughts, and beliefs become normal between the couple become what is *expected* from them. They learn to hone their typical sexual dance so well that it stops being interesting and fun; they always know what (or who) is coming next. In the language of neurophysiology, we say that they have neuro-pathways and learned chemical responses that encourage them on the same cycle over and over again.

That's fine for moving through an arousal cycle, but over time, sex starts to feel like eating the same ice cream every day, because it eventually captures their senses less and less.

Most married couples have had sexual encounters where they've become bored enough during sex to withdraw mentally into fantasy or some other form of distraction. This type of fantasy (unlike fantasies that a couple might create and share in together[1]) serves only to disengage them from the moment and from each other. For couples who yearn for a deeper spiritual experience, that kind of detachment only makes it harder to experience divine love through the encounter. Many couples have also learned to rate whether an encounter is "good" or "bad" by whether a certain *behavioral* goal is reached—usually intercourse, or orgasm in particular.

But deeply satisfying sex has more to do with the *quality* of the connection than with behaviors or positions, and it involves bringing the *whole* self to one's partner, not just the sexual organs, and not just the body, with other parts disengaged.

While it tends to happen slowly, as a couple falls out of tune with each other, a kind of malaise falls over them, both individually and collectively. That spark of creativity they had when their relationship was young or in a juicier state can get lost somewhere between work projects, laundry, and unending e-mails. The partner they used to pine for and anticipate that next rendezvous with now only brushes their teeth next to them each morning and night. Instead, anticipation is now synonymous with anxiety and wrapped up in job security. Life starts to feel like a big list of chores. The dynamic connection that felt so life-giving between them in those early days has faded like a guidepost that has been shrouded by a dark cloth. The pathway toward experiencing passion with each other feels dimmer and dimmer, and seeing the way clearly toward intense connection seems to take more effort. The creative juices that stirred within each for the other in their lovemaking, both in and out of the bedroom, have turned cold as lovemaking has devolved into transactional, routine sex.

In this chapter and in Chapter 8, I am going to offer ideas that will invite clients to leave their old habits of sexual relating that do not engage their whole being and do not draw them deeper into the experience of love—God's love and the love of their partner. With practice, your clients can learn new ways of touching and loving that are deeply nourishing to their whole selves and to the relationship, and leave them feeling satiated on every level.

Like anything new, these concepts and exercises will take practice, and they can feel odd at first, so you'll need to try to make the idea that "this feels unusual" the new normal for your clients. They'll need your permission to admit that they may feel strange the first several times. They'll need your guidance to know that it's okay to feel that way. Above all, they'll need your encouragement to hang in there. This challenging journey can usher them into sacred, ecstatic experiences that they never knew were possible. In time, they will wonder how the gift was kept buried deep in the vault of our collective history, and having gotten a taste of it, they're likely to find themselves wanting more.

A New Sexual Paradigm

In this section we will discuss what I have come to call the "Anatomy of Intimacy." This is a series of seven elements adapted from the work of David Taylor and Lana Holstein, physicians who after ten years of marriage went in search of their own marriage restoration. They discovered some of the practices I will share in the next two chapters and articulated that intimacy was an integrated whole of seven elements. They found that intentional investment in intimacy through integrated practices that engage the body, mind, soul, spirit, and relationship has the capacity to keep sexual intimacy deeply satisfying, pleasurable, and connecting for both partners (Holstein and Taylor 2004, 43–69).

To set the stage, you'll first need to help a client to establish how the "undercurrents" of their relationship currently work, the "Anatomy of Intimacy." If it is a couple, in their relationship together, both sexual and otherwise, what are their strengths, and where is there room for growth? For example, maybe they're really good at clearing their calendars to make regular time for sex (strength), but not so good at staying "in the moment" and focusing on each other when they are touching (weakness). Or perhaps they have a pattern of relating to one another with dependability in day-to-day living (strength) but tend to avoid conflicts when they arise (weakness). As you talk with your clients, there will be several areas to inquire about their continuum of intimacy on each domain.

If you're working with a single client, the Anatomy of Intimacy process involves asking him or her to think critically about their desires in a relationship and how to evaluate a person's relational skill-set whom they may be dating. Early in a relationship, it will be the chemical attraction that will reign supreme and help to incentivize their growing closer together, but the feelings don't last forever. Ultimately, it will be the health of these relationship currents that provides the foundation to build a durable eros. You can ask single clients to reflect on these dynamics—what they like, what they tend to avoid, and so on—to help them to gain a sense of what their assets and liabilities are in how they relate to the significant people in their lives. You will want to assess how they are individually living into each of the elements as well.

Anatomy of Intimacy

Conceptualizing the elements of intimacy can be a challenge, which is why I am grateful to Holstein and Taylor for this model and the way it helps to explain a complex human experience. I refer to their model with many couples who struggle with intimacy. Each of the seven dimensions of the Anatomy of Intimacy are placed on a continuum of positive, negative, and a quality that lies between, what I call "slack-tide." Placing each dimension on a continuum helps us to see more of the complexity of each area and allows us to help our clients to think through their relationship in more detail.

As we review these seven elements, think about a couple (or a single client) whom you're seeing, and ask yourself how you would place them on each continuum. Then, ask what kinds of interventions might come to mind to help them to move further toward health. If you are working with an individual client, ask questions about how they examine their emotional intelligence on each continuum.

Continuum 1: The Anatomy of Body Intimacy[2]

The physical body is the embodiment of the heart/mind core of us. According to the Judeo-Christian story, human life began in the primordial Garden of Eden with God breathing the breath of life into the bodies of Adam and Eve (see Genesis 1–2). So it is with us: we live from first breath until we breathe our final breath at the end of our lives. In between, we live in communion with our body and with the breath of life (God's breath) flowing through us. The body, every bit of it, is the vessel of our erotic love, and so it's very important that we think carefully about how well it's being maintained and how well it works in general.

The first continuum in the Anatomy of Intimacy, then, looks like Figure 7.1.

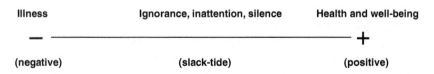

Illness	Ignorance, inattention, silence	Health and well-being
—		**+**
(negative)	(slack-tide)	(positive)

Figure 7.1 Continuum of the Body

Building toward the positive pole means knowing and understanding the physical body and striving for health and wellness. For your clients, it also involves knowing the sensuality of their own, *whole* body, including the fine details about what it likes and dislikes and why. Every facet of the body's experience matters here: what sights, smells, and tastes does a person's body enjoy? What kind of erotic touch does a person's body like, and what does it dislike? What about the partner's body? Can each person in the couple accurately describe what will make the other person's body "sing," and what will make it yawn? The key here is about self-knowledge, understanding what brings you pleasure, and knowing what brings your partner pleasure, all built on a foundation of basic knowledge of how the body and its systems work in the first place.

People who find themselves in the slack-tide area (ignorance, inattention, and silence) do not have this basic understanding, either of their own bodies or of their partners'. One of the most common symptoms can be a sense of distraction or apathy during lovemaking, or simply not knowing what kind of touch or sensual experience the other person wants or likes, or even what they themselves want or like. But couples do not have to remain in the slack-tide. Aside from learning to be fully present through practice, to move toward the positive pole requires learning to talk to each other—openly, honestly, and in detail—about what brings them pleasure. They have to learn to ask, to listen, to go slowly, and to check to see if they have the details before acting on them.

The most common mistake couples make in communication is that instead of talking, they assume they already know what their partner wants or likes, not realizing that most of the assumptions we bring to the bedroom come either from mass media or from what *we* tend to like. For women, it often means giving her man a slow massage, and for men, it usually means that he goes straight to her clitoris. Neither route is usually a good way to bring sexual satisfaction to the other.

No matter how awkward or difficult it is, couples need to learn to talk to one another. It's important to coach your couples to say things like, "I might like *this* kind of touch," or to ask, "Is there another way I could touch you that would be more pleasurable?" They'll need help learning to be kind and gracious with each other as they learn the process, and as they become more aware of each other's likes and dislikes over time. Whatever they say to each other may not "come out right" the first several times they try, and that's completely okay. Talking honestly about sexual preferences is a very vulnerable task and takes enormous courage, grace, and patience, and they'll be looking to you for encouragement.

Some of the people you'll encounter in your practice will be situated at the opposite end of the pole: illness. Having worked with many couples who were in the middle of chronic or life-threatening illnesses, I've learned that sacred sexual and erotic encounters do not have to end when the body is failing. The body does become limited when it is ill, and the simple fact of aging brings bodily changes that must be contended with. But when you remember that erotic lovemaking isn't ultimately about just the *body*—that it's about *using* the body to give and receive deep love—it's easier to understand that it's completely possible to make love in sweet and powerful ways even when the body is limited. Some of the most moving stories of lovemaking I have heard in my career have come from those who felt their days with their lover were limited because of an illness. Even with a frail body, touch was electric and filled with profound meaning.

For single clients, learning to place oneself on the continuum is a chance to get to know the body and all of its marvelous senses. Encourage your single clients to become familiar with every inch of their skin and what each location likes—that is, which kind of touch works best in each location, or which lotions, scents, or textures are the most pleasurable in different regions of their body. In addition to learning different regions and types of touch, encourage your single clients to know their arousal cycle and the many ways they can enjoy self-pleasuring.[3] Single folks can also find activities to do that allow them to move in their bodies and appreciate their strength and agility, such as playing in water, listening to music, taking an ecstatic dance class, hiking in the woods, or savoring food. Invite them to imagine God dancing with them, loving them, nourishing them in and through the body, because the more they inhabit their body, building its health and strength, the more sensually alive and intentional their engagement in the world and the more attuned they will be to fully loving themselves and others. Whether single or partnered, erotic loving begins here, in learning to love and appreciate oneself—every part—as God's beloved.

Continuum 2: The Anatomy of Sensuality

The sensual dimension of relationship and lovemaking is pleasure. As a species, we are hard-wired for connection and pleasure. Why else would we be so driven toward sexual touch? Part of the reason why pleasure can be so powerful for us is that it can play with all five of our senses at the same time. Plus, regardless of whether we're aware of it in a given moment, we are constantly taking in the "data" that our senses are giving us, which explains why we can remember intense experiences in fine detail, or why memories from a distant time can suddenly engulf us when we hear a particular song on the radio or smell a particular aroma. I experienced this firsthand once while in a duty-free store on a trip, when a man walked past who was wearing the same cologne my high-school boyfriend had worn years before. All *kinds* of memories of that relationship came flooding back in an instant!

Listening to our various senses takes discipline, just like learning how our bodies work. The second continuum of the Anatomy of Intimacy looks like Figure 7.2 on the next page.

People on the positive end of the sensuality continuum have practiced noticing everyday pleasure and have cultivated a slow enough pace to soak in

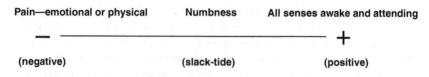

Figure 7.2 Continuum of Sensuality

the sweet moments of life when they happen. Most of us are so busy running on the day-to-day hamster wheel that everyday pleasures like wind on one's face, the warmth of the shower, and the smell of a lover's skin go completely unnoticed. Many artists, on the other hand, have spent their lives cultivating this level of attentiveness to the detail of beauty around them—shape, size, texture, line, color, light—and putting it down carefully on canvas or in words. Dancers, whose very bodies and the spaces they inhabit are both paint and canvas, are especially good at this, and so you might encourage a client or couple to take an ecstatic dance class. The more your clients learn to cultivate an ability to savor on that level, the better, more attentive lovemakers they will become at home.

Actually, a heightened awareness of pleasure is self-perpetuating, because it tends to ignite a desire to cultivate *more* pleasure. When a person has learned to bring this level of sensual cultivation into their sacred spaces with their lover, it has the effect of making pleasure "expand" in all directions within the relationship at the same time, a cascade effect of ushering lover and beloved from one form of pleasure to another to another to another, the senses fully and yet somehow *increasingly* awake and charged with each new touch, sound, taste, and sight—a torrent of pleasure.

But maintaining that level of pleasure-making does not come easy, quickly, or without sustained practice. People often find that they're able to experience pleasure like this at the beginning of a new relationship, when everything is novel, all things are possible, and they're on a kind of high. That's why even a brush of the hands can send electric bolts of pleasure through the body. In time, however, as the unfamiliar becomes familiar, the volume turns down on our sensory radar and we take in less and less until, if we're not careful, we may not take in anything at all. This is the point at which couples start to get bored and lovemaking loses its sense of play. That's why inviting your clients to stop, look, listen, breathe, and drink deep of pleasure in the moment is so important.

"I have entered my garden, my treasure, my bride!" says one of the speakers in the Song of Songs, reflecting exactly this kind of sensory attentiveness and play. "I gather myrrh with my spices and eat honeycomb with my honey. I drink wine with my milk." "Oh, lover and beloved, eat and drink!" reply their chorus of friends. "Yes, drink deeply of your love!" (Song of Songs 5:1 NLT).

On the other end of the sensuality continuum, the negative pole is pain. Pain can be physical or emotional and can ruin a sexual encounter, melting all desire in an instant. If it's a simple pain, like a position that aggravates one person's hip or a recent discomfort in the neck, pain may be temporary or avoidable. Emotional pain, on the other hand, can be all-encompassing and is generally more challenging to deal with, such as when there is an unresolved issue in the relationship, or when there is grief. One of the most devastating kinds can be when a person has experienced sexual trauma in the past, such that a part of the body "holds" the memory of the assault and brings it to the fore of the mind whenever that body part is stimulated. For persons who have been traumatized in the past, it's important to remember that wounds of the heart and body can heal, and that professionals are available to facilitate that healing. You may need to remind your clients many times, gently, not to be afraid to ask about why their physical reactions are being triggered, or to describe the way they feel. They deserve to be out of pain and to experience the full measure of pleasure that their senses can bring them.

In the slack-tide of the continuum is numbness, a lack of awareness of the sensations of the body. It can occur when someone has an emotional wound and they have shut off the awareness of what is going on, such as when they are protecting themselves from fear and pain. More commonly, numbness is being "off somewhere else" in one's head during a sexual encounter, free from pain but devoid of pleasure, too. Clients may describe thinking about work, or planning for Christmas, or worrying about money, or being lost in some sexual fantasy far away from the here-and-now. This is the phenomenon of being absent from one's own sexual encounters: the body may be having sex, but the person—their presence and attention—isn't really there at all.

The best way out of numbness is to learn to awaken oneself to sensory pleasure and to love—to notice and enjoy, to talk and adapt, then to notice and enjoy again, and talk and adapt again, and so on, gradually becoming fully awake to life, the surrounding environment, one's lover, and all that is wonderful in lovemaking.

Here again, the key is helping clients to slow down, to watch and savor the pleasures in an encounter, even talking about them aloud if necessary to fully notice them. Offer suggestions, such as "I want you to imagine using only your hands and eyes to make love to your partner (without bringing them to orgasm). Your hands and eyes are to speak your love and give pleasure to his/her whole body. There is no goal of orgasm or moving him/her through their arousal cycle—only the desire to give them pleasure and to show your love for at least 20 minutes."

Or you might give them this assignment, to help accentuate their sensory intake of taste. "I want you to blindfold your partner," you might tell them, "and feed them delicious-tasting treats that he/she doesn't know are coming, one after the other, allowing them to focus on receiving the pleasure of tasting." You can even invite them to add an element of fun by teasing each other, allowing them only to smell something delicious but delaying (for a moment) the gratification of tasting it. That small step can often help to expand one's ability to receive pleasure, and in all cases, by isolating the sense of sight, you will expand the sense of taste.

With your single clients, design an evening or a weekend exploration into the senses. Spa treatments are great for this, because they often involve isolating senses, such as having one's eyes covered while the body is massaged. Invite your client to pay particular attention to what kinds of sensations they enjoy when they go for their treatment. Have them spend time thinking about what they enjoyed in each of the five senses, one by one, and to think about what they might like to do next time to explore even further. If going to a spa isn't a good fit, invite them to do a "spa-in" at home, starting with a hot bath and candles, music, maybe their journal or a good book. Then they should run a good lotion or oil on their skin after the bath, appreciating the sensuality of the experience.

Continuum 3: The Anatomy of Desire

We often think of desire when we think of sex. "Desire" is the word we use to describe things like drive, passion, longing, aching, excitement, attraction, and wanting. It is the core of God's life force or breath within us. It's the electricity of erotic sexuality. The third continuum of the Anatomy of Intimacy looks like Figure 7.3.

For people at the positive end of the desire continuum, the qualities of attraction, passion, and sexual life force are in two locations. The first is the sense *within oneself* that "I am a passionate, vital, and sexual woman/man. God created me with this essential energy." A person who can make a statement like that, and say it with confidence, is probably a person filled with levity, who is passionate and present in their encounters with others, and known as loving and full of life. Generally, they carry themselves tall and seem comfortable in their own skin. Crucially, while they feel passion and desire in life, they are also very clear about *how* and *when* they choose to express desire; often it is inside of a committed relationship of some kind. For many, this is the place where they let their desire and passion fly completely free.

The other place where desire locates in a relationship is *for one's lover.* Many people don't realize that the expression of desire for one's partner is dependent on the first aspect, feeling passion and desire within oneself. If a person

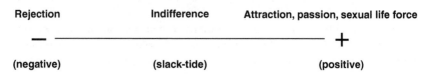

Figure 7.3 Continuum of Desire

cannot see themselves as passionate and desirable, then nothing their partner does will convince them. The energy of their desire, stale as it may be, will still emanate such that their partner will sense it clearly, and the person with low desire is likely to project the emptiness onto their *partner*—seeing their partner as less than desirable. A dynamic like that can lock the relationship into a downward spiral of decreasing desire and increasing misery. Under these conditions, a sexual encounter will suffer from a kind of emptiness as a result, which can be disorienting for couples, since they will have described amazing levels of passion at the beginning of their relationship before the vicious cycle started.

But there's good news: even if one or both of the people involved don't see themselves as desirable, they can still develop a story of great desire. In the beginning of a relationship, we have two emotional "helpers." The first is what I call the "urge-to-merge" chemicals that flood the brain for approximately the first four years of a relationship. These are powerful brain hormones like dopamine, adrenaline, serotonin, and oxytocin, and they make connection feel desirable and satiating. The second is our tendency to take our blank slate of self-worth and to project onto it how much the other person seems to want us and to see us as desirable. Essentially, we say to ourselves, "Well, if *she* (he) wants me this bad, then I *must* be hot!"

But over time, both of these "helpers" fade away, and we're back to where we started. If we do not see ourselves as desirable and loved passionately by our Creator *and* learn to live into that reality, the passion at the beginning of the relationship will eventually fall flat and the downward spiral of dissatisfaction will begin. Instead, in order for one partner's desire to resonate with the desire of the other partner such that an overriding desire grows to encase them *both*, each person needs to come to the encounter having made peace with the part of him or her that is hot, sexy, and longing to be erotically alive.

As we've seen throughout this book, many clients, and conservative Christians in particular, will bring beliefs from the past that may subtly block the flow of desire, beliefs such as "desire is bad" or "desire is dangerous" or "desire will get me into trouble" or "desire will pull me away from God" or "my sexual wants and desires are perverted" or "I am perverted." As long as these beliefs run free in a person's mind and body, he or she will keep returning to the slack-tide of indifference. But if a client can be invited into feeling *their desire as good* and feeling their desire for *their partner as good*, appreciating the desire, and deciding if and how to express it in a way that honors their core beliefs and values, it can be a nourishing gift. They will come to enjoy how alive, empowered, and creative they feel, and soon they will see what a gift desire is and how it can add excitement to their lives.

In spiritual terms, a person's desires are their passions, the most authentic and exciting parts of who they are, akin to the breath of God. Passions are the very place where all of human innovation comes from, whether it's athletic, creative, sexual, recreational, or loving. It is our inspiration, which literally means the "in-breath." Your clients were not created to be afraid of or victimized by their desire. They have the power to decide where, when, and how to act on desire, in ways that honor what they most value and believe. The challenge is that the most sexually traumatized Christians are paralyzed by fear to act outside of the rigid rules they grew up with. In response to listening to or trusting their values, you will hear things like "I cannot cross that line," or "What is going too far?" Be patient and gently explore the fear. You might want to ask questions like "How might you imagine engaging your sexuality in tangible ways in this stage of your life that are more informed by your values than by rules?"

On the negative end of the desire continuum is rejection, the flipside of feeling empowered. When our passions are shut out, shut down, shamed, ridiculed, or denigrated, we usually feel personal rejection. This is because there is something deeply personal about a passion or desire. Rejection is the feeling of being deflated, unwanted, and devalued. It is one of the relational experiences we are most afraid of, and one of the reasons we shy away from love and attachment. In part, we fear that someone else will confirm the lies that shame has been telling us all along, that we really are unworthy of love and belonging. Our fear of rejection and our experience of it are triggers for shame. When we are lost in our rejection and shame, we are cut off from the creative life force of desire, which is why we so often see connections between rejection, deep shame, and depression. If people are rejected and treated as unworthy, their natural physiological and emotional response can be depression.

Men and women tend to experience rejection differently. For women, the most common culprits seem to be exhaustion, anger, and fear, a reality that I see play out all the time in my office. Women, especially mothers, are notorious for working and not eating or sleeping enough, driving themselves into exhaustion, and then being angry at others for how they feel. They have what I call "low body awareness" and "low permission tolerance." They have a hard time reading how exhausted, hungry, burned out, and depleted they are getting, and once they do become aware, they have a hard time giving themselves permission to do anything about it. They can have the most supportive partners and yet remain unskilled at changing how they nourish themselves. When women are depleted, they feel flat inside, devoid of desire for pleasure. If they desire anything, it is for sleep and silence.

Women need to take time to renew, restore, and process through issues of frustration, and to take charge of their overall health if they are to keep feeling their passion for life and sexuality. When women put everyone else in front of them, they get exhausted, angry, and afraid, and passion can dry to a slow trickle or evaporate completely. Women need to develop clear and strong voices about what they need in order to remain vital and engaged in life, a critical first step if women are to keep feeling hot and juicy in their eros.

When I work with a depleted or rejected woman, I might ask questions like these: When do you feel the lowest sexual desire? When do you feel the highest? When do you have the lowest creative energy? When do you have the highest? What do you think is the connection between creative energy, playfulness, and sexual desire? What would need to happen to free up more creative energy for you? Whom is sexual desire for? When has sexual desire been for you and about you?

For men, sexual desire can drop significantly when he is humiliated (at work or sexually) or when he encounters financial loss—any situation where his power, vitality, and sense of importance are deflated. Men can learn over time to see setbacks as a condition of life and not a reflection of self, but they also need people they love and respect to remain steadfast in their love and admiration of them and their belief in their competency and worth. Rejection by a partner around sexual intimacy comes in many forms, ranging from statements as innocuous and honest as "Not tonight, I am feeling really worried and preoccupied about the situation going on at my office," to something more rejecting of the whole person, like "Why I would want to have sex with you?" Usually, however, what I tend to hear from couples is a kind of indifference or couched apathy. It can sound something like "I don't have the sex drive he has," or "I have sex with him when I know it has been too long and he is starting to pull away," or "I just get it over with to make him happy." In these scenarios, while sex does happen, the woman's *want* of the man is not there, and he doesn't feel desired, needed, or important to his partner. He may be physically accepted, in the sense that there is physical interaction between both people, but he will feel emotionally rejected during the encounter. Sex may still happen; arousal cycles may even fire and orgasms may spill over; but authentic desire is blocked, and the reality is that both people end up slightly rejected and neither person gets fully nourished. They will each end up feeling unfulfilled and unconnected.

I'll often ask men, "When have you felt most wanted by your partner?" or "When have you felt most seen and appreciated?" or "What does your partner do or say that gives you a sense of being desired?" I hear responses like "I love it when she greets me when I get home at night," or "It means the world to me when I do something for her and she lets me know that it made a difference for her."

When couples fail to deal with whatever is blocking desire and instead withdraw their sexual energy from the relationship, desire becomes more and more faint. If this goes on for a while, it can take a great deal of effort to re-ignite passion. Dancing around blocked desire, or pretending that it is not there or not a big deal, will continue to erode love, trust, and passion, and it will kill the opportunity for a fulfilling sex life.

For my single clients, freeing sexual desire is akin to releasing them from sexual shame. In addition to using the Frame, Name, Claim, and Aim processes (see Chapter 6), we work around body awareness, body image, body movement, body pleasure, sensual awareness, and sensual experimentation. We try to open them up to an awareness of their body in the world and the stories that come up as they try to be more intentional with their body and their sensuality. Questions in therapy might include examples like "What excitements or hesitations emerge for you as you focus on something sensual, like savoring a delicious meal, or a massage, or sleeping in?" Or another example: "In your opinion and experience, what constitutes physical decadence, and why?"

Continuum 4: The Anatomy of the Heart

Just as the physical heart is at the core of our body, our emotional heart is the nourishing vibrancy at the core of deeply satiating sex. Heart is the essential foundation of intimacy. If a couple has many other strengths but does not have a heart connection, the relationship may not stand the test of time. On the other hand, if a relationship has a strong heart foundation, there is usually hope for renewal.

Have you ever been around a couple with a strong heart connection whose love flows easily? I've noticed that when I'm in the presence of people who have a strong emotional connection, somehow the love that binds them flows out to me as well, such that I can feel the sense of goodwill and play that exudes from the way they interact with each other.

A heart foundation is all about love, and when the heart is open, love emanates out. In a healthy body, the physical heart and the physical brain help each other in their work: the brain modulates the heart, and the heart supplies blood and nutrients to the brain. The emotions of the heart work the same way. Healthy individuals are able to keep the heart in constant communication with the brain, a two-way conversation in which both parts help each other to regulate the thoughts and feelings of life.

Similarly, just as the physical heart cannot be separated from the emotional heart, sex separated from love ultimately flatlines, like a physical heart does when disconnected from the brain. The current hookup culture is an example of this kind of emotionless sexuality in practice (see Stepp 2007). While it emerged as a response to life and career demands and a gradual delay in the age of marriage, research is now suggesting that hooking up carries unforeseen consequences, such as a growing sense of doubt in the very existence of true, love-borne intimacy at all (Stepp 2007). That doesn't bode well for our culture's understanding and experience of sexuality. Intimacy is an essential ingredient in the nourishment of a passionate and compassionate life, and a core element of how God made us. Continually having sex with no love or care for the person is like slowly turning off an oxygen valve, and the effects on a person's (emotional) heart can be roughly the same. The fourth continuum of the Anatomy of Intimacy looks like Figure 7.4.

People on the positive end of the of the heart continuum describe intentional experiences of giving and receiving love, often demonstrated by romantic gestures like cards, loving texts, romantic dinners, and other forms of affection. Early romance often leads toward a life-commitment ritual—a wedding ceremony—that publicly declares, "As real life sets in, we vow to

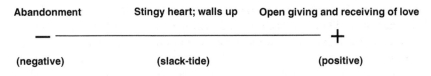

Figure 7.4 Continuum of the Heart

keep an open heart toward each other." But that can't be the end of the story. Just as we saw on the previous continuums, the heart requires discipline, nurture, and care in order to grow stronger and more durable over time.

I can't overstate the importance of what happens in the heart for lovemaking. At its deepest level, when two cultivated, well-nurtured hearts begin to run over with love and desire for each other, the result is manifested sexually in the form of lovemaking—what the Hebrew Scriptures call becoming "one flesh" (see Genesis 2:24). Their devotion to each other, their love for each other, their desire for each other, their appreciation for each other, and their mutual acknowledgment of God's communion and ordination of their love can melt into sacred, erotic ecstasy. *This* is what is meant by "making love," as opposed to its counterfeit twin of only "making sex." In lovemaking, love is actually *created*, *made*, on the uncontrollable, nuclear power of well-cultivated hearts that yearn for each other.

On the other pole of the heart continuum is *abandonment*, something most people have experienced at one point or another. Many clients can tell stories of the parent who couldn't love, the mother who died when they were children, the girlfriend who cheated, the ex-husband who was abusive. Whatever the form of abandonment, these wounds, if left unhealed, can close the heart and make it impenetrable to love inside or out, like a city under siege.

I've encountered clients with "closed" hearts, unable to give or receive love, and it always makes me feel profoundly sad, not because I don't appreciate the devastation of what may have caused the heart to close—I do—but because I also know that healing is possible, even though the man or woman sitting before me may not believe it anymore.

In the slack-tide of the heart continuum is what we might call the "stingy" heart, one that keeps score and settles old ones given half a chance. Rather than openly giving love, these clients tend to keep an accounting of who is giving more and who is giving less. They might make scorekeeping remarks like "I never get to go out with my friends, but he does every weekend," or "the last time she wanted to make love was my birthday, two months ago." Therapists might also hear that "she spends more on clothes than I spend on anything" or that "the last time I got flowers was before we were married."

This kind of thinking, aside from being an isolating force by its nature, is self-reinforcing and easy to perpetuate. As we saw in Chapter 3, our consumer culture trains us to focus on what is *not* working so that we can get the new version. In my office, I see many couples whose initial language to describe their partner and their marriage is in precisely this stingy, closed-hearted way. They are holding themselves and their relationship hostage behind a wall of entitlement and expectation, and the worst part is that nothing in the accounting or wall-building system is actually protective of the person or their relationship. If anything, it serves only to damage the fabric of trust between each person, because the one may learn to be always wondering what their "score" is with the other person, or may withhold certain favors or pleasures if they feel that they are "owed" something.

Here, especially when working with clients from conservative Christian backgrounds, it's important to remember a concept that was attributed to Jesus himself: "It is more blessed to give than to receive" (Acts 20:35). It is only when *both* partners have opened their hearts and actively forgiven each other that love can grow. An open heart loves, forgives, extends grace, empathizes, enjoys, and extends itself. For my own part, I think it's because our hearts already know on some level that remaining open is *good* for the heart, as well as good for the relationship. This is almost impossible at times in a marriage, of course. But it is exactly in this near-impossible place, where we learn how to love like Jesus loved, that we begin to see and feel a bit of how far God's love extends to reach us in our faults and imperfections. I often call this the spiritual side of loving; it is when loving is difficult that we are given the best opportunity to learn about ourselves and the biggest opportunity to grow.

With your single clients, explore how they manage emotional hurts in their closest relationships (family of origin, closest friends, past significant relationships). What were their triggers? When and how did they close their hearts? Did they tend to keep score? How did they deal with conflict? Were they overt or covert? Were they conflict-avoidant, reactive, or proactive? With your couples, explore similar questions but in the history of their relationship. See what you can find out about their patterns of the heart.

Continuum 5: The Anatomy of Trust

Intimacy is fundamentally built on trust and can grow only when we reveal ourselves to each other—the good, the bad, and the ugly—in a relationship environment of safety. When a relationship has high levels of trust, one partner will receive with grace what the other one tells them, and they will respond with compassion and interest, keeping an open and loving heart all the while. This is a major part of what the therapist is providing in the therapeutic space—a nonjudgmental, confidential, fully trustworthy "Other" to hear the inner thoughts of another person. Likewise, in an intimate partnership, when people are loving and trustworthy, the heart of the relationship beats strong and true. Trusting our lover is critical if we are going to walk into the fullness of our vulnerability, into the risk of loving deeply and exploring the limits of erotic ecstasy. We can go only as deep as we trust our lover, or otherwise, we are holding back. The fifth continuum of the Anatomy of Intimacy looks like Figure 7.5.

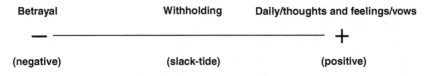

Figure 7.5 Continuum of Trust

In *Your Long Erotic Weekend*, Holstein and Taylor describe the notion of trust by breaking it down into three areas. The first area of trust is in the day-to-day operations of life, like house maintenance, grocery shopping, shuttling kids around, finances, and so on. We need to trust that what we have agreed on, or what we have said we will do, will in fact be done unless we hear otherwise. We want and need to count on our partner in the everyday logistics of life (Holstein and Taylor 2004, 43–69).

The second area is honesty, the need to be able to trust our partner to give us their real opinions, thoughts, and feelings about life together. Here we trust our partner not only to speak what is true for them but also, just as importantly, to be able to hear our truth without judgment. This is what keeps safety at a high enough level that a person can feel safe enough to speak up (Holstein and Taylor 2004, 43–69).

The third area is honoring the exclusivity of the relationship. Here, we count on our partner to hold certain private aspects of our life in confidence, to keep their promises, and to give us their truthfulness about our deeper lives and their deeper selves (Holstein and Taylor 2004, 43–69). Secrecy is seen as a potential solvent of intimacy, and it is evaluated very carefully for its potential effects on trust. In this space, we learn to think before we say or do anything that would be a violation of the privacy of our partner or our shared life together. If in our gut we know our partner would not want us doing or saying something to someone else, we're probably dealing with questions of privacy.

On the negative pole of the trust continuum is betrayal. Small forms of betrayal will erode trust over time, and larger forms of betrayal, like affairs, can cause irreversible damage to a relationship. Shirley Glass, a leading expert on infidelity, says that marriage is like a house. The windows and doors of the house have different purposes. Windows let those who are inside see what is outside and those who are outside of the house see what is inside—which, in marriage, consists of the information that we share with others. Doors, on the other hand, keep what is outside the house on the outside and keep what is inside the house inside. In marriage, this is what the couple has decided is private between them, typically consisting of private information, intimate thoughts and feelings, and "just-between-us" behaviors that are not to be shared with those on the outside. When doors become windows and a person within a couple begins sharing private information with someone on the outside, and when they then keep the transgression a secret from their beloved, the slippery slope into betrayal has already begun (see Gilbert 2010, 108ff.; see also Glass 2003).

"I don't know how it happened," clients sometimes tell me. "I never intended to have an affair." Often, an affair will have begun because over time, the client had started turning doors into windows one by one until there were only windows. The intense damage of an affair usually requires professional support if there is to be hope of recovery from the pain and disillusionment that comes— another reason why a history of a strong heart connection is critical for hope of reconciliation and restoration. It's hard work, but I have seen many couples come out stronger on the other side.

In the slack-tide of the trust continuum is withholding. When couples stop sharing their life or their truth with each other, an insidious, almost imperceptible slide toward distance and distrust can take place. As couples keep more and more of their lives tucked away from the intimacy of knowing and being known by their partner, the distance between the two of them will grow and grow until they become strangers. Withholding can be a sneaky companion, as I've seen many times in client families that are stretched thin with kids and careers and who have never learned to make their intimate lives a priority. The genesis of an erosion of trust can begin with something fairly small, like an argument where someone's feelings get hurt but he or she decides to tuck the hurt feelings and anger inside rather than speaking what is true. Instead of fighting for intimacy they avoid conflict, tuck the pain away, and let the conflict go unresolved, while the distance grows between them. Soon, one or both has forgotten what the argument was about and why the distance is there, but a vague distrust is still there on a seismic level. In order to nurture trust together, clients have to be willing to courageously speak their *whole* truth, holding onto themselves and standing in the fire of misunderstanding and pain until they can find their way out together, united. This is another place where couples therapists and sex therapists can be a critical resource, because it can be immensely helpful and comforting to a struggling couple to have someone else guide this difficult and vulnerable process.

In addition to being committed to sharing difficult thoughts and feelings, couples have to be invited to keep sharing their dreams and hopes with each other. It is their passion and purpose in life that often ignite passion and purpose in another. Couples that are well connected often get noticeably energized when their partner talks about their life callings—their hopes, passions, and purposes in life, and in their relationship together. This kind of conversation is nurturing to a relationship and to intimate connection, and yet it's often one of the key conversations that are silenced by busy schedules. Help your clients to remember to carve out time for this. It will help them to build a passionate connection to each other and to their life calling.

Remind your single clients that in these foundations of body, sensuality, desire, heart, and trust, they have the opportunity to examine how well they have developed these skills in their own life. They can ask themselves, "How committed am I to the practice of a healthy body, an awareness of all that is sensual around me, of the energy of attraction and sexual stirrings, of living with an open heart, of being trustworthy?" And equally important, "How savvy am I at examining the strengths or weaknesses of these qualities in those to whom I am romantically attracted?" We practice these skills in all of our key relationships, not just with a lover—with our closest friends and family members, with God, and in relationship to the self. The more practiced our clients are in living and noticing these elements of intimacy, the more this will guide them in the dating process, should this be a part of their desire. This is part of learning how to choose a partner well. Helping our clients to know themselves and know the kind of person they want to weave their mind, body, soul, and future with can make all the difference in quality of life. As a single person, they are in an ideal place to be intentional about choosing who and what they want in building a lifetime of sacred sexual intimacy.

Continuum 6: The Anatomy of the Aesthetic

The aesthetic dimension of intimacy opens us to the deep pleasure that comes from beauty. Plato spoke of eros as the coming together in beauty of body and soul (Plato 1973). This is deep beauty, not the surface beauty that our consumer culture sells so often. It is the beauty that takes our breath away and deeply roots us. If you've ever been moved by a sunset, a landscape, the laughter of a child, or a musical piece, then you've experienced the aesthetic quality of eros. It's the beauty that is within you and encompasses all of you, the core beauty found in the presence of love, and the beauty of your beloved—the beauty that is ignited when your love is stirred. The sixth continuum of the Anatomy of Intimacy looks like Figure 7.6.

In sacred lovemaking, the positive pole of the aesthetic continuum opens us up to seeing all the beauty that is around, within, and beyond us. It invites us to delight in the beauty in the creation of our expressions of love, in the making of love, and in the nourishment of gratefulness.

On the negative pole of the aesthetic continuum, we find judgment and shame, qualities that place a condemning eye on us and on our partner. Judgment and shame can preoccupy us with what is condemned and can eclipse the dance of beauty that is happening all around us. There is no delight or gratefulness that can be felt or nourished in a landscape of shame and judgment. Henri Nouwen once wrote that "self-rejection is the greatest enemy

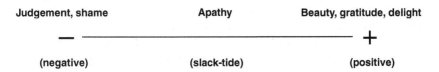

Judgement, shame   Apathy   Beauty, gratitude, delight

(negative)   (slack-tide)   (positive)

Figure 7.6 Continuum of the Aesthetic

of the spiritual life because it contradicts the sacred voice that calls us the 'Beloved.' Being the Beloved expresses the core truth of our existence" (Nouwen 1992, 26–8).

In the slack-tide of the aesthetic continuum is apathy. The word *apathy* comes from a Greek word *apathea*, meaning "absence of passion." In modern times, it is considered a state of indifference, but it wasn't always considered a bad thing. For the ancient Stoics (approx. the third century BCE through the fifth century CE), apathy was seen as a desired state of indifference to earthly passions in service of the mind and reason (Fleming [1857] 2006, 34). Later, the idea of apathy was reappropriated by many Christians, who adopted the term to express contempt for all earthly concerns (Farley 2006, 38–9). This was yet another way that Christianity invited people away from desire, passion, beauty, and love, away from the very breath of God within us. Apathy can be a quiet emotion, but when we see it at work in the center of our clients' relationships, it is an urgent warning sign, a signal that some crucial part of the relationship is dying.

When working with couples and individuals, you might ask them when and where they've been particularly struck by deep beauty in their lives. You might explore a time when they saw deep beauty in the eyes or face of their lover and deconstruct the context around that time. What opened their heart to see that beauty? What kind of presence did they bring? What kind of intention?

With your single clients, you might ask them to tell you stories of what captures deep beauty. What stirs their soul in a deeply beautiful way in each of their different senses? When they imagine sexual expression to be beautiful, what comes to mind? What would make it beautiful in an aesthetic way? How would they discern if someone else had an appreciation of the aesthetic beauty of sexual expression?

Continuum 7: The Anatomy of the Ecstatic

The seventh and final foundation of the Anatomy of Intimacy model is the continuum of the ecstatic. We have now moved from our beginnings in the body and sensation, through the core emotional qualities of intimacy, into the spiritual dimensions of sacred love. The seventh continuum of the Anatomy of Intimacy looks like Figure 7.7.

If we want to expand our lovemaking experience into a deeply spiritual encounter, we first must believe it is possible to do so. That may sound

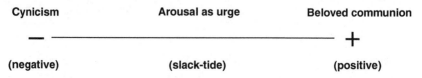

Cynicism	Arousal as urge	Beloved communion
(negative)	(slack-tide)	(positive)

Figure 7.7 Continuum of the Ecstatic

simple, but it's not as common as it may appear. Many people have had at least one sexual experience that felt deeply spiritual, but most of the time, those who have experienced it believe that it was a wonderful, mysterious surprise, a pleasant fluke, and they have no idea how to increase the likelihood of more of these experiences.

But it is precisely the belief in profound, spiritual-sexual communion, and the commitment, preparation, and spiritual discipline of growing our sacred love, that can bring all seven of these continuums into concert and harmony with each other and that can usher a couple toward many more sacred sexual encounters in the future. Couples who have experienced encounters like these have talked about feeling themselves in the presence of God during the sexual encounter, or feeling overwhelmed by love and awe—a true sense of ecstasy.

On the negative pole of the ecstatic continuum is the belief that sexual desire and arousal are simply animal instincts to be satisfied as needed, or that they're actually profane, disgusting, wrong, and worldly. (We saw this in our discussion of Christian sexual history in Chapter 2.) Both of these ideas share the belief that sexual desire and sexual expression are *human* instincts, and they imply that those instincts have nothing to do with God.

In the slack-tide of the ecstasy continuum is a consumer mind-set toward sex. This is quid-pro-quo sex, an eroticism that says, "I'll do you, you do me; I'll have an orgasm, you'll have an orgasm; we'll both be happy." This is a body-focused, transactional approach, a sexual *exchange* that leaves the heart out, along with concerns for the quality of the relationship and all spiritual dimensions of the two people involved. Many couples don't realize that this kind of sex is but a small sliver of the pleasure and power that can be created through the gift of sexuality, and most people who are stuck in the slack-tide don't even know that something better is possible until we tell them and they finally experience it.

With both single and coupled people, I'll often ask clients to write down a description of a sexual experience they had that felt spiritual in some way or a spiritual experience that felt sexual or sensual in some way. I ask them to describe the environmental circumstances, their mind-set at the time, their heart-set at the time, and other factors that come to mind for them as they reflect on their experience of all five of their senses. I also ask them questions like these: What was going on in their life at that time? What might have opened them up to that experience? What was their intention like on that day? What was the quality of their attention on that day? What was the quality of their presence on that day?

Building on Our Foundation

Each of the seven elements of the Anatomy of Intimacy builds on the others and expands the pleasure and connection experience of sexual intimacy. Our culture has tended to focus on the body, and the questions that people ask in early sessions in my office tend to sound like "How often should we be having sex (i.e., intercourse)?" or "How do we have mutual orgasms?" A wife might say, "I need to give this to my husband" (meaning intercourse), or a husband might say, "We are not having enough sex" (also meaning intercourse). Young people are coached to "wait" until marriage for sex (yet again, meaning *intercourse*). As we've seen, this is a narrow view of sex, and it composes only a small portion of the pleasure and connection that God intends. It's no wonder that when sex is focused on the body alone, desire often fizzles out over time. In order for sexuality to stay nourishing and exciting, it has to go beyond coitus and orgasm to the level of actual love*making*, a process that requires all seven of these dimensions of intimacy cascading into the larger picture of how a couple connects together (Figure 7.8).

As you help your clients to appreciate and attend to all of these elements of sexual and intimate energy, an amazing array of opportunities to enhance connection will become available. Many couples may feel as though they've

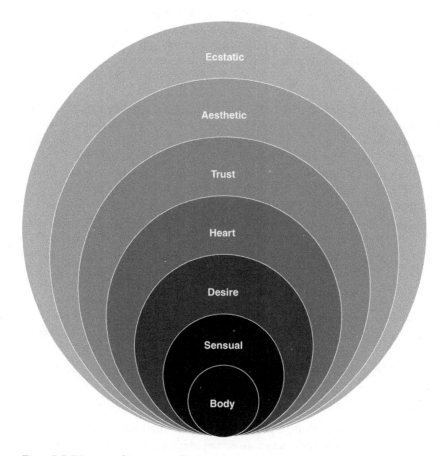

Figure 7.8 Diagram of Anatomy of Intimacy

removed blinders from their eyes. They will become aware of where they had been inadvertently undermining their relationship simply out of a lack of awareness. For others, thinking through the elements will give them ideas as to how to enhance their connection together. The key involves intention and daily attention. This is what I work to help my clients appreciate so that they can find their way back to the intention they had when they first got together. What kind of relationship did they intend to create? What kind of attention is needed to create that kind of relationship? What is the spiritual discipline needed with each element that will help them attain this kind of connection?

Here's one suggestion for how to get started living into these seven dimensions daily.

What's in a Hug and a Kiss?

It's impossible to overstate the importance of the daily "long hug" and "juicy kiss." Research shows that the happiest couples still kiss and hug almost daily. They also are known to say "I love you" to each other, to practice public displays of affection, and to be happy with their sex lives. This is all contrasted to unhappy couples, who tend to rate the opposite on all of these measures. The daily kiss and long hug can be simple, crucial, accessible steps toward building a connection together that lasts and grows deeper over time (Northrup, Schwartz, and Witte 2012, 60).

To understand what a long hug or a juicy kiss can look like, it's important to note that we're not talking about a "fly by," a peck on the lips, or a side-shoulder-hug lasting no more than a fraction of a second. We're talking about a *real* kiss and *real* hug—the kind that can integrate all seven elements of the Anatomy of Intimacy all at once (the body, sensuality, desire, the heart, trust, aesthetics, and ecstasy). Here are the directions I give my clients for how to practice this kind of daily hug and kiss.

The Whole-Being Hug (2–3 Minutes)

I encourage clients to practice this hug every day, whether inside or outside their sacred space, and typically without any intention to make love. In fact, I recommend that couples do this at least *twice* a day.

Here's how it works. Ask the couple to walk into a hug and wrap their arms around each other. Have them place one hand on their partner's upper back, behind the heart, and the other deep on the lower back above the tailbone. Have them pull each other close and get a firm, balanced stand (or whatever feels comfortable for them). Now have them slow their breathing into deep, four-count breaths—inhale, exhale. They should let their shoulders drop and their bodies relax.

Ask them to imagine that they are sending any concerns, worries, and preoccupations "out" on their exhalations, and breathing *in* pure love on the inhalations. Have them feel their body let go. Next, let their breath either match their lover's or alternate (either is fine, as long as they're in sync). Have them try to imagine that they are accessing the infinite well of divine love. Then, on the exhalation, ask them to imagine *sending* that love into their partner's body such that it flows through every cell and fiber. On the inhalation, invite them to imagine that they are capturing, in their body, all the love that their partner is sending to them. Remind them to have their body relax further.

Invite them to feel *how* and *where* their bodies are touching, tracing the line with their mind's eyes, to take in all that their body is absorbing. Remind them to be fully present in the moment, to feel love relax and unite them. Remind them that *this person* is their beloved, *this place* is their safe place, a place with an infinite supply of love to nourish and heal both of them.

When they feel fully present and satiated, have them pull slightly away from each other and to meet each other's eyes for a moment before they end and say "I love you" with their facial expression. It should take two or three minutes to do the whole hug. If my clients have little kids, I always say, "Long enough for all the kids and animals to be in between you."

The Savory Kiss

This practice ushers lovers into the luscious and tantalizing world of kisses.

Kissing is a forgotten art form, often tossed aside in marriage by the drive for orgasm. The lips are a wonderfully sensuous and sensitive part of the human body. They can read the body nearly as well as the eyes can. Kisses can be soft or firm, shallow or deep, light or hard, and every inch of a lover's body can be fair game for the attention of loving lips.

I like to invite couples to avoid "fly by" kisses, and instead to really "plant one" each time they are kissing each other hello or good-bye. They should *mean it* every time, and to try for one special, *juicy* kiss each day.

If it has been a while since a couple has been actively kissing each other, I invite them to play a game to get them used to touching and playing with their lips again. I ask one of them to be the active one and the other to be passive. I ask the active one to think of a flavor that they enjoy, like a fresh, juicy strawberry, for example, and to imagine rubbing it over their lover's relaxed lips. (You can do this with a real strawberry if you'd like.) Then, they should act like they're trying to lick it off of their partner's lips until every molecule of flavor has been savored off. Then they should do the exercise a second time, but this time, they should nibble it off. The third time, they should softly *kiss* it off. By kissing in all three of these ways, both partners will gain experience in the complexity of the different kinds of kissing that are possible, and they will learn the art of slowing down and enjoying each other's lips.

I instruct them to show each other how they like to kiss by exploring together. As before, one person can be active and one passive in this sensual "show-and-tell." I ask my clients to make it a game and to have fun, to pretend to be teenagers again. Doing so usually helps people to get silly, which provides a doorway into talking about how to bring more kissing into daily life and lovemaking.

When a couple makes it a daily practice to intentionally and sensually hug and kiss, they can activate all seven dimensions of the Anatomy of Intimacy at once. In bringing each other close and synchronizing their breath, they are purposefully embodied and sensually aware. Each allows themselves to relax and make space for desire to bubble up. The desire can be enjoyed because it is not expected to initiate any other sexual behavior, but instead, it's there only for the purpose of being felt and savored. As it is enjoyed, the couple's relationship is likely to see an increase in trust and intimacy, in addition to increased physical pleasure. This in turn deepens the heart connection between the two of them and raises the likelihood of there being a seismic, thrilling love between them.

In Chapter 8, I will introduce more explicit clinical interventions for expanding the integration of spiritual intimacy. How can sexual touch be used to heal and celebrate the gift of the body, desire, sensuality, love, intimacy, trust, and a deep commitment to loving over time? How can we help our clients to take the power of the erotic and use it to serve their lives, their intimate relationships, and their spiritual life, rather than having them feel opposed or separated? This is the final frontier of sexual and spiritual liberation, a place where the sexual and spiritual can merge together and even act as a form of grateful worship.

Notes

1. A fantasy a couple creates together might be a role play. For example, the couple might make an agreement to meet at a designated place, arrive separately, pretend to be strangers, talk to the people around them, pretend to be meeting for the first time, and pick each other up.
2. Throughout this chapter, I am greatly indebted to Holstein and Taylor (2004, esp. 52–69).
3. Some people from conservative backgrounds may have difficulty with the acceptability of self-pleasuring. I have written about this on my blog and would refer you there for how to speak about it in a faith-honoring way. See Schermer Sellers (2012).

References

Farley, Margaret A. 2006. *Just Love: A Framework for Christian Sexual Ethics*. New York, NY: Continuum.

Fleming, William. (1857) 2006. *The Vocabulary of Philosophy, Mental, Moral, and Metaphysical*. Reprint. Whitefish, MT: Kessinger.

Gilbert, Elizabeth. 2010. *Committed: A Sceptic Makes Peace with Marriage*. London: Bloomsbury.

Glass, Shirley P., with Jean Coppock Staeheli. 2003. *Not Just Friends: Rebuilding Trust and Recovering Your Sanity after Infidelity*. New York, NY: The Free Press.

Holstein, Lana, and David Taylor. 2004. *Your Long Erotic Weekend: Four Days of Passion for a Lifetime of Magnificent Sex*. Gloucester, MA: Fair Winds.

Northrup, Chrisanna, Pepper Schwartz, and James Witte. 2012. *The Normal Bar: The Surprising Secrets of Happy Couples and What They Reveal about Creating a New Normal in Your Relationship*. New York, NY: Harmony.

Nouwen, Henri J.M. 1992. *Life of the Beloved: Spiritual Living in a Secular World*. New York, NY: Crossroad.

Plato. 1973. *The Symposium*. Translated by Walter Hamilton. Harmondsworth, UK: Penguin.

Schermer Sellers, Tina. 2012. Masturbation, Desire, Want . . . Good or Bad? (blog post). http://tinaschermersellers.com/2012/02/18/masturbation-desire-want-good-or-bad, accessed September 10, 2014.

Stepp, Laura Sessions. 2007. *Unhooked: How Young Women Pursue Sex, Delay Love and Lose at Both*. New York, NY: Riverhead.

Whitman, Walt. 1855–56. I Sing the Body Electric (Poem). In *Leaves of Grass: A Textual Variorum of the Printed Poems*, vol. 1, edited by Sculley Bradley, Harold W. Blodgett, Arthur Golden, and William White, 30. New York, NY: New York University Press.

8 Sex Therapy Interventions

The Practices of Intimacy

How fair and pleasant you are,
  O loved one, delectable maiden!
You are stately as a palm tree,
  and your breasts are like its clusters.
I say I will climb the palm tree
  and lay hold of its branches.
  —Song of Songs 7:6–8

We're discovering a whole new capacity to our lovemaking. Being aware, being open, believing in God's sacred blessing, and taking time to enjoy our space, our time, and every inch of skin has made each time together different and wonderful.
  —Roger, client

Practices That Prepare and Open

Before I have clients practice the touching part of any shared sacred sexual experiences, I ask them to spend time learning how to open their heart and body to each other and to God. In doing so, we're fighting uphill against centuries of mind–body dualism, so it takes time and preparation just to *begin* the process together, and a willingness to have *tons* of conversations with each other. That may seem a bit odd; we begin the touch by first *not* touching but moving inside to test the waters of the spirit of our touching. I like to begin the opening-up process by having clients write a series of letters, in an effort to help them to integrate God's deep love for their whole person, including their body and sexuality.

Instructions for Client Letters

Here are some sample instructions that you might give to your clients for practicing between sessions.

1. Write a love letter from your Creator to you—imagine that God wants to write you a love letter, but needs you to be the scribe. So you must

write down whatever you hear God saying in the silence of your listening heart. What does God see in you? Why has God fallen in love with you? There are aspects of you that are breathtakingly beautiful and stir the heart of God. What are these aspects? Let God answer these questions. Try not to let shame, embarrassment, or false modesty get in your way. Write down whatever you hear. Give God a chance to express love for you. For ideas, you might refer back to Chapter 4 and its discussion of the Song of Songs, or take a look at *Revelations of Divine Love* by Julian of Norwich (2013), *The Book of Love: Poems of Ecstasy and Longing* by Rumi (1998), or *Ecstatic Poems* by Mirabai (2004).

2.   Write a letter *to your body*, expressing your appreciation for its health, uniqueness, and desires for connection. Extend grace and reconciliation to any past thoughts or actions that were hurtful to the sacredness, goodness, and beauty of your body. Tell your body how much you love it, how much you *like* it.

3.   Write a letter *to your Creator* expressing gratefulness for yourself—body, mind, soul, spirit, relationship, and ways of being in the world. Try to express gratefulness for each area you value about yourself, along with the areas you are still learning to value.

4.   Write another letter *to your Creator*, expressing any fears, concerns, or risks of entering into a lovemaking partnership with another person or into a fully engaged life. Ask for what you need for sustaining courage, strength, and honesty in the process.

Writing these letters will take time, so your clients will need to move slowly and savor the process. You may need to remind them that it is in *experiencing* the letter-writing, not *completing* it, that the transformation occurs. I instruct my clients to keep writing until they have nothing more to say, then to put their letters down and take a break. Then I invite them to spend a little time each day for several days in walking meditation with God—perhaps walking around the neighborhood or around a local park, or going on a run—in listening, looking for evidence of the Divine in creation, using their senses to experience God in smells, sounds, tastes, what they see, and what they feel through their skin. After the meditation, which should last at least 30 minutes, they should pick up the letters again and to ask themselves whether they have anything that can be added to them. Finally, invite your clients to bring their letters into session and read them aloud, so that you can bear witness to their healing.

The letter-writing process is crucial groundwork for the practices that follow, a kind of "plowing" before you plant the seeds of a new lifestyle of intimacy through the assignments you'll give them. Don't skip the letters. If you do, the "soil" of their self-respect and self-love will probably be too brittle for them to truly engage the practices and grow to their next level of development. Once the letters have been written, meditated over, and read aloud, you'll be ready to move to the next step: orienting the heart.

Orienting the Heart

These first practices will help your clients to prepare their minds and hearts to "open up" to giving and receiving love between each other and with the Divine. This will open the door to deep connection and pleasure and will help to take away any walls that may have kept their hearts separated from each other, their body separated from God, and God separated from their sexuality.

If you are working with an individual client and not a couple, it is good to talk about how to grow intimacy with self during this season of their life, and also to expand the conversation into how intimacy shows up in any other areas of life, like on the job or among friends. If you can, you might also host conversations around how to bring others into their circle of support who share their values around integration and intimacy, and who would encourage their continued growth.

Attention, Intention, Presence, Breath, Eyes, and Love

For couples, through all of the exercises that follow, you'll want to invite them to attend to each of six elements: attention, intention, presence, breath, eyes, and love. *Attention* is the ability to focus on the fullness of the experience and on one's beloved—to stay "in the moment" without the mind wandering off. *Intention*, which needs to be established prior to lovemaking, is a shared sense of purpose in the encounter, a kind of agreement that each party makes that this is sacred time, lovemaking time. There are many ways to share intention. The couple can have a brief conversation beforehand, where one partner tells the other that she intends for her beloved to feel her love through her eyes and touch. Intention can also be shared through prayer or meditation, dedicating the time, such as when the two pray aloud to ask God to keep their hearts open to God's love in the form of pleasure together. Clients can express intention any way that makes sense to them; the crucial thing is to make sure that there's a clear expression that the lovemaking encounter is going to be deliberate and on purpose.

Presence is about "showing up" to each other emotionally and spiritually. This goes beyond simply paying attention; presence has to do with an openness of heart and mind, bringing one's whole self to the encounter. The heart is open, as is the mind, and each person is fully available for whatever the moment will bring.

Breath involves a commitment to stay "in" one's body, remaining aware of its sensations and communicating with the other person throughout the experience. Male clients often tell me how much they appreciate hearing their lover express what they like and guiding them, saying things like "that feels nice," or "yes, more there," or "a little softer." Each person should also allow themselves to share vocalizations (e.g., moans) as part of the communication between the two persons.

Finally, the element of the *eyes* involves a commitment to gaze into each other's eyes often throughout the experience of making love. There is a strong connection between looking someone in the eye for a long time and opening one's heart and body to them. Eye contact is a profound expression of trust and vulnerability, and so it's a critical element of intimacy. Because of the high level of vulnerability required to maintain eye contact, especially while naked, it is natural for most people to close their eyes during love-making and to disappear from their partner. Trying to maintain eye contact can bring fears of rejection and shame to the forefront of one's mind, and many people shut their eyes for fear of seeing that rejection realized during an encounter. But it's also possible to learn to self-soothe one's fears and to meet the other person's loving glance. When a person keeps their eyes open and sees their lover's love cascading from *their* eyes and bathing them, the experience can be a powerful opportunity for healing that fear of rejection, allowing the body to experience the power of sexual arousal, climax, and release. There is no other place in life where people are more seen, known, loved, and accepted than in the complete embrace of one's beloved in sacred lovemaking, but it takes tremendous courage. With practice and guidance, it's possible to summon the strength to share with each other in this way and to experience the healing power that loving eye contact can bring amid an erotic encounter.

The element of *love* involves mindfulness beyond the elements of attention, intention, and presence: *love* involves a deliberate focus on the desirable qualities of one's partner and an intentional gratefulness for the other person's existence, all as a form of lead-up and preparation for the sexual encounter that's about to happen. It's a little like turning one's heart toward the "true north" of the other person—the things about him or her that led to sexual and emotional desire in the first place—and away from other forms of distraction, all before crawling into bed. Spending some time before an erotic encounter focusing on love is part of the process of aligning the heart, mind, and body in the same direction.

As we move into the practices that follow, take note of which practices you might recommend for clients in your office as you guide them through designing a preparatory ritual for their sacred lovemaking. There is room here to be creative and to modify the practices for particular people and situations, but in all cases, the important thing is to make sure that attention, intention, presence, breath, eyes, and love each make it into the encounter. Also bear in mind that the goal of these practices isn't orgasm or ejaculation: it's connection and pleasure, pure and simple.

Awakening the Body and the Senses

In these first practices, we introduce clients to the idea of slowing down and opening up their awareness to sensations of love and blessing in everyday life. This is a critical beginning, because our culture tends to reduce erotic love to a set of behaviors rather than the quality of the experience or the relationship. Many couples have learned to move themselves through the arousal cycle to orgasm by closing their attention to anything beyond their genitals, moving inside the self and away from the other, and focusing on genital sensations at the expense of all the other senses—taste, sight, sounds, smell, and touch elsewhere on the body. Here are some ways to help clients to slow down and be *with* each other in the moment.

Priming the Senses

To help clients prime their senses and add levity and fun to their lives, have clients do one or more of the following exercises, adapting them as you see fit. (Many of these practices can be adapted for individual clients as well.)

Sensual Practice 1

Have your clients spend a day paying attention to anything sensual that emerges in the regular course of everyday life. They should take note of anything that they find beautiful, moving, tasty, or aesthetically pleasing among the regular sounds, smells, tastes, and touches of an average day. Talk about these things together, and highlight the similarities and differences between what resonated with each partner. For example: how does the crunch of the corn flakes feel on the tongue at breakfast? How does the warmth of the first sip of coffee make the throat and stomach feel as it goes down? What color are the trees beside the highway on the way to work, and how do they move in the wind? How does the acceleration of the subway or automobile seat make the body feel? What kind of music was playing on the stereo at the grocery store? How did it feel to take your shoes off when you got home from work?

Have your clients make these observations in regard to their partner's body, too. In a moment when she wasn't even trying to be erotic, what did you notice was enticing about your wife's body when she casually stepped through the door after a day of work apart? What parts did you notice first, and how did your body react? How would you describe the scent on your husband's neck when you gave him a long hug?

Sensual Practice 2

Have your clients prepare items of sensory delight for their partner to be used in a sacred sexual encounter. Have them blindfold each other one at a time (after negotiating the parameters and gaining permission beforehand, of course) and surprise the other person's mouth, nose, skin, tongue, and ears with experiences from their repertoire of sensual inspiration. Examples could include things like: a sudden morsel of dark chocolate or red wine on the tongue; an essential oil waved gently in front of the nose; a toasty blanket wrapped around the feet; warm oil caressed into the upper back; or a drip from an ice cube. Invite each partner to imagine these delights nourishing every cell of the body and filling it with erotic bliss. Both of them will need to move slowly, savoring the experience and describing the encounter to each other in as much detail as they can.

Preparing a Sacred Space

Your clients' lovemaking space—the actual, physical room—should be an oasis from the crazy demands of life, a place that gives each partner a sense of peace, calm, and delicious anticipation when they enter. Talk about the lovemaking environment together. How can they make the room feel "sanctified," set apart from the rest of the home's living spaces? How can the physical environment of the room emphasize that it's a room for grown-ups only, for people who are lovers (as opposed to just friends, or coparents, or business partners)?

Izzy and Jaci had two teenagers and were spread so thin that lovemaking was almost nonexistent. They saw each other every day and night, but they both missed each other (and their now-elusive sense of connection) terribly and wanted more from their marriage than just to feel like parents.

When I asked them *where* in their house they wanted "more action," they both said their bedroom, and then burst out laughing. I asked them to tell me about their laughter. Izzy said that her office was in the bedroom, and it was a mess. Jaci added that the kids loved their bed for watching TV and goofing around, so they were always in there. There was no lock on the door.

Izzy and Jaci were feeling that there was no sense of boundary on the space, nothing to communicate that "this is a special place, *only for us lovers.*" To hear them talk about the room, it sounded like it was basically a workplace, a lounge for teens, and a dressing room with a revolving door—hardly a place for two lovers' eroticism. The last thing that came to mind when Izzy and Jaci thought of their bedroom was sexual pleasure.

(There may be seasons in a family's life, of course, when children are small and need to be in the parents' bedroom for convenience. The important issue, though, is that over time, they come to respect a firm sense of boundary that entering the bedroom is a once-in-a-while privilege that requires an express invitation and is *never* an entitlement.)

In a family, the cultivation of love is the foundation of the family's life and health, but there are very few places in our culture where the parents can be reminded that they are a couple, that they are lovers. Kids certainly won't remind them to take care of their relationship, nor will work, the media, or probably even family and friends—so why on earth would we let them into a lovemaking chamber? Walking through the threshold of that space ought to remind the couple that their love, their time in private, their naked and sacred space, is there to nourish and to revitalize them.

Whether it's the actual bedroom doesn't matter; the sacred space can be another room in the house, designated as sacred to the love between the couple. Wherever it is, it needs to be a space that they can count on. I try to remind couples that it's a hard thing to do, just like most things in life that are worthwhile. Even Gary and I have to keep striving to make our bedroom sacred, and we are constantly cleaning up after each other and ourselves. It doesn't always work. But we've learned to give each other the benefit of the doubt and to do what we can to keep the space special, even amid the very busy lives that we both lead. For us, this process has taken time, planning, and ongoing attentiveness, but the relationship that we're cultivating over time has been worth every ounce of effort.

Elements in Your Sacred Space

First, a sacred lovemaking space should offer a sense of protection from the urgency of everyday life. It should have distinct qualities that set it apart as a place of stillness, beauty, sensual delight, elegance, privacy, and worship. It doesn't need to be expensive, but it does need to be intentional.

Invite your clients first to simply clean up the space. Get all the clutter out, along with any reminder of the outside world of work, demands, bills, and obligations, until the only things that remain are items that facilitate romance and sensual pleasure.

Next, have them bring elements *into* the room that help to inspire the sensual and spiritual elements they want to have in a time of connecting. Remind them to think about when they were children and made a fort or some other special, hidden place for play. That's the spirit they need to tap into here. Invite them to bring that same playfulness and imagination to the room. They might decide, for example, to bring silky fabrics, photographs, flowers, candles, sacred mementos, Scripture or special quotes, plants, art, music, pillows, blankets, fruit, massage oils, beverages, lubricants, scented oils or sprays, feathers, or other sensual objects. I myself am fascinated by black-and-white photography of the naked human form, so the space that Gary and I have made includes an array of over 30 photographs around the room, in addition to some of the other elements I mentioned. The pictures remind me of God's love in the elegance of the human body and help me to remember the magnificence of the gift.

Initial Intimacy Practices of Body, Mind, and Spirit

Once your clients are ready to enjoy an intentional time of lovemaking, here is some of the coaching you can give them as they go home. First, invite them to take a shower or a bath beforehand, to relax and ready their body, heart, and soul. (This can be done separately or together, as long as it's relaxing.) The next step is to wrap themselves in something soft and silky, like a bathrobe or a very large, soft towel. As they enter the room, they should let themselves savor the sights, sounds, scents, colors, and textures that meet them (it's been carefully crafted in advance, remember), in an effort to become fully aware of what their senses are telling them. Invite them to stand together in the center of their sacred space, to join hands and take a couple of deep, relaxing breaths, and to ask their Creator to come and fill them and the room with love, making divine love manifest between them. Invite them to thank God for joining them in the beauty of their union and for God's desire to commune with them as they commune with each other. Ask for divine blessing to be bestowed on their lovemaking and on their relationship itself, and to guide them in knowing more of the depth of God's love and the image of God within each of them as they create something special together in the moments that follow.

These steps of preparation may seem like a lot of work "up front" for making love. But a ritual of presence and intention like this actually helps to enhance the experience of togetherness and can often result in much better sex and deeper intimacy. Ask your clients to think about which other moments in their lives have occasioned this level of intentionality in something, like a first date, or when they made their marital vows. Ask them to think about what difference it makes when they bring their full attention and planning to an endeavor of loving, and to reflect over time on how their lovelife is changing as they learn to practice this kind of intentionality.

Grounding Practices

"Grounding" practices might be what a couple would do at the initial phase of their sacred time together to set an intention and to connect with each other slowly and carefully. Here are two examples.

Becoming a Vessel of Love (3–5 Minutes Minimum)

Have the couple sit cross-legged on a bed or on the floor with their backs against each other. (They may want to put a pillow under their tailbones to make it more comfortable.) They can be clothed or naked; it's up to them.

The couple should take a couple of deep breaths, inhaling from the top of the lungs down deep into the abdomen, *slowly*. I often recommend a four-count breath (four counts in and four out). They should try to imagine the breath gathering from God's love and radiating up throughout their body—through the legs, genitals, belly, heart, throat, and head—such that it saturates the body, heart, and soul. As they exhale, they should imagine gathering even *more* of God's love as the exhalation travels back down the body, through the lungs, into the genitals, and down through the legs before radiating out from the feet.

As they breathe in again, they should imagine divine light and love filling their bodies on the inhalations, and stress and burdens leaving their bodies on the exhalations. They should feel their partner's back next to their own, a symbol of their hearts being aligned. Invite them to feel a sense of rooted-ness, like a tree, giving a solid center to their being. Then, as the light and love flow through the body on the inhalations, each person should imagine it bathing their partner as well. As they exhale and imagine life's stressors and distractions leaving the body, they should imagine creating a swift current, coaxing their partner's stressors out of their body as well.

The couple should do this for three to five minutes, or until they can feel their bodies slow down and relax, their hearts lighten and expand with love, and a sense of connection develop between themselves and each other and with God.

Engaging the Soul (5–7 Minutes Minimum)

Have the couple sit facing each other, either knee-to-knee, in two chairs, or with one of them sitting in the lap of the other with their legs and arms wrapped around each other. Invite them to put their heads as close to each other as possible while still being able to see the other's face clearly.

The couple should begin this practice by first spending 2–3 minutes sim-ply breathing, in order to quiet their hearts and center themselves and the relationship, and to open their hearts to each other and to God. The couple can choose to close their eyes at first if they want, but after a time, they should look deeply into each other's eyes as they begin to synchronize their breathing, inhaling and exhaling together. Ask the couple to pay attention to the synergy that will grow between them for a few minutes as they do this.

Next, they should begin to alternate their breathing, such that one person inhales as the other exhales and vice versa. At the same time, each of them should look into the other's *left* eye while imagining that with each inhala-tion they are "gathering in" all the love they have ever received in their life, and with each exhalation that they are *sending* that love back into the soul of their partner.

As they stay in this posture for several minutes, each of them should think back on times when they have received great love. Invite them to let the body, the mind, the heart, and the soul recollect what happened and what they felt in the moment—emotions like gratefulness, deep joy, or any other deep, positive feeling they had at the time. Then invite them to intentionally "send" that love to their partner across the connection, as though their heart were broadcasting or uploading it directly into the other person's body or soul. No words need to be exchanged during the "transfer."

Ask the couple to notice any part of them that might be withholding love during the exercise. If so, invite them to open their heart and to try to give fully anyway, remembering that love is not finite but infinite. Invite them to let go of any conditions on their love; tell them that there will always be enough love for each person, even when they give it all away. As each partner breathes into the other, the receiving person should do their best to accept every ounce of love he or she is being sent, and to imagine themselves receiving it directly into their heart. They need to *feel* the depth of their partner's love, and to be reminded to think of the love as a form of God's love, too. Ask them to notice any places where they are rejecting or doubting the gift. If they find this difficult to do, let them know that through practice and with time, God will begin to heal self-rejection and open them up to receive love. This can all be somewhat difficult at first, especially for clients who didn't grow up hearing that they were beloved; they may have years of defensiveness and walls built up around them. That's why it's important to practice this until it starts to feel more natural.

Clients should do this for three to five minutes or until their hearts are open to gratefulness, generosity, and love from each other. When they're ready to conclude, each of them should put their right hand on their own heart and their left hand on their partner's heart. Then, they should touch their foreheads together and say, "I love you and the image of the Divine in you."

Perhaps you're asking, "You can't possibly be expecting people to go through these opening rituals every time they want to make love, can you?" Of course not. I just encourage them to be aware that sometimes, they may struggle more to become fully present, slowed, and focused in their lovemaking. Sometimes, life's demands simply won't allow for detail like this, and sometimes we frankly just want a "quickie!" That's all fine. But I encourage my clients to give themselves and their relationship this kind of luxurious loving at least twice a month. Doing so can play an important role for vitalizing their marriage, their spiritual relationship, and the degree to which they're able to extend more love into the world. The more devotion they bring to these practices, the more transcendent and transformative their lovemaking, as well as their sense of connection to that which is greater than them.

Lavishly Enjoying Each Other

When we think of sex as more than just behaviors, something whose purpose is rooted in relationship and intimacy, it becomes easier to feel a freedom to touch in all kinds of ways, including ways we hadn't thought of before. Many people tend to expect that both partners will give and receive pleasure at the same time through mutual orgasms and intercourse, but in fact, there is often more intense pleasure when a couple takes turns, alternating between giving and receiving. But since most have never experienced one-giver-at-a-time sex, most people don't realize how true that is, and as a result, they miss something of the art of how to give well, or the humility and wisdom in *receiving* while opening up to one's beloved.

The following sexual practices are included to help your clients learn to alternate the roles of giver and receiver, slowing down the sexual process and helping each person to savor the intimacy more as a result. Think of it as the difference between a monologue and a dialogue. In a monologue, both people talk over each other (trying to give and receive at the same time), but in a dialogue, one person listens while the other shares (one person gives, the other receives), and then they switch. You probably know from experience in conversation that the depth of communion is much deeper when two people aren't talking over each other. The same can be true with making love. Though there are many ways to make love, it is the freedom to be creative and to match the experience to the desire one has that gives life to lovemaking. Do they both feel a bit daring? Are they in a hurry, ready for some playful fun? Does one of them want to lavishly bless the other? Do they both want to go slowly and see where the next moment leads without any preconceived ideas? Each lovemaking experience is up to the couple to create, based on what they desire and feel ready to do. It is a cocreated experience.

The alternation between giving and receiving does not need to be rigid. For example, one partner does not have to give an exercise and then receive the exact same exercise immediately afterward. What counts is that both partners stay conscious that they *each* have ample time in the giver role and ample time as the receiver *over time*.

Single adaptations: many of the ideas that will be shared ahead can be modified or expanded. I want to encourage those folks who are single to take this time to thoroughly learn and delight in the gifts of your body and sexuality. Learn about yourself on all seven dimensions of the Anatomy of Intimacy. For women, read books like *For Yourself* by Lonnie Barbach (2000), *Come As You Are* by Emily Nagoski (2015), and *The Enlightened Sex Manual* by David Deida (2007). For men, read books like *The New Male Sexuality* by Bernie Zilbergeld (1999), *The Multi-orgasmic Man* by Mantak Chia (1996), and *The Way of the Superior Man* by David Deida (1997).

Awakening Love

I will describe this exercise with the man as the giver and the woman as the receiver.

> **Items needed:** warm massage oil; poetry, or something he has written for her

INSTRUCTIONS TO THE GIVER

Make sure the sacred space is nice and warm and that you are both comfortable. Ask your beloved to lie on her tummy. Rub your hands together to warm them, and then slowly pour the warmed oil down her spine from the base of her neck to the base of her backbone. Place a hand firmly at the top of the spine and the other at the base, and just hold there for a moment. Imagine sending your love and God's love through your hands into her body, filling her with warmth and safety. Proceed to massage her whole back.

Next, place your mouth very close to her spine, and gently blow warm air from the base of her spine, upward this time, to the base of her neck. Do this two or three times, and then move to kissing and nibbling the back of her neck, around her ears, and on her shoulders. Keep thinking of yourself as sending love into her heart with each touch.

Next, provide a firm massage around her hips and on her sacral space around and below the base of her spine. (Especially if she, like the majority of women, has been hurt sexually in the past somehow, this motion can carry a great message of safety and care. In fact, acupuncturists often focus on this area to help release and heal sexual wounds.) Massage deeply, using your thumbs and firm pressure, and keep imagining that you are sending healing love and joy into her sacral space.

After a few moments, slowly add oil down the back of her legs, and massage down to her feet. Use long strokes, moving down the back of her legs and up the inside of her legs. Be slow and deliberate. Then ask her to turn over, and slowly hold a kiss over her heart. Let your kiss tell her of your love. Take some oil, massaging the front of her body, but leaving the breasts and genitals for last. Hold the image that you are sending love, yours and God's, through this touch of pleasure. When you do get to massaging her breasts and genitals, remind yourself that this touch is for sacred pleasure and love. It is touch that is entirely for her, not for you (except to marinate in the joy of her pleasure). If you are not sure if the touch is pleasing to her, ask her, "Is there any other way I could be touching your breast/sacred space (vulva)/clitoris/sacred spot (G-spot) that would be more pleasing to you?" Try different touches, kisses, and sensations, and watch her response. Ask, "Would you like more of this?" Be sure to provide the safety for her to say no. A "no" is just as important as a "yes." It is not a rejection: it's a direction—a lesson as she teaches the map of her body, the map of her pleasure. She is completely unique. When she gives you a "no," thank her for her courage and remind her that you want to know her body and her pleasure. You're here to study her, to be her master lover. Most women have never been given permission to be honest about their plea-sure, so your reassurance is critical. Being a receiver is harder than it looks, so if guilt or shame well up for either person, remind them to wrap each person in reassurance and love, allowing the touch to heal the shame throughout the experience. Remember, there is no expectation that you will bring her to orgasm. Allow yourself to feel the full measure of the pleasure in giving—opening, softening, and filling with love. If she starts to move toward climax, let her spill over naturally. This is fine and wonderful, but not the goal, just a wonderful gift. Then, at the close of the exercise, either lie facing each other, or spooning, or sit up and face each other. Tell her what you appreciate about her, and read her the words of love you have found or prepared. Savor the feeling of being complete and together; love has been made and added to the universe. The world is a better place because of what you have just added to it.

A word of caution: for most heterosexual Americans, it's very difficult to think of this activity as anything other than foreplay, but this exercise isn't intended as a precursor for intercourse. It's meant to stand on its own. She needs to know that the entire exercise is a gift *for* her and *because of* her, not as a prelude to something for the man. If it becomes an appetizer to their typical sexual banquet, she is likely to discount the authenticity of his love-gift to her. Remember, she needs to feel his loving *intention* and loving *attention*.

When this exercise is reversed (in a heterosexual couple), it can also feel odd to give lavishly to the man without an expectation of orgasm. I usually recommend to women that when they get to the point of genital stimulation, they should consider focusing real love on his penis. I also recommend that as they stimulate him, they do so manually while looking into his eyes and asking him to tell her when he is close to ejaculating but before he is at the point of no return. I recommend that she take him to *the point before* and hold the penis gently but firmly while asking him to pull all that loving energy up into his heart. When he has a sense that the energy in his penis has dropped down, she can begin stimulating him again if he would like. I recommend that she do this four or five times if it's something that is bringing him pleasure and connecting her to him.

This process does three things: it allows him to connect his heart to his sexual experience, stay in pleasure with her longer, and increase the strength of the orgasm when and if he decides to have one. Again, this is not the goal, but it may be what happens. For some men who practice this skill, eventually they will begin to have the orgasmic contractions prior to ejaculation, thus allowing them to have controlled and sustained orgasms (Chia and Arava 1996).

Blessing Your Beloved

I will describe this exercise with the woman as the giver and the man as the receiver.

Items needed: warm massage oil

INSTRUCTIONS TO THE GIVER

Make sure the room is warm and comfortable for you both, and have your beloved lie on his tummy. Begin massaging his back and legs. As you make sure to touch each inch of skin, offer up an ongoing, silent prayer of thanksgiving for his body. As you complete the back of your lover's body, lower your chest onto his back and place your head on his upper back. Send your prayer deeper "into" him with your heart and mind, with your body touching his, and ask God to bless him with vitality and well-being.

After a few moments, have your beloved roll onto his back and move yourself to his feet. Begin rubbing oil into his feet, one foot at a time. As you massage his feet, begin a blessing—something like, "Creator of Heaven and Earth, bless these feet that have held this man I love tall for all these years.

Bless these feet that have carried him up mountains, into his life's work, and into my arms. Please keep these feet strong and sure as he faces the next steps in his life." (You can invite your clients to adapt this blessing to suit what they know of how the receiver's feet have facilitated meaningful moments in his life, and in whatever ways best fit their beliefs.)

Next, move to his ankles, calves, and knees, and up the rest of his body. Take time at each area of his body, offering a blessing, thanking God, and asking for the protection and strength of *this particular* area of the body. Have clients be as specific as possible in their words of honor, gratefulness, and hope for that particular area. Make sure not to forget the hands, which have often been crucial in life experience, or the sensory features of their face and head. Let their final blessing be upon his head.

A note about the genitals: they are an important aspect of the body, and a physical location that has not often been blessed but instead has been defamed by culture and the church. Ask your clients to think about how they can bless this part of his body. Both men and women often have shame in regard to their genitals, and it can be profoundly healing to have their beloved spend time finding specific ways to bless their genitals for the pleasure, life, and health that they have provided, while also offering acknowledgment for the years of being ignored, mistreated, and vilified.

(Note: Some people like to spend time in advance thinking up particular blessings for each part of the body, and others like to let what arises in the moment be perfect. Either way is fine.)

For single clients: taking the time to bless each part of your own body is a wonderful exercise. Invite your clients to think about what they like about each body part, and what each part of their body has done in contributing to their memories and life experience. Ask them to think about how they could incorporate this kind of careful appreciation into a creative ritual of thankfulness for the gift of their physical self.

Sharing Desire (15–30 Minutes)

(I will describe this exercise with the man as the giver and the woman as the receiver.)

> **Items needed:** warm massage oil; feathers, silk, or other soft, sensual items

This exercise not only increases intimacy but also often helps in healing shame and improving a couple's ability to communicate during and around sexual touch. Since so many people grew up in sexually silent or shaming homes, many have never developed comfort or skill in communicating openly about their desires in specific, intimate touch. So while they may desire certain forms of touch, they may find it nearly impossible to put those desires into words or to speak them out loud to each other. Many also do not know what kind of touch they like outside of the narrow behaviors of customary sex. Remind your clients to be patient, compassionate, and playful in this exercise, especially if they can see their lover struggling to speak. This exercise can use many forms of touch or sensation. Have them gather supplies ahead of time if they would like to use oil, feathers, silk, or anything else that they think would create a pleasurable sensation for their lover.

INSTRUCTIONS TO THE GIVER

First, have your beloved lie on her tummy. Begin by touching her in some way that you think she would enjoy receiving and you would enjoy giving. After about 30 seconds, ask, "Is there any other way I could touch you in this area that would be more pleasurable?" She can answer with a "no," which means "keep going for now, this is feeling great!" Or she could answer with a "yes," and then explain how: "I think I would like you to touch me in *this* place or in *this* way."

Here is an example, using sensual props: The giver says, "Is there any other way I could touch you in this area that would be more pleasurable?" The receiver replies, "Yes, I think I would like for you to run that feather across my bottom." The key is to repeat the question about every 30 seconds, eliciting lots of feedback and information.

The giver may change the location or manner of touch at any time. As the giver, it's important to give touch that you enjoy giving. Both of you need to avoid getting into spaces where you are merely putting up with a particular touch to be polite, or where you're giving a particular touch out of obligation or because you "should," as these tend to shut down desire and curtail the flow of love. We can actually intuit when someone is giving touch out of obligation rather than out of love. Desire is a fragile visitor, and she will leave when she's not treated with generosity, so don't underestimate the importance of doing what you actually enjoy.

This practice has the advantage of allowing your clients to learn the intricacies of what the *beloved* finds pleasurable through the constant feedback. For the receiver, and especially for women, allowing herself to speak in this kind of detail and to receive this kind of focused giving can raise all kinds of uncomfortable thoughts and feelings. It's common for women to feel that they "don't deserve to get this kind of attention," or to find themselves thinking, "I have never spoken this before and feel very vulnerable saying what I'd like," or that "It's wrong for me to allow myself this kind of pleasure," or that "I feel very exposed that he is studying my body like this." A powerful and common form of projection (i.e., when she puts on him the uncomfortable feelings *she* is having) is the idea that "he can't really want to be doing this" (projecting onto the giver) or that "God can't be here with us if I am being this explicit" (projecting onto God). You may need to gently point out those lines of thinking as they emerge, and to invite the receiver back into a space of complete receptivity. It should get easier over time. For example, if she gets defensive and mentally pulls back in some way, the giver may need to reassure her by saying something like, "I want you to try to receive my touch and my love. This is my gift to you because I love you; I love to touch you and give you pleasure!"

When I use this exercise with my clients, I repeatedly remind them to be patient and compassionate. If they can tell that their lover is struggling to get the words out, invite them to offer words of encouragement, like "It's okay, sweetie. Take your time. I love you and I want you to feel my love through touch that you enjoy. I want to learn you."

A few more words of instruction to the giver. You may ask her to turn on her back at any time, if you choose, but keep the focus on giving pleasure, not on orgasm or intercourse. After about 15 or 30 minutes, hold her against you; she can be facing toward you or away from you, whichever feels more comfortable to her. Tell her what you value about knowing more ways to touch and love her. At first, this exercise can require a lot of courage and trust in each other. Like all of these practices, be sure to switch up being the giver or receiver at some point, either that same day, or very soon after, as long as both of you get to practice both giving and receiving.

Daily Prayer (5 Minutes)

Items needed: You may need lubricant nearby.

Being mindful is a critical part of orienting and recommitting yourself to your partner and to your communion with the Divine. The Daily Prayer practice is usually done as a stand-alone exercise at the opening or closing of the day and at a time when the couple has agreed *not* to have sex, because like all of these practices, it is important that they aren't seen as a precursor to something else (orgasm, intercourse, etc.).

Some couples find the Daily Prayer practice so healing that they begin or close each day this way. This practice or prayer is done with the body, not with words, so that the couple does not intellectualize their commitment. Instead, they demonstrate it mutually.

To begin, the woman lies on her back with her knees bent and legs apart. The man lies between her legs in the missionary position while she or he places his penis inside her vagina. (The penis can be erect or flaccid; it doesn't matter. Only the head of the penis needs to be inside her.) Then she wraps her legs around his back or legs, whichever is more comfortable, and wraps her arms around his back so that they are locked together. They connect their arms, legs, mouths, and genitals. Together, they relax and let go in this position—no movement, no expectation to have an erection or to have inter-course or an orgasm. With the arousal cycle and orgasm set aside, each person's heart, mind, soul, and body are better able to focus on their love and bonding, because there are fewer goal-oriented distractions. Have the couple bring their attention, intention, presence, breath, and love, prayerfully (and silently) recommitting to their union with each other and with God through the simple, silent language of their unmoving embrace. Nothing else matters at that moment: this embraced connection is their highest priority and their highest good.

As you instruct your clients on how to do this exercise, tell them to let themselves sensually appreciate each place of connection along the body and to notice all of the pleasurable sensations that come and go. If the mind drifts, they can gently bring it back to the body-prayer. In all cases, let any disconnection or disharmony melt away. Be in God's belovedness for a five-minute mindful body-prayer.

The Paradox in Practices

After walking through these practices several times, clients can adapt them in ways unique and special to them, and they can design times of intimacy that suit what they want, based on what state their energy, emotions, spirit, body, and relationship are in at that moment. They're free to make these practices their own over time, and to expand on them, add elements, and give them a flavor that is unique to the two personalities between them at that given time. Long-term relationships evolve over time, and so does the sexual relationship. It needs a varied recipe book and refrigerator full of options for creating the meal that suits them in that moment. Very few couples are satisfied having the same meal over and over, again and again for years. The more a couple is able to talk, adapt, and create together, while also bringing their intention, attention, presence, eyes, breath, and love, the more vital and satisfying their sexual life will be.

In sacred sexual celebrations, there is a paradox that is worth mentioning. In the midst of all the intentional preparation and planning, surprising and spontaneous experiences frequently emerge. As your clients bring their full attention to learning these practices, let them know to be prepared for the spontaneous invitation to let go of fear and restraints and be carried away by the sacred ecstasy and synergy that may fill them. There can be virtue in letting go of control, of relinquishing the need for things to look a particular way. Invite them to open up—to allow themselves to melt fully into the experience and awareness of all that is present in that loving moment. Sometimes, edges disappear in the process of making love, and cocreation happens differently than expected. If both partners feel connected, invite them to go with it.

It's hard to predict how a couple's practice will look, and that's part of the beauty of it. They may find themselves being wild, or tender, or playful, or serious, and the best part is *it doesn't matter what tone they set* as long as they are connected and in sync. It's in those moments that they, their beloved, and God will become one flesh, recreating in the moment and improvising a new song of body, mind, and soul together. Here's to learning to show up to each other, to relax, to focus—and then to play the music of each other's love in a new, beautiful, unpredictable symphony of divine creativity and erotic play, rooted in a deep connection of mindful, intentional love.

I have had previously conservative couples ask me if such-and-such "edgy" sexual behavior is okay (i.e., morally or theologically acceptable for them to practice). While I might spend time deconstructing their beliefs and values to show how they evolved, I'll often refer back to the Hebrew vow of 'Onah and say, "If it is truly okay with each of you, and if it is legal and safe, it is okay." I tell couples that they are cocreating *their* love and *their* lovemaking. It is *their* choice.

Weaving It All Together

These practices demonstrate a particular kind of attention, intention, and level of communication going into times of intimate touch. They can be playful, serious, quick, slow, tender, silly, focused on just one person, or sharing the pleasure. Their touch can involve both of their arousal cycles, or neither of their arousal cycles; one or both of them having an orgasm, or neither of them having an orgasm. It should be whatever they feel up to. The key is to approach each other out of a desire to share pleasure and connection, not to be serviced by the other. If pleasure and connection are shared between them, then we say that they have truly made love!

Holding Wisdom

Remind your clients that these practices are not ends in themselves. They will do nothing if the couple has ignored its heart connection, damaged the trust between them, disengaged from their vitality and creativity, or locked God out of their sexuality and sexual expression. Sexual practices are only as intimate and sacred as the rest of their relationship.

Instruct them to *nourish* the relationship, to give it the time and attention it deserves and to facilitate its ability to be a place of communion with the Creator. From this devotion and communion will come a flowing stream of vitality, life, purpose, and God's infinite love, coursing through both partners and overflowing into our world. That's the *lovemaking lifestyle*.

References

Barbach, Lonnie Garfield. 2000. *For Yourself: The Fulfilment of Female Sexuality*. New York, NY: Putnam.

Chia, Mantak, and Douglas Abrams Arava. 1996. *The Multi-Orgasmic Man: Sexual Secrets Every Man Should Know*. San Francisco, CA: HarperSanFrancisco.

Deida, David. 1997. *The Way of the Superior Man: A Spiritual Guide to Mastering the Challenges of Women, Work, and Sexual Desire*. Boulder, CO: Sounds True.

———. 2007. *The Enlightened Sex Manual: Sexual Skills for the Superior Lover*. Boulder, CO: Sounds True.

Julian of Norwich. 2013. *Revelations of Love*. Edited by Grace Warrack. Overland Park, KS: Digireads.com.

Mirabai. 2004. *Ecstatic Poems*. Versions by Robert Bly and Jane Hirshfield. Boston, MA: Beacon.

Nagoski, Emily. 2015. *Come as You Are: The Surprising New Science that Will Transform Your Sex Life*. New York, NY: Simon & Schuster.

Rumi, Jalal al-Din. 1998. *The Book of Love: Poems of Ecstasy and Longing*. Edited by Deepak Chopra. New York, NY: Harmony.

Zilbergeld, Bernie. 1999. *The New Male Sexuality: The Truth about Men, Sex, and Pleasure*, rev. ed. New York, NY: Bantam.

Epilogue
Are You a Renegade Therapist?

We deeply seek to be seen, known, loved, and accepted—quests that are as much sexual as they are spiritual.

Gwen was running into a brick wall, and it was clear that her couples therapist wasn't going to be any help to her or her husband. In fact, their therapist was a big part of the problem—and it's sad that stories like Gwen's are so common.

Married for 30 years and now in their fifties, Gwen and Dan were active participants in a church from a conservative branch of Christianity similar to the one they had each known when they were growing up. Over the previous year, they had been seeing a couples' counselor for help with their relationship, which was growing more and more distant by the day.

Gwen and Dan each felt estranged from the other, and their stated goal in counseling was to get closer. Each of them reported a different problem, neither of them very unusual from a therapist's point of view. Dan wanted Gwen to make more time for him, and not to put other commitments first, as he felt she had been doing. Gwen, on the other hand, wanted him to be more romantic, more affirming, more loving. She described a kind of "dance" between them; when he wasn't what she wanted or didn't behave the way she liked, she would become distant and preoccupied and withdraw from intimacy with him. Both of them felt alienated from each other, and that it was getting worse over time.

While the two of them were in couples' counseling, Gwen was also seeing a second therapist on an individual basis (per their other therapist's recommendation and with Dan's knowledge) out of a desire to get help with handling her attention-deficit disorder and how scattered she felt in her daily life. On their second individual session together, Gwen happened to mention to Tracy (her individual therapist) that she and Dan were having sex about once every month or two.

She got lucky. Not only had Tracy done lots of work with clients from conservative Christian backgrounds before, making her very familiar with the nuanced challenges of working with the population, but also she was trained in sex therapy and spiritual intimacy. Their couples' counselor hadn't been trained in either of those ways.

Being comfortable with the subjects of sexuality and Christian faith, Tracy began to ask Gwen questions about her experience with sexual pleasure, her satisfaction with the kind of sexual touch in their relationship, and how she felt about her body and her sexuality. Surprised by the directness of Tracy's questions, Gwen decided to take the plunge and talk about her sex life, revealing the paradoxical shame and disdain she had for sex, her body, self-pleasuring, and all things erotic and physical. It was the start of exploring a new dimension in therapy for her.

Sex, said Gwen, was supposed to be something a wife "gave her husband" when she wasn't punishing him for not being what she wanted. But while she believed that sex was overtly acceptable in marriage, it was hard to free herself from an idea that Christian culture had implicitly taught her throughout her life: that on some level, sex was still basically sinful. She never felt completely at peace when having sex, thanks both to all the baggage of her church culture and to her increasing sense of alienation from Dan in general.

To therapist Tracy, Gwen's comments just reaffirmed how sexuality and spirituality were deeply woven together and how there would need to be a careful deconstruction and reconstruction of her understanding of sex and spirituality if Gwen and Dan were ever going to experience the kind of attachment, sexual healing, and playful pleasure they were created to enjoy.

Gwen was beginning to discover how the body, the spirit, and the mind are integrated together, and it was all because Tracy had been trained in how to work with conservative Christians to help them reclaim their sexuality in a way they could relate to in the language of faith, like we've been exploring in this book. Tracy wasn't the brick wall. It was Mike, their couples therapist, who would prove to be the problem.

When Gwen and Dan sat for their next marital session together with Mike, Gwen mentioned Tracy's line of questioning, and how intriguing and helpful it had been for their conversation together. Mike's response was telling. "Oh, that's just Tracy," he said. "She's a sex therapist, and she's much more into *those* topics. I won't be bothering you guys with *those* things here."

Can you imagine sitting on the brink of isolation from your spouse, and asking your therapist for help in bridging the divide between you in your erotic life—only to be told that the therapist wasn't even "into" *entering* those spaces in the conversation? Can you think of what it would be like to desire closeness with someone you love, only to be told by a so-called professional that the most embodied aspect of life and love, sexuality and eroticism, isn't even a factor in how you'll be guided and treated?

For countless couples today, a situation like this one isn't hard to imagine. Gwen and Dan's experience with their couples therapist is a typical example of how the fields of psychotherapy and marriage and family therapy tolerate inadequate training. By assuming that it's possible to treat couples through looking at emotional issues alone, never addressing physical intimacy and sexual issues, many of the symptoms and root causes of dysfunctional intimacy aren't even addressed. As we've seen throughout this book, that kind of avoidance only reinforces our culture's unhealthy approaches to the body and intimacy, and it doesn't allow clients to explore the deep ways that their sexual patterns are wrapped up in their beliefs about what the body is and how it should behave.

There are implications for us as a community of therapists, physicians, and counselors, too, because when we allow this level of ignorance and lack of training to persist in our own professional development, we are doing an active, far-reaching disservice to our patients. Like Mike, we may even be standing directly in the way of the healing process, preventing our clients from experiencing the connection and intimacy that they were made for and reinforcing any religious sexual shame and ignorance that came through their communities of faith. Our silence may be causing profound damage to marital harmony.

For these reasons, I am convinced that in order to practice couples therapy well, a therapist must also be trained as a sex therapist. Good sex therapy provides an opportunity for profound personal growth, both for individuals and for couples. Since much of sexual growth is profoundly tied to one's spirituality, there's all the more reason for therapists to know how to approach conversations with clients who come from a faith background. But it takes training and credentialing of a kind that most of us have never been given.

NO MORE AVOIDANCE!

Anytime clients walk through our office door, they come to us as multidimensional creatures, people who are biological, social, psychological, sexual, and spiritual, all at the same time. Why, then, do our therapeutic training curricula often require no training in sex therapy at all? How can it be acceptable not to be trained in how to relate sexuality to the rest of the whole person, and to the whole relationship, in intimacy counseling, when so much of a person's being involves some element of sexuality? How does it make sense to chop off the physical aspect of a relationship, when the body is the vessel we humans have been given for relating to each other? How does any of this make sense?

After working with couples on these things for years and hearing the pain that conservative Christians carry in their sex lives because no one has hosted these conversations with them, I am convinced that it's time to raise the bar in our field and to encourage each other to become adept at sex therapy and spiritual intimacy. In some states, therapists and medical doctors are required to take only a single course in human sexuality in graduate school; in some states, there's no requirement at all. How can we expect our clinicians to be any more comfortable or knowledgeable about sexual issues than the clients they serve if they're just like the rest of us, getting most of their information from mass media?

FINDING A NEEDLE IN A HAYSTACK

These aren't hypothetical questions. Many clients migrate from counselor to counselor, unsatisfied with their treatment, not realizing that it's probably because no one has really dealt with their bodies and their faith backgrounds, helping them understand how to relate the one to the other.

A few years ago, I met a classic example of just such a couple. Phoebe and Jack were trying me out as their fourth therapist in five months. As I typically do, I saw them as a couple for their first session to hear about them and their attempted solutions and goals, and then saw each of them individually to hear more of their story and for a full sex history. After those three initial sessions, I brought them back together to put together a plan, all of us.

Phoebe and Jack clearly had a lot of smarts between them, and at 16 years of marriage, they had been together long enough to get to know each other fairly well. She was outspoken and bright; he was quieter, and a brilliant computer engineer at a major aerospace firm. After getting the whole story of their relationship, I remember thinking how hopeful their situation was. "This isn't rocket science," I said to myself! "Why did it take three other therapists before they got to me?"

Here's what it looked like. Phoebe and Jack had four kids, ranging in age from 6 to 13, and life was very busy, which made it a challenge to stay connected to each other in their marriage. Phoebe was the high-desire partner and the pursuer in the relationship, and Jack tended to withdraw if Phoebe became too assertive. Their pattern of activation, I discovered, was tied to childhood relationships and losses that were pretty clear to both of them, and easy for me as a therapist to map out. Plus, both Jack and Phoebe had a strong Christian faith and many friends who were of great support in their lives, as did their kids. So where was the issue? It all seemed so clean-cut to me—and I was pretty sure I knew what to do. Why had therapy been so evasive for them?

The issue was that none of their other marital therapists had known how to deal with the sexual issues between them. At that moment in their relationship, the primary challenge was Jack's disclosure of a fur fetish, and Phoebe's sense of insecurity that his fetish was of greater desire for him than she herself was. None of this was new territory for me as a sex therapist— but none of their three previous therapists had had any idea what to do with the fetish or with their Christian faith, or the dynamics of how the two factors were interacting in Jack's and Phoebe's thinking. Each therapist had been thrown, such that either they didn't deal directly with the issues at hand, or they would make suggestions that failed to take their Christian faith into consideration. Jack and Phoebe had moved on in frustration, thirsting to have conversations that respected their faith and took the fetish seriously at the same time.

In four joint treatment sessions together, the three of us looked at the conditions under which Phoebe felt connected to Jack and felt secure in their emotional and sexual relationship, along with the things that negatively impacted their attachment pattern. We also talked about how to understand the history of Jack's fetish—the comfort it provided, how it functioned, and what he needed from it. I explored whether the fetish might be in conflict with the theology of either person, and surprisingly, both were okay with it, provided that it was not a secret between them and Internet pornography was not secretly involved. We discussed times in the past when Jack had gone "underground" with his fetish and how doing so had impacted Phoebe. This discussion seemed to clear the air and make space for establishing new ground rules that honored what they both named as "integrity" in their marriage. They both said that setting ground rules was important for living in a way that was congruent with their faith values.

From their new sense of clarity, Jack and Phoebe were able to negotiate a way for the fetish to have a place in Jack's life that he was pleased with and didn't cause undue insecurity for Phoebe, and Jack came to understand Phoebe's need for connection to him and how to provide it. At the same time, Phoebe came to understand the fetish without feeling threatened by it, and she grew in her understanding of how to approach Jack instead of triggering him.

The story of Jack and Phoebe is a common example of how we therapists *cannot* separate the emotional from the relational, from the spiritual, from the sexual, from the developmental. For one thing, Jack and Phoebe showed their first three therapists that they were willing to vote with their feet and find someone else when their needs weren't being addressed. But more importantly, they were suffering needlessly because of our common practice of failing to receive training in the issues that people hold most dearly—their faith and their sexuality. It was all there in one story. The problem had nothing to do with the therapists' desire to help; it was only a matter of familiarity. Three different licensed therapists only lacked training, or else they could have helped Jack and Phoebe find a solution that best suited them. They deserved better. All of our clients do.

Who Writes a Book Like This?

Many people ask me how I got so passionate about the intersection of Christian faith and sexuality. How did I come to question the Western church, American culture, and psychotherapy's mishandling of sexuality?

People who ask me this question sometimes assume that I also grew up in a conservative Christian environment, but this was not the case. Not that I wasn't part of Christian culture in some way. In my adolescence, I was part of a church during the "Jesus movement" (that wild time in Southern California in the 1970s that I mentioned in Chapter 2) and I have been part of different church communities in my adult years. Culturally, my Christian experience has involved communities where a wide array of theological ideas are allowed and discussions are rich. But that's been a relatively new reality for me, because church involvement wasn't a major part of my childhood years except for cursory Easter visits to our neighborhood Lutheran church where I had been baptized. Perhaps because of my childhood, the kind of Christianity I practice has been particularly sensitive to issues of justice for those marginalized and without voice in our community and the world at large.

For many people, their sense of professional calling is inspired by some significant life experience in their childhood. But oddly enough, my childhood was nearly opposite from the experience of those who grew up immersed in purity culture: it was my growing-up years, in fact, that gave me my basic comfort with the field of sexuality in the first place, as I wrote in the introduction to this book.

What really catalyzed my interest in sexuality and faith was when I began to encounter the stories of the first students to grow up in the purity movement, especially after the year 2000 or so. Their stories, sitting against the backdrop of how sex-positive my own family culture had been, completely broke my heart. But it also was because of my respect for their faith, and my belief in a loving God, that I believed that the pain of their religious sexual shame was not only an injustice that had been done to them but also indicative of a narrative that wasn't even loving, healing, or even truly Christian in the first place.

How a Swedish Heritage Can Shape a Therapist

Let me tell you a bit about my childhood so that you can understand the backdrop by which I held the stories of my students and clients. I grew up inside a big Swedish immigrant family that included my grandparents and four great aunts all living on a huge piece of property in the Pacific Northwest. I spent most weekends and every holiday running from house to house and down to the beach to play. My maternal grandfather ("Papa") had come to America as a 17-year-old soccer player determined to bring his family over and find his American dream. For him, family was of enormous importance, and I saw this reflected in our boisterous celebrations and family times while I was growing up. While my Papa loved America with all his heart, his Swedish cooking and, more importantly, his Swedish love of the sensual permeated how we all did family time: eating and laughing and talking and joking and poking fun at one another in love.

One element of this was an open and ongoing conversation about bodies and sexuality that happened naturally among all members of the family and at all times. I grew up watching married people flirt, giggle, and sit on each other's lap; even sexual joking was part of our rowdy family dialogue. But because family was central, so was respect. I didn't know until I was well into my thirties that I grew up in what I came to call a "sound-bite sex home." I can't remember one single conversation about sex because it was an ongoing, open, age-appropriate conversation that I had with my parents, grandparents, and aunts and uncles along the way. It is because of this comfort in my family that I grew up comfortable with the field and study of sexuality and intimacy. I give all the credit to my Swedish heritage and especially my wild extended family. Their openness was such a gift to me.

My first passion in my career was working with adolescents, so my first job was as a science and Latin teacher for junior and senior high students at a private college prep school. I taught their sex ed program and had such a blast that I found myself unable to understand why more teachers didn't jump at the opportunity, not yet realizing that I'd grown up in an unusually sex-positive family. By this time, I was also married and a new mom, and I was getting my first shot at passing down the heritage of an open conversation about sexuality as a woven-in part of life for my children as my family had done for me.

Teaching adolescents and learning how their home lives affected their ability to learn led me to graduate school to become a marriage and family therapist. After I graduated and started my practice, I was asked by one of my past professors if I would teach the human sexuality course in the program I had just finished. I jumped at the chance. "What could be more fun?" I thought. That was 1991. Six years later, I found myself teaching full-time for the school, directing its medical family therapy program and continuing to love my human sexuality course.

Part of my human sexuality curriculum involves asking students to write their own sexual autobiographies, and in about 2000, I began to see an increase in sexual dysfunction and religious sexual shame and trauma in the narratives of students from a religiously conservative background. It concerned me greatly and I began to keep research notes on what I was seeing. Each year, I would be in tears over the pain and sexual dysfunction in the stories I was reading. I began to see a marked increase in pelvic pain; vaginismus; erectile and ejaculatory dysfunction; out-of-control sexual behavior; self-condemnation; profound fear of sexuality, of sexual desire, and of the other gender; and extreme, unrealistic expectations for marriage and sex. In 2006, I wrote an article titled "Christians Caught between the Sheets—How 'Abstinence Only' Ideology Hurts Us" (Schermer Sellers 2006), published online in *The Other Journal: An Intersection of Theology and Culture*. The article went viral and I realized I had struck a nerve.

I heard from people all over the globe—scores, hundreds, even thousands of individuals who were suffering under religious sexual shame and trauma. But I couldn't find anyone speaking about these issues in the public arena or naming what was going on. So I decided to start researching, writing, and speaking about what I had been learning about religious sexual shame in more venues. I started a blog, a community-based website (ThankGod-ForSex.org), and intimacy retreats for couples.

In my personal life, my first marriage had long been over. After nine years as a single mom and two months after I published that first article, I met a man named Gary who would later become my husband. Six months after we met, we dove headlong together into the exploration of sexuality and spirituality by attending a conference on those themes in Santa Fe, New Mexico. I was already knee-deep in trying to learn everything I could from all perspectives, and I had met my match in Gary. I believed in what I had read about the merging of hearts, minds, spirits, and bodies in intentional sexual union, but I had not personally experienced it firsthand. I wanted this for my clients and students, and somewhere in the recesses of my heart, I wanted it for myself, too. I had long done my work to heal from the pain of my past marriage and any sexual wounding, but I had yet to experience what I believed was possible when two people commit to bringing their bodies, hearts, minds, souls, and vulnerability to each other, with a willingness to let the edges dissolve, being truly seen, known, loved, and accepted in the presence of their Creator.

Over a decade has gone by since I wrote that first article, and I am finally finishing this book. I have talked to over a thousand people affected by Christian purity teaching or other conservative religious movements. I have walked with many people as they have done the hard work of reclaiming their bodies as beautiful, their sexuality as pleasurable, their minds as trustworthy, and their hearts as loving. I have watched them set themselves free to create a new relationship with their God as a Creator who is passionate and loving, not punitive and restrictive, a Creator who deliberately made them embodied, sensual, and sexual, and who desires to give them all that love has to offer. I have watched clients work hard to give themselves permission to make decisions that feel in line with a loving God, not dictated by a punitive, hierarchical church that has taught them to doubt the trustworthiness of their heart. This has been courageous work for them, and at times, they have felt it dangerous, and it has cost some of them friends or loved ones and has exposed them to ridicule and criticism.

But in the end, they have claimed *their* voice, *their* power, *their* faith, *their* body, *their* sexuality, and *their* relationship with a loving God. Over and over, I hear about how grateful they are for the work, how right their relationship with God finally feels, and how delicious life, liberation, and erotic pleasure are. They tell me about how the spiritual discipline of learning to give and receive love with their body, mind, heart, and soul is the place where they have come to experience the very face of God.

This is why I care. And I invite you to join me.

Reference

Schermer Sellers, Tina. 2006. Christians Caught between the Sheets—How 'Abstinence Only' Ideology Hurts Us. *The Other Journal* 7. http://theotherjournal.com/2006/04/02/christians-caught-between-the-sheets-how-abstinence-only-ideology-hurts-us/.

Index